# POLITICIZING ISLAM IN AUSTRIA

# POLITICIZING ISLAM IN AUSTRIA

## The Far-Right Impact in the Twenty-First Century

FARID HAFEZ AND REINHARD HEINISCH

RUTGERS UNIVERSITY PRESS
New Brunswick, Camden, and Newark, New Jersey
London and Oxford

Rutgers University Press is a department of Rutgers, The State University of New Jersey, one of the leading public research universities in the nation. By publishing worldwide, it furthers the University's mission of dedication to excellence in teaching, scholarship, research, and clinical care.

Library of Congress Cataloging-in-Publication Data

Names: Hafez, Farid, author. | Heinisch, Reinhard, 1963- author.
Title: Politicizing Islam in Austria : the far-right impact in the twenty-first century / Farid Hafez and Reinhard Heinisch.
Description: 1. | New Brunswick : Rutgers University Press, 2024. | Includes bibliographical references and index.
Identifiers: LCCN 2023031268 | ISBN 9781978830448 (paperback) | ISBN 9781978830455 (hardcover) | ISBN 9781978830462 (epub) | ISBN 9781978830479 (pdf)
Subjects: LCSH: Islamophobia—Austria. | Islam—Austria. | Muslims—Political activity—Austria. | Muslims—Cultural assimilation—Austria. | Austria--Ethnic relations.
Classification: LCC BP65.A9 H345 2024 | DDC 305.6/9709436—dc23/eng/20230921
LC record available at https://lccn.loc.gov/2023031268

British Cataloging-in-Publication record for this book is available from the British Library.

rutgersuniversitypress.org

# CONTENTS

# PREFACE

In this book, we analyze the politicization of Islam in Austria, a prosperous and peaceful democracy in Central Europe known for Habsburg splendor, bucolic landscapes, and socioeconomic stability. Austria is not generally associated with Islam and Islam-related politics, nor does it have a past colonial history outside of Europe comparable to the Netherlands, France, or the United Kingdom. As a neutral country following the end of World War II, this placid country has no obvious connection to the events and debates that shape the Muslim world and its relationship with the West. Yet, Austria is indeed a country with a sizable and growing Muslim population. Moreover, Austria has a historical relationship with Islam that was once considered generally tolerant and progressive, dating back to the time of imperial Austria. Yet, as this book explains, Islam became politicized and so-called political Islam even criminalized. Austria is thus an unlikely case full of unexpected twists and turns. As we show in this book, the causes are complex and in some ways indicative of developments that unfold across Western democracies.

Austrian society has been undergoing a rapid transformation toward greater diversity over the past half century. In Vienna, a city with a population of about two million, the number of people calling themselves Roman Catholic has declined to about 584,000, while the number of Muslims has risen to 200,000. In the whole county, the number of Muslims has increased to over 700,000, representing 8 percent of the total population but less than 2 percent of the citizenry. Much like the rest of Western Europe, Austrian society has become extraordinarily diverse. By 2020, within only a few decades, the share of the country's foreign-born population had increased to about 20 percent. In fact, almost one in three people between the ages of thirty and forty-four has a so-called migration background (defined as having at least one parent who was born outside of Austria).

Despite, or precisely because of these trends, cultural diversity and immigration are a subject of denial and a source of radical political mobilization. The hurdles to naturalization remain high, and members of cultural minorities are seen as potential problems rather than sources of enrichment. Like most countries in Western Europe, Austria grapples with its societal and cultural transformation, but from a more insular perspective than countries like Britain and the Netherlands, all of which have long histories of immigration and have developed more global outlooks.

However, the Austrian story is also complex and paradoxical. On the one hand, Austria is a country struggling to define and hold onto its identity, as most of today's Austrians are the descendants of the German-speaking population in a multinational empire. Muslims are seen as "the Other" and a large share of the population believes that Muslims are not compatible with European society or that they need to show greater effort to integrate themselves into society. In Austria as well as in other European countries, the populist radical right emerged and subsequently rose to prominence by attacking immigration and the cultural Other. The shift in discourse on Islam by the populist radical right, as we argue in this book, has led to a general shift in the view and debate among political elites about Muslims, ultimately culminating in a deterioration of the legal privileges enjoyed by the Muslim community in Austria. On the other hand, Austria has had one of the earliest and most progressive legal frameworks for granting full and equal religious recognition to Muslims since the days of the Habsburg Empire. Against all odds, the Austrian Republic has maintained this framework and indeed provided an example of a tolerant Islam policy in a Western country. This book tells the story of what happened. It traces the politicization of Islam in Austria and the shifting agendas of all actors in this process—the political parties, the government and the ministries, ambitious political leaders, and of course the representatives of the Muslim community and the media.

We hope that this book helps in better understanding Austria's politics in connection with Islam and the activities of the government, interest groups, and other political actors that have shaped the political ramifications of Islam and the Muslim community in Austria. Against the backdrop of historically tolerant state regulation of Islam and Muslims, we explain how recent changes in anti-Muslim mobilization by the populist radical right and the subsequent co-optation of these strategies by centrist parties have changed the Austrian legal tradition to frame Islam and Muslims in Austria as a threat.

The book consists of eight chapters. After the introduction, we briefly present the context of Austria's relationship with Islam and Muslims and the emergence of the populist radical right in the country. The next five chapters deal with different policy fields and the electorate attitudes among Austrian voters. We analyze in chapter 3 the discourse about Islam among the political elite. In chapter 4, we look at the changing legal regulations of Islam. Chapter 5 discusses the regulation of the headscarf, and chapter 6 discusses the changes in the security apparatus in dealing with Muslims from the perspective of security politics. In chapter 7, we look at quantitative data of the perception of Islam in the Austrian electorate. In chapter 8, we wrap up our analysis and discuss the conclusions to be drawn from our findings.

# ABBREVIATIONS

| | |
|---|---|
| AbwA | Abwehramt (Counterintelligence Service) |
| BR | Bundesrat (Federal Council) |
| BVT | Bundesamt für Verfassungsschutz und Terrorismusbekämpfung (Office for the Protection of the Constitution and Counterterrorism) |
| BZÖ | Bündnis Zukunft Österreich (Alliance for the Future of Austria) |
| DSN | Direktion für Staatsschutz und Nachrichtendienst (Directory of State Protection and Intelligence) |
| FPÖ | Freiheitliche Partei Österreichs (Freedom Party of Austria) |
| HNaA | Heeres-Nachrichtenamt (Army Intelligence Office) |
| IGGÖ | Islamische Glaubensgemeinschaft in Österreich (Islamic Religious Society in Austria) |
| IKG | Israelitische Kultusgemeinde (Jewish Community of Vienna) |
| Kultusamt | Cultural Affairs Office of the Republic of Austria |
| MP | Member of Parliament |
| NEOS | Das Neue Österreich und Liberales Forum (New Austria and Liberal Forum) |
| NR | Nationalrat (National Council) |
| OGH | Oberster Gerichtshof (Supreme Court of Justice) |
| OPEC | Organization of the Petroleum Exporting Countries |
| ÖVP | Österreichische Volkspartei (Austrian People's Party) |
| SPÖ | Sozialdemokratische Partei Österreichs (Social Democratic Party of Austria) |

# POLITICIZING ISLAM IN AUSTRIA

# 1 · INTRODUCTION

When the 9/11 attacks provoked a wave of sympathy for the United States among Austrians, hostility toward Muslims was generally absent from the country's public political response. The then Austrian head of state, Thomas Klestil, a member of the Austrian People's Party (ÖVP), reiterated a position widely shared among the Austrian political elite, stating at the opening of a Muslim book fair in 2002 that "Austria is . . . proud of . . . having special ties to the Arab region and Islamic culture" (Klestil 2005, 345). In 2006, the president of the main chamber of the Austrian Parliament and a senior member of the ÖVP known for his conservative positions, Andreas Khol, made public statements such as "Austria knows no clash of civilizations. . . . Our Muslim citizens are an important part of our society" (Khol 2006). The populist radical right Freedom Party of Austria (FPÖ), which was in a coalition with the ÖVP in 2002, made an attempt to politicize Muslim life in Austria when, following debate about banning the hijab in France and Germany, one of its deputies called for a similar ban in Austria. However, the response of the then chancellor and ÖVP party leader, Wolfgang Schüssel, was unequivocal: "We do not have to import all the debates that take place in Germany" (*Profil* 2003). When the public debate about implementing a hijab ban in schools erupted in 2004, the Ministry of Education issued a decree establishing the right to wear the hijab on the basis of the freedom to exercise one's religion (BMBWK 2004). This decree had been drafted in consultation with the Islamic Religious Society in Austria (IGGÖ) (Anas Schakfeh, interview with Farid Hafez, 7 July 2011) and reflected the long-established practice in Austria of cooperation between policymakers and stakeholders from the communities affected by government action.

More than ten years later, the difference could not be more striking. In 2017, a coalition government formed between the ÖVP and the FPÖ implemented a ban on the full-face veil in 2017, followed by a hijab ban for children attending kindergarten and primary school in 2018. The government later planned to extend this ban to secondary schools, but the coalition's term in office ended prematurely. When the Conservatives formed a new coalition government with the Greens in 2020, they went so far as to call these measures a top priority. Gone were the days of cooperation between state authorities and Muslim representative institutions. The government framed these initiatives as successful attempts to crack down on what the ÖVP had begun to label "political Islam." When the IGGÖ criticized the coalition program of the ÖVP and the Greens for reflecting a "hostile attitude" toward Muslims and invoking terminology that encouraged the stigmatization and criminalization of Muslims (IGGÖ 2020), interior minister and later chancellor Karl Nehammer (ÖVP) responded by saying that "religious freedom is important and therefore not touched, of course. However, it is absolutely clear that political Islam is a threat" (ÖVP 2020). Similarly, the then party leader and chancellor Sebastian Kurz went so far as to state during the subsequent COVID-19 pandemic, "We have to fight two challenges: firstly, the Corona pandemic and secondly, the even tougher fight against terrorism and radicalization in Austria and Europe" (BKA 2020a). This significant shift in political discourse raises the question of how to explain such a change. How is it possible that a mainstream Christian Democratic party that had previously expressed deep respect for religious values, cherished interfaith tolerance, and actively promoted compromise and cooperation between different social interests would take such a hard-line position on an issue that had relatively little relevance in Austria and offered minimal traction in political campaigns? Even more striking is the fact that Conservative politicians began to parrot the previously expressed views of the populist radical right, but not immediately after the events of 9/11, which would have provided these politicians with an electoral opportunity, but years later. Finally, why did the left-wing mainstream parties, especially the Greens, who had explicitly committed themselves to multiculturalism and liberal values, not do more to counter the anti-Islamic policies of the political right? How best to explain the acquiescence of the Austrian political class to a political course that so clearly affected on a personal level the second-largest religious group in the country and about 9 percent of the population? These are the questions at the heart of this book.

What is more, Austrian politics and society had not been characterized by sociocultural polarization until then, so "culture wars" have been almost entirely absent from political discourse since the end of World War II. Austrian governments have prided themselves on their excellent relations with the Middle East, in particular with Arab countries and Iran. Moreover, Islam has been an officially recognized religion for at least a century. In fact, Austria was one of the first European countries to grant this status. Finally, the vast majority of Austria's Muslim population arrived as labor migrants from the former Yugoslavia and Turkey and never engaged very seriously in political activism. In sum, the causes and timing of the shift in Austrian Islamic politics represent a puzzle of sorts that this book seeks to investigate. This exploration is also a revealing account of how the political agenda and discourse launched by the radical populist right slowly but decisively penetrated mainstream parties, or at least found favor with certain mainstream political currents, while other established political groups did little to come to the defense of a beleaguered religious community.

In this book, we want to explain Austria's politics of Islam and the politicization of Islam. By this, we mean the activities of the government, interest groups, and other political actors in shaping the political conditions and perceptions of Islam and the Muslim community in Austria. While Austria is not typically associated with Islam-related issues, Muslims in Austria have continued to gain significant cultural influence while still being denied adequate political influence. This discrepancy between their cultural influence, which some perceive as a threat, and their weak political influence, which leaves Muslims with few political allies, is at the heart of Austria's Islam politics. However, the Austrian case is also one of a progressive and tolerant legal tradition that has allowed the Austrian Muslim community to manage its affairs autonomously. The argument we advance in this book is straightforward. For a century, Austria had a relatively progressive and tolerant approach to dealing with Islam and its Muslim community. Uncharacteristic as this approach was for a Catholic and socially conservative country, it was maintained throughout the waves of labor immigration including those from Turkey and Bosnia, acts of Palestinian insurgency affecting Austria in the 1980s, and the events on 9/11 and the aftermath. Indeed, Austrian elites often used these incidences to remind people of the importance of tolerance and mutual understanding. However, within a decade this changed markedly in terms of both official discourse and policies that have been adopted. We show in this book that the shift occurred when the populist radical right Austrian Freedom Party split, resulting in two parties on the far right that were competing with each other. The radical discourse that ensued and the issues that were introduced into public debate began affecting the discourse of other political parties. Especially the Conservatives, whose political fortunes had stalled, began embracing anti-Islamic identity politics, which further politicized Islam and resulted in the attempt to criminalize something called "political Islam."

A second important theme of this book is the way the Austrian state and the Muslim community had appropriated a framework of institutional mediation where the state respected the autonomy of the religious community to govern itself and certain aspects of cultural life. Thus, traditionally, relations between Muslims and the Austrian state were good, and social conflicts over culture and religion were largely absent. However, the rise of anti-Muslim mobilization with the help of the populist radical right and the subsequent co-optation by centrist parties (first and foremost, the centrist right) has fundamentally changed Austrian Islam politics. Gone is the Austrian legal tradition of tolerant inclusion. When combined with the general reluctance to grant citizenship to most migrants, Muslim or not, an increasingly large group is deprived of political representation. In addition, large segments of the population consider Islam incompatible with the Austrian lifestyle and are uncomfortable with the way they perceive society as changing. These different perceptions feed into the agendas of political actors and continue to shape the country politically.

## BACKGROUND

Religion had been a neglected area of political research for a long time until Samuel Huntington's concept of the "clash of civilizations" gained widespread attention in the early 1990s (Huntington 1993). Views on the role of religion in politics present in social science studies have since changed (for an overview, see Casanova 2011), and political scientists have gradually come to regard religion as a crucial area of analysis (Wald and Wilcox 2006; Kettell 2012). While this is especially true in the United States, it is also increasingly the case in German-speaking countries. In the latter case, the long pause in academic engagement with religion was the result of ideological and epistemological considerations based on the notion that secularity was indispensable for humanity to achieve social progress, an argument that has since been contested, if not refuted (Asad 2003; Taylor 2007). The growing importance of religion in shaping politics in many parts of the world has also led to a shift in the field of political science in German-speaking countries (Lynch and Schwarz 2016; Hafez 2017c).

In Austria, the role of religion in the context of politics was viewed much as it was in Germany. The main difference is that in Austria, the perception of religion had been shaped almost exclusively by political Roman Catholicism before 1938, when the country was annexed by Nazi Germany. In that earlier period, Austrian Catholicism had clearly authoritarian and militant tendencies, which underpinned an Austrian fascist regime that came to an end as a result of the Anschluss (Pyrah 2007). After Austria emerged from the ravages of World War II, it was seen as a country that had undergone a delayed secularization, but nevertheless it fit the familiar Western European pattern of religion experiencing a sharp decline and losing its political importance (Bischof, Pelinka, and Denz 2005). Consequently, neither public debate nor social science research in Austria has considered religion to be a particularly relevant concern in explaining postwar and contemporary politics.

Although since the 1960s there has been a steady influx into Austria of Muslims who arrived as labor migrants from the former Yugoslavia and Turkey, this has not been considered a cultural or religious phenomenon, but a matter for the labor market and social policy. Consequently, the Austrian case has generally been neglected in the growing literature on Islam-related policies (Bader 2007; Koenig 2007; Monsma and Soper 2009; Loobuyck, Debeer, and Meier 2013; Kastoryano 2004; Haddad and Golson 2007; Maussen 2007; Laurence 2006; Modood and Kastoryano 2006; Bleich 2009). This book is the first comprehensive attempt to fill this gap in the literature.

We argue that Austria is a significant case that deserves more attention for several reasons. First and foremost, Austria is unique among the countries in the region in that it granted full legal recognition to Islam as early as 1912, during the Habsburg monarchy. Although this move was largely a consequence of Austria's imperialist ambitions when the annexation of Bosnia-Herzegovina meant that a large Muslim population had to be incorporated into a largely Catholic empire, the law nevertheless signaled a rather unusual level of multicultural acceptance at a time when nationalism and Catholic orthodoxy were flourishing. The 1912 law granted the status of equality before the law to the main religions of Austria: Catholicism, Protestantism, Judaism, and Islam. Henceforth, Christian clergy and imams were serving equally in the Austro-Hungarian military. Thus, unlike most other Western European countries, Austria had created an institutional framework that could accommodate Islam long before the first Muslim immigrants arrived as "guest workers" in the 1960s and early 1970s.

While previous studies had focused on only one or two aspects of Islam-related politics, we have followed a broader understanding by conceiving Austrian Islam politics as the sum of discourses, institutions, laws, and administrative measures that aim to regulate and define Islam in Austria. This includes political demands, claims, and programmatic positions on Islam and Islam-related issues by political actors, parties, interest groups, and government officials. The "politicization of Islam" refers to the introduction of a religion and religious and cultural practices, religious institutions, and practitioners as objects of political competition and mobilization.

Richard Traunmüller (2014) confirmed such a regulatory trend across the twenty-seven European Union (EU) member states during the period between 1990 and 2011. As Jonathan Laurence shows in his research focusing on the period from the mid-1990s to the mid-2000s, "Gone were the ad hoc responses . . . and in came the creation of corporatist-style institutions and the establishment of 'state-mosque' relationships" (Laurence 2012, xix). Especially since the 9/11 attacks, European governments have been more interested in gradually appropriating their Muslim populations, as this gives them "unique influence over organizations and leadership" within this elusive minority (12). By influencing how Islam should be presented, national governments have aimed to create "the institutional conditions for the emergence of an Italian or German Islam, for example, rather than merely tolerating Islam 'in' Italy or Germany" (13). This reflects two objectives that matter to the state: first, the objective of "liberating" Muslims by disconnecting them from foreign policy agendas and, especially, from the influence of embassies in their countries of origin; and second, the objective of "moderating" Muslim organizations with transnational links to Islamist movements (13). Many authors agree that states sought to establish a domesticated "democratic European Islam," which occurred in the context of national debates about Islam as a potential threat to "security" (Cesari 2010), "integration," and "European values" (Bader 2014). Related research also problematizes the racial dimension that relates to these governmental strategies (Hafez 2018a; Hernández Aguilar 2018).

In most European countries, these initiatives to develop "state-mosque" relations have come from interior ministries, which have institutionalized "dialogue platforms" with Muslim actors to discuss issues related to Islam, society, inclusion and extremism (Laurence 2012). For Muslim civil society actors, the main objective of participation in these state initiatives has been to negotiate the institutional incorporation of Muslim institutions within the political system and the accommodation of the Muslim religion, as Luis Manuel Hernández Aguilar has shown in the case of Germany (Hernández Aguilar 2017, 2018). While several studies have analyzed these policies at the European level (Silvestri 2009), from a comparative perspective in different European countries (Fetzer and Soper 2004; Bader 2007; Laurence 2012; Joppke 2013; K. Hafez 2014; Koenig 2007), or in individual countries such as Germany (Amir-Moazami 2011; Teczan 2012; Hernández Aguilar 2015), France (Kuru 2009), and the United Kingdom (Birt 2006), the political science literature on Islam-related policies in Austria has focused only on specific issues, such as headscarf regulations (Gresch et al. 2008; Rosenberger and Sauer 2013). However, as noted above, the Austrian case is often neglected in the study of Islam and politics in Europe.

One of the most acclaimed works in political science on politics and Islam is Fetzer and Soper's (2004) comparative study of the accommodation of Islam in Germany, France, and Britain. Using social movement theory approaches, the authors argue that historically established church-state relations in these countries tended to prestructure the reception of Islam. Incidentally, this conclusion is clearly consistent with the explanation based on historical institutionalism, which views the relationship between the state and Islam as dependent on institutional path dependencies (see Kastoryano 2004; Modood and Kastoryano 2006). Fetzer and Soper argue that the history of church-state relations has played a more important role in determining the accommodation of Islam in European countries than other salient factors, such as those proposed by social movement theories (e.g., resource mobilization, political opportunity structure, and ideology). This historical institutionalist approach has also been used in studies of the institutionalization of Islamic religious education in Germany (Pratt Ewing 2000; Hofhansel 2010; Triadafilopoulos and Rahmann 2016; Euchner 2018) and beyond (Ciornei, Euchner, and Yesil 2021).

Other scholars, however, question the idea that historically developed patterns of church-state relations have determined the place of Islam in European countries. Loobuyck, Debeer, and Meier (2013), for example, demonstrate that church-state regimes did not have an impact on the institutionalization of representative Muslim organizations. This is an important critique of Fetzer and

Soper's work, as it points out that states treat Muslims differently than adherents of the state's respective dominant religion. Loobuyck and colleagues find in their analysis of Belgium, France, Germany, and the United Kingdom that "several states have abandoned their traditional methods in dealing with the institutionalization of Islam" (Loobuyck, Debeer, and Meier 2013, 71). The authors note a trend that "transcends disparate regimes and relies primarily on other factors, such as recognition of Islam, security, and integration policy" (73). The evidence for this claim lies in the timing of these policies following certain political incidents, and the policies' explicit references to deradicalization, or, at the very least, "dialogue" and the "call for a 'European Islam' to replace various Islamic trends and traditional Muslim cultural practices in Europe" (73). This approach draws on the work of other authors who have argued that it would be imprudent to overemphasize the role of historical state-church relations (Laurence 2006, 2012; Bleich 2009; Haddad and Golson 2007).

How does this debate influence our approach? This book aims to provide a comprehensive account of the politics of Islam in Austria based on the insights of the institutionalist approach. It takes into consideration the argument that other factors can be identified as central aspects in the "discursive field of Islam," including the country's recognition of Islam and its security and integration policies (Halm 2008). However, it also goes further and differs from other such studies in two main ways: (1) by examining Austrian Islam politics from different perspectives, such as state bureaucracy, party politics, legislation, and demography; and (2) by using multiple theoretical and methodological approaches to understand different aspects of the history of Austrian Islamic politics, such as institutionalism, discourse analysis, and legal analysis. The main question of this book is, how can we conceptualize and explain the Islam politics in Austria from 1945 to 2022, and specifically the politicization of Islam? Since this is a long period of time, starting with the end of World War II, our aim is not only to describe these politics, but also to theorize and explain their evolution, especially the changes that have taken place since the restoration of Austria in 1945.

## WHY AUSTRIA MATTERS

The Austrian case study offers several important insights and lessons for understanding the role of Islam politics in contemporary Western democracies. In many ways, Austria is representative of countries whose encounters with a growing Muslim population are not associated with a history of transcontinental colonialism. As a stable and prosperous liberal democracy, albeit with a relatively homogeneous population, Austria was economically well equipped to handle immigration. In comparison with the Scandinavian countries, which have similar overall profiles and comprehensive welfare states with institutionalized relationships between the state and interest groups in areas such as labor relations and social policy, Austria is predominantly Catholic and socioculturally less liberal. As such, the country shares many characteristics with its northern neighbor, Germany.

Although Austria and Germany are also connected through a history marked by Nazism and the Holocaust, Germany was much more in the international spotlight after World War II. Austria, by contrast, was confronted with its own fascist legacy decades later, which in turn often obscures the fact that the Nazi regime in Austria from 1938 to 1945 was preceded by a homegrown version of fascism that relied heavily on political Catholicism. Like its Central European neighbors to the east, Austria is not immune to identity politics and political impulses that see modernization, European integration, and economic liberalization primarily as threats (Heinisch 2002). Although Austria is a relatively successful member of the European Union, the country's accession to the EU and its subsequent integration have been marked by political conflicts. As in neighboring Italy and Switzerland, an electorally successful radical far-right populist party emerged in Austria earlier than in most other European countries. As early as the 1980s, the Freedom Party had begun to shape the political discourse on immigration and globalization (Heinisch 2003).

As in Germany, but unlike in Scandinavian countries, Austria's socially conservative traditions are one reason why Austria's political elites chose to import foreign labor rather than increase the number of domestic female workers when the rapidly growing postwar economy began to suffer from labor shortages. Consequently, Muslims came to Austria as labor migrants during the years of economic boom, beginning with the recruitment of low-cost labor from Turkey and the former Yugoslavia by Austrian and German industry in 1966. It should be noted, however, that Turkish and Bosnian labor migration was not labeled "Muslim" until much later, in the context of the rise of far-right identity politics (Bunzl 2005). Another factor that contributed to the realization that there was indeed a growing Muslim population in Austria was the increasing demand for religious services when workers were finally able to bring their families into the country. A third reason why labor migration eventually became associated with Islam was the emergence of a younger generation born into immigrant families and raised in Austria. However, the growing cultural presence of Islam and the related need for religious services was neither generally noticed nor perceived as particularly relevant by Austrian society. In fact, the political mainstream in Austria paid little attention to Muslim culture until the populist radical right Freedom Party took up the immigration issue and portrayed it in a completely negative light. In this context, it is also important to note that the FPÖ did not initially focus on the issue of Islam per se, but rather on the aspect of competition for labor and resources. Only later, in the context of rising identity politics in their election campaigns, were Islam and Muslims increasingly seen as a cultural and political threat to Austrians.

Although the populist radical right began to engage in Islamophobe identity politics in other European countries as well, the case of the FPÖ stands out, since it was invited to join the government four times by mainstream centrist parties. The first invitation came from the Austrian Social Democratic Party (SPÖ) in 1983 resulting in a coalition government that lasted until 1986. By the time the FPÖ joined that government it had evolved ideologically from far-right German nationalist formation into a more liberal direction. Shortly therafter, it repositioned itself as a radical far-right populist party. Subsequently, it served as a coalition partner of the Christian Conservative ÖVP, twice from 2000 to 2005 and finally one time from 2017 to 2019. The FPÖ's mobilization against Islam went hand in hand with its claim to defend Western Christianity and traditional Austrian religious culture—a curious turn for a party with a distinctly anticlerical and anti-Catholic history. In earlier times, German nationalists, who were the forebears of the FPÖ, had seen Austrian Catholicism and the Catholic Habsburg state as the main obstacle to an all-German national unification of Austria and Germany.

In the following chapter, we will discuss in some detail how it happened that the anticlerical right rebranded themselves as defenders of European Christendom and how the ÖVP came to adopt key aspects of the FPÖ's rhetoric and agenda, which became especially evident when the two parties formed a coalition from 2017 to 2019. Although on two occasions ÖVP-FPÖ coalition governments collapsed due to the radicalism and internal problems of the Freedom Party (Heinisch 2003), the FPÖ has had a lasting effect on the Austrian political system (van Dijk and Wodak 2010; Hafez and Heinisch 2019) and the way in which contemporary Austrian politics deals with Islam and Muslims.

Austria is also an interesting reference case compared to the much better-known German example because history has given the former a rather ambivalent national identity, which seems to reinforce the fear that it is particularly threatened by people who are seen as cultural "Others." After World War II, Austria faced the political necessity of distancing itself from Germany, with which the majority of Austrians share cultural, political, and historical roots. Since imperial Austria was neither ethnically nor linguistically defined, but was the domain of the ruling Habsburg dynasty, in which the German-speaking population was the dominant but not the only cultural group, a significant part of this population shared the desire to be part of a unified Germany. The exclusion of those Austrians from the process of German national unification in the second half of the nineteenth century was perceived as a trauma by many forebears of contemporary Austrians, as was the idea of power sharing with other ethnic groups in the later Habsburg Empire. Only the experience of Nazism, the war, and the Allied occupation managed to foster among Austrians the strong desire for complete national independence from Germany and to be no longer perceived as another (Catholic) version of Germany. After all, the Allies had promised in the Moscow Declaration of 1943 that Austria would be restored as an independent republic after the war (Steininger 2008). For Austrians, therefore, it was politically useful and culturally desirable to lay claim to an ancient and distinct imperial heritage to underscore Austria's independence from all things German. In reality, the complexity of Central European history, its multiethnic character, and its crucial political outcomes, which were largely determined by outside powers, make identities like Austria's inherently ambivalent and also precarious. What distinguishes Austrians from Germans? What historical developments can today's Austrians claim for themselves? What sets them apart from their neighbors to the east and southeast, with whom they have shared a common political but also cultural history? In a country whose developments have so often been shaped by the accidents of history, there is a tendency to look backward and to emphasize local identities and customs.

Even after World War II, it took decades before most Austrian citizens were able to unequivocally embrace an Austrian national identity (Tschiggerl 2021). However, when asked what constitutes an Austrian identity, people often respond by referring to lifestyle and cultural traditions as well as universal values rather than particular national values or shared national achievements. This, in turn, makes the question of immigrants' assimilation to an actual or supposed *Leitkultur* (leading culture) important. It also underscores the cultural significance of religion in the sense that it matters not because of its spiritual or doctrinal dimension, but because of the cherished traditions and practices that many people have grown up with and that, for them, constitute the essence of being Austrian. For this reason, even an increasingly secular society maintains a Christian Catholic tradition.

A further interesting aspect of the Austrian case is the institutionalized system for accommodating organized religion. Based on the 1933 concordat with the Vatican, the country created a legal framework that initially recognized the Catholic Church as a body with autonomous rights and duties, capable of independently regulating affairs within its own sphere, particularly with regard to internal organization, rulemaking, and education. This approach was extended to other religious denominations, which had already been legally recognized in the late nineteenth century as a consequence of the increasingly multicultural character of the Habsburg monarchy (Potz and Schinkele 2016). Similar examples can be found in Germany, where, as in Austria, organized religion is linked to the state, political parties, and the political sphere in general. Only in Austria do these arrangements also include Islam and the Islamic community and its religious association.

Another special feature of the Austrian political system is the strongly institutionalized tradition of mediating interests within the framework of the so-called corporatist system of governance. This applies above all to the labor market and economic policy, but also generally to a kind of consensus politics focused on compromise and the sharing of benefits and sacrifices. A key feature of this system is the state's willingness to grant interest groups autonomous regulatory powers in their respective areas of responsibility (Plasser and Ulram 1995). This system, also known as social partnership, was intended to prevent a return to the radical politics of competing interests and ideological polarization that character-ized Austria in the interwar period and ultimately led to the end of Austrian democracy in 1933. We will also show that this institutionalization of consensus politics is a characteristic of the Austrian state's approach to Islam policy. This means that we need to understand how this consensualism was created and main-tained with regard to Islam and why it was then rather abruptly abandoned.

Austria did not have a postcolonial intellectual elite that could have served as a mouthpiece and cultural rallying point for ethnic and cultural minorities. In the absence of such an intellectual and political tradition, the impression is often created both at home and abroad that a society like Austria's remains unchanged and culturally homogeneous. This image is reinforced and reproduced by a dom-inant culture that prefers unity to division and whose international image and commercial interests, especially in tourism and hospitality, depend on the pro-jection of certain cultural clichés and a particular identity.

In reality, Austria was not as unified and homogeneous as it is often portrayed today. Historically, the urban bourgeoisie and the Catholic camp in the country-side were quite hostile to the socialist and largely nonreligious working class. This division dates back to the last decades of the Habsburg monarchy and continued into the First Republic. It culminated in an armed conflict between these two groups, the establishment of an authoritarian state, and the armed suppression of the organized left even before the Nazis came to power. This trau-matic experience also explains the pervasive postwar desire for national unity and the establishment of a consociationalist political model. The prevailing view was that the conflict that had to be mitigated was not cultural or religious but social and economic. Austrian postwar democracy was constructed around the idea of internalizing and managing socioeconomic conflict. Political Catholi-cism was finished as a political model, and the postwar political leaders saw the causes of fascism primarily in the realm of economic deprivation and less in sociocultural cleavages.

## AUSTRIAN SOCIAL SCIENCE SCHOLARSHIP ON ISLAM POLITICS AND THE AIMS OF THIS BOOK

Austria is unique among Western European countries in having recognized Islam as a religious denomination more than a century ago. Because of this early inclusion of Islam in the political system, unlike in Germany, for example, where such recognition has remained controversial, Muslims in Austria have enjoyed the benefits of a legally recognized Islamic religious society that serves as an organ of organized advocacy for the religious needs of Muslims vis-à-vis the Austrian state.

Although political scientists have addressed the special legal status of Islam in Austria, their findings largely reflect the conclusions reached by legal scholars in their work on Islam-related issues (Prainsack 2006), and recent research on this issue also reproduces these assumptions (Gresch et al. 2008; Rosenberger and Sauer 2013). While these findings are innovative and insightful in some respects, for example in matters concerning gender, some of the underlying assumptions made by legal scholars regarding Islam-related politics clearly can be challenged (Kalb, Potz, and Schinkele 2003).

One of the most comprehensive political science sources on politics and religion in Austria, a chapter of the same name (Prainsack 2006) included in the leading handbook on Politics in Austria (Dachs et al. 2006), confirms that most of the referenced literature is indeed based on the work of legal scholars, who for a long time were the only ones to study the relationship between law and religion. However, much has changed in the last fifteen years, and researchers have increasingly turned to analyzing religion from a political science perspective (Hafez 2017c). At the same time, the political science literature is still not well connected to the legal and administrative science literature, reflecting the traditionally low recognition of the social and political sciences outside their respective fields in Austrian academia (Biegelbauer and Grießler 2009; Ehs 2011; Biegelbauer, Konrath, and Speer 2014). This tendency is even more evident in the field of Islam-related politics. Our book therefore aims to fill an important gap in the literature by providing a comprehensive analysis of Islam politics and regulations as well as party and public discourses in Austria in the context of the current democratic system and its policies. Its main goal is to illustrate how a prosperous, politically stable, and largely secular modern democratic society with a generally efficient administrative apparatus and a history of centrist politics deals with Islam. In this way, Austria is also an example of those European societies whose populations have become more heterogeneous and culturally complex as a result of modernization, but which generally do not receive the same attention as larger countries, especially those with a history of transcontinental imperialism.

How then can we explain Austria's approach to regulating the organization and practice of Islam and to developing and maintaining relations between the state and the Islamic Religious Association? At this point, we should recall our earlier brief discussion of the Austrian approach to dealing with social division and divergent group interests. In the field of industrial relations and social policy, an institutionalized social partnership helped to translate social and economic interests through an institutional framework into broad consensual solutions (Plasser and Ulram 1995). A central aspect of this consociational model is the relative autonomy of interest groups, which act independently within their sphere of competence and expect the state to recognize their decisions and compromises.

This organizing principle carries over to the way the Austrian state deals with other important social cleavages. In particular, Catholics and secular socialists used to view each other with mutual suspicion and feared that if one side controlled the state, it would impose its ideological preferences on the other. For Catholics, therefore, a degree of relative autonomy from the state in important areas such as religious education, the hiring and training of priests, and control over doctrinal issues was deemed necessary to maintain their religious practice. For other religions, all of which have historically been small minorities in Austria, including the various Protestant and Christian Orthodox denominations, this autonomy also meant that they did not have to fear that an overbearing Catholic Church would impose its religious agenda on them. For secular society, this autonomy meant a quid pro quo in that the Church would henceforth stay out of politics, something it had not done in the First Republic in the 1920s and 1930s.

From another perspective, the early recognition of Islam in Austria through the 1912 Islam Act created one of the oldest and, for a long time, one of the most progressive relationships between the state and Muslims in Western Europe. This law fully recognized Islam as an equal religion, and from it grew important institutional patterns and policies in Austria's so-called Second Republic after World War II. It is the persistence of these patterns and policies that we wish to examine here in light of the growing presence of Islam in Austria, in the wake of the increased use of identity politics, and in the context of the politicization of Islam in party politics across Europe.

In order to understand both the long duration of Islam-related politics in Austria and the changes in these politics over the past decades, we will examine the relationship between the state, political parties, and Islam, particularly from an institutionalist perspective. Institutional path dependence and the institutionalized autonomy and mediation inherent in Austrian consociationalism explain the persistence of the long stable relationship between the state and the Islamic community, whereas party competition tends to account for the recent changes in the state's Islam politics, especially at a time when consociationalism has been in decline (Crepaz 1994; Bruckmüller 1994; Tálos 1993). Specifically, we will examine Austria's Islam-related policies by comparing Islam-related legislation over time, tracing the processes responsible for these policies, and attempting to explain the relevant policy outcomes and their effects.

Austria's approach to Islam during most of the Second Republic can be explained using historical and sociological institutionalism. Based on the main mechanism of path-dependent institutional development and the logic of appropriateness, the actions of Austria's policymakers followed the consociationalist institutionalist pattern from the moment Islam was first recognized as a divisive issue. Later, the rise of identity politics, driven by far-right political actors, increasingly shaped party competition. In this context, Islam and religion and their impact on culture and society became a point of contention that could be successfully used for political mobilization. In this way, the old consociationalist institutional pattern was broken and Austria's Islam policy was pushed in a different direction by shifting the conflict away from institutions back into society. This was most evident in the creation of the 2015 Islam Act, which represented a shift toward the agenda of the populist radical right party, the FPÖ. Islam and its religious expressions were thus presented as a growing problem for Austria's security, political stability, and culture in the context of immigration. The debate has led actors outside the radical and populist right to adopt programs and rhetoric that are widely considered populist and similar, if not identical, to those of the populist radical right.

Our book is organized as follows. The first chapter introduces the main research question and presents the theory and approach we have used to explain the pattern of Islam-related politics as it has emerged in Austria. Chapter 2 summarizes the position of Islam in the specific context of Austria and highlights the role of religious denominations in relation to Austrian consociationalism and the historically evolved relationship between church and state in Austria. It also presents the crucial role of the FPÖ and shows how the party adopted an Islamophobic discourse for the purpose of political mobilization in party competition. The subsequent chapters discuss the changes in Austrian Islam policy against the backdrop of party competition in four different areas. Chapter 3 is devoted to an analysis of elite discourses on Islam, examining how the FPÖ's discourse influenced the positions of other parties on both the right and left. Chapter 4 looks at changes in the legal status of Islam, comparing the 1912 Islam Act with the new 2015 Islam Act. Chapter 5 analyzes the regulation and debate over the hijab, which used to be a nonissue in public and political debate but is now increasingly in the spotlight and subject to various legal restrictions. Chapter 6 discusses the changes in the security policy of the state, which no longer sees Muslims as partners in the fight against extremism but as a potential risk. Chapter 7 is devoted to the demand side and looks at the opinions of the electorate. Finally, in chapter 8 we summarize our findings and present our conclusions.

## THEORY AND METHODOLOGY

To show the change in Islam-related policies in Austria, especially in the government's policy response, we will present three strands of analysis. First, we show that Austria's institutionalist tradition, along with its consociational political culture, contributed to its fairly progressive treatment of Islamic organizations by allowing Muslims to fully participate in the legislative process. Second, we note a change in this policy that is related to developments in Austrian party politics, leading to a change in elite discourse about Islam in particular. Third, we show that this change has taken place in the core area of regulation of religious practices and that a before-and-after effect can be detected here as well.

In our theoretical approach, we rely on the theory of new institutionalism as the main explanatory framework. Following Hall and Taylor's (1996) delineation of three new institutionalisms—the rational choice, the historical, and the sociological varieties—we consider the latter two to be particularly relevant for the Austrian case, both in terms of the long, consistent development of Islam-related policies in Austria and the importance of sociological-institutionalist explanations for policymaking in Austria in general (for an overview, see Heinisch 1999; Lehmbruch 1984; Paster 2013; Obinger 2002).

The main advantage of applying an institutionalist framework is that it allows us to understand how institutions emerge and change and helps to explain the construction of relationships between institutions, the behavior of institutions, and the actors operating within them (Hall and Taylor 1996; see also Peters 1999). In functional terms, institutionalism provides us with an explanation of why institutions evolved in the first place, for it is not readily apparent why governments would willingly relinquish the power to regulate labor markets or religious communities were it not for the possibility of lower transaction costs, greater conformity, and the greater potential to reduce social conflict. Historical institutionalism draws attention to structural conditions beyond the initial rational calculus that explain why institutions persist even when the conditions under which they were created no longer exist. Institutions have a certain inertia and create a logic of appropriateness that shapes the behavior of those individuals who have been socialized into certain roles and patterns of behavior. Thus, the Austro-Hungarian monarchy may have had good reasons to accommodate the new Bosnian Muslim population, especially in the context of a multiethnic military. However, for post-World War II Austria with its majority Catholic population, these initial conditions and their functional rationale clearly no longer applied. Moreover, the influx of Muslims from the former Yugoslavia and Turkey was not perceived as an immigration of people with a different religious background and thus did not represent a particularly new problem. Rather, these people were seen as temporary workers who could be accommodated by the existing system. As a result, the institutional arrangements from the time of the Austrian monarchy remained in place, which will be discussed in more detail below. It therefore makes sense to look at Austrian Islam relations and Islam politics through the institutionalist lens. The institutionalist approach emphasizes path dependence, unintended consequences, and power asymmetries (Hall and Taylor 1996). The sociological variant of institutionalism draws on a more constructivist concept of culture and therefore defines institutions in a broader sense, additionally including the symbol systems, cognitive scripts, and moral templates that generate meaning for actors. In this context, culture is redefined as an institution in itself. Accordingly, institutions are viewed as cultural signifiers that affect the behavior of individuals. Sociological institutionalism emphasizes the interactive and mutually constituting nature of this relationship. Thus, social legitimacy in a cultural setting is central to the possibility that institutions will emerge and change (Hall and Taylor 1996). Although Hall and Taylor do not call for a synthesis of the three varieties of institutionalism, they do emphasize the importance of integrating their insights and drawing on their respective strengths.

How can this be applied to the Austrian case? Here we must remember that Austrian society was divided not only between the bourgeoisie and the working class but also along confessional and cultural lines (Catholic and prochurch versus anticlerical, secular, and socialist). It is therefore not surprising that Austria applied its tried and tested institutionalist solutions based on the consociationalist model to dealing with Islam in a majority-Catholic country. In Austria, political support for internalizing potential areas of conflict by transferring decision-making powers to designated institutions, regulated by a mutual give-and-take, has a long and successful tradition (Scharpf 1991; Crouch and Traxler 1995; Heinisch 2000, 2001; Paster 2013). Especially during the heyday of Austrian corporatism and consociationalism (Lijphart 1977; Lehmbruch 1984, 1985; Katzenstein 1976, 1985; Crepaz 1994), it would have been rather out of character for political actors to engage in political mobilization based on religion or attempt to aggravate existing societal cleavages.

This type of response to cleavages in society is observable in other European countries, such as the Netherlands, which also featured a corporatist model of labor relations (Wolinetz 2002) and encouraged institutionalized relationships between religious denominations and the state, albeit this did not initially concern Islam but rather relations between Protestants and Catholics. What emerged was a so-called pillared society (*Verzuiling*), denoting the vertical politicodenominational segregation of society and the creation of separate institutions, ranging from political parties to universities, along confessional lines to engage in interest negotiations at the top end of the pillarized structure and arrive at mutually satisfactory arrangements (van Schendelen 1984; Deschouwer 1989; Knappskog 2001). Although pillarization has substantially declined in the Netherlands due to secularization, it has not disappeared. In fact, and in a fashion similar to the Austrian situation, Muslim immigrants in the Netherlands have availed themselves of the legal opportunities created in a society that once had a highly pillarized structure. For example, the government treated the Muslims who initially arrived from the colonies and those who came later as migrant laborers as a new pillar (Kaag and Tabarki 2010, 37–38).

As in the Netherlands, consociationalism and corporatism have significantly declined in Austria since the 1960s and 1970s, when this approach was the predominant mode of policymaking (Heinisch 1999). This could lead to the premature conclusion that the weakening of Austrian corporatism (e.g., Karlhofer and Tálos 1999; Lehmbruch 1985; Tálos 1993; Crepaz 1994; Tálos and Kittel 2001; Heinisch 2000, 2001) simply carried over to Islam politics (Hafez and Heinisch 2018) and is thus connected to general ideological shifts and the growing populist zeitgeist (Mudde 2004). However, the problems of Austro-corporatism date back to the 1980s. For example, Austria's noted political scientist Peter Gerlich wrote about the issue in *Social Partnership in Crisis* some thirty years ago (Gerlich 1985). However, this preceded the changes in the institutionalized relationship between the state and the Muslim community by nearly two decades and hence cannot explain the government's recent about-face on Islam-related politics. Instead, we will see that the reintroduction of Islam as an issue of party-political contestation is crucial for understanding the shift in Austrian Islam politics. Although we can date this development fairly precisely, it is important to recall that it did not occur in connection with the 9/11 attacks but rather later, when the populist radical right Freedom Party decided to make Islam an issue. The party had undergone a split and dropped out of government in 2005. It was in that context that the FPÖ moved sharply to the right and pursued a radical voter-seeking course that heavily emphasized identity politics to distinguish itself from the slightly more moderate new splinter party called Alliance Future Austria (BZÖ).

Once Islam was reintroduced as a political issue, party competition helps explain the subsequent changes in the discourse about Islam and related policy measures rippling through the Austrian party system. There are several well-established explanations as to why and to what extent parties pay attention to certain issues while ignoring others altogether. Leading scholars on the topics of party behavior and the rise of the right such as Tim Bale (2003) have shown that center-right parties often engage in immigration issues because they share common positions with radical parties. This is especially the case in Austria.

Odmalm (2011), by comparison, argues that parties only turn to immigration if they need to accommodate opposing ideological positions such as, in the case of Conservatives, market liberalism and value conservatism. Leftist parties, by contrast, do so when facing trade-offs between international solidarity and welfare-state/labor-market protectionism. To bolster a Conservative party's core competencies and avoid unintentionally supporting competitors from the radical right, the former have to think carefully about whether to make immigration a central political issue (Odmalm 2011, 1071). While most of the literature argues that adopting ambiguous issue positions is predominantly a costly strategy, Rovny (2012) has shown in an analysis of 132 political parties in fourteen Western European party systems that the choice of party strategy—whether a party decides to emphasize or blur the lines of certain issues—is determined by the degree of party involvement in the political issue dimension. Emphasizing core competencies may be the rule, but blurring one's position may also be a beneficial strategy if applied to the appropriate issue dimension to attract a broader section of the electorate (Rovny 2012). We argue that the center-right's engagement with Islam, in which Conservatives compete with the populist radical right, came about after Islam was successfully introduced as a divisive political issue by the latter.

To summarize our argument, we first claim that Islam in Austria was initially assigned by political actors to the consociational-institutionalist framework founded on the legal basis of 1912 and subsequently established in Austrian post-war politics, as this was the standard approach to dealing with social divisions. This can be seen in the establishment of representative institutional bodies, the recognition of these bodies as formerly equal negotiating partners, the endowment of these bodies with some veto power over new rules binding on members of their community, and finally the mutual adoption of rules to resolve cleavage-related conflicts. Second, we argue that this pattern changed decisively later when Islam was introduced as a point of political contestation, which in turn allowed political actors to use it successfully in party competition. In the following chapters, we will present empirical evidence of these relationships in the form of public statements, party platforms, and legislative changes.

Methodologically, we conduct our comparative case study by tracing the processes and analyzing the public and parliamentary debates, as well as interviewing the key actors involved in the legislative process of the 2015 Islam Act. Our process-tracing approach focuses on the factors that explain relatively sudden changes in government policy after long periods of political continuity. Despite debates about its analytical strength (for a fuller discussion, see Bennett and George 2005; Muno 2009, 125; Collier 2011, 824), we find this methodological tool particularly useful. It allows us to analyze stable patterns of behavior punctuated by critical junctures that either lead to long-delayed policy outcomes or produce abrupt policy changes, even though neither the composition of actors nor their power relations changes significantly. As such, it fits well with our institutionalist approach and our emphasis on opportunity structures that reshape both the interest-based calculus of actors and the logic of appropriateness.

As chapter 2 shows, institutional solutions in the form of the creation of the legal and institutional foundations—that is, the 1912 Islamic Law and its policy implications—represent the preferred outcome in a multinational and multicultural monarchy for political actors who were motivated to treat different groups as equally as possible while welcoming a new (in this case, Muslim) population into their fold. Institutional inertia, disinterest, and the functional need to maintain some continuity between the Austrian monarchy and even the postwar democratic republic ensured the continuation of the political regime, but they are not sufficient to explain why it took decades for there to be a recognized Islamic society that officially advocated for the concerns of Austrian Muslims. Looking at the changes in opportunity both in the otherwise asymmetrical relationship between Muslim representatives and state actors and in party competition helps explain abrupt improvements in Islam policy, as in the 1970s, and abrupt negative changes, as after 2005.

# 2 · THE CONTEXT

## Islam and the (Radical) Right in Austrian Politics

Austria was long known for its tolerant policies toward the Muslim community. In contrast to other Western European countries, there were neither restrictions on Muslims' freedom of religion nor (national) parliamentary debates with the purpose of introducing such limitations (Gresch and Hadj-Abdou 2009) before 2015. This favorable situation was clearly a consequence of the legal status Muslims have enjoyed since 1912, when Islam became fully recognized as one of Austria's established religions (Kalb, Potz, and Schinkele 2003). This status guarantees Muslims important rights pertaining only to legally recognized churches and religious societies (Heine, Lohlker, and Potz 2012). The long-standing consensus on the integration of Islam and its inclusion in a "we," constructed in terms of a national identity within the ruling political elite, was, however, challenged by a resurgent radical right to which other political parties reacted (Hafez 2014b).

The situation changed after the crisis of the political coalition that governed Austria from 2000 to 2005. At that time, the Conservatives (ÖVP) formed a coalition with the populist radical right FPÖ. However, in 2005 the FPÖ became embroiled in an internal conflict and broke with its Conservative coalition partner. The party also split, and the remaining bulk of the FPÖ became a radical opposition party (Hödl 2010). A smaller group that wanted to remain in government formed a new party called BZÖ, which continued in the coalition with the Conservatives. This meant that two far-right populist parties were now competing with each other—one that remained in public office and was more moderate, and one in opposition that was more radical and wanted to raise its own profile. A race for the title of the most Islamophobic group thus began, which led people on the radical right, but also parts of the political center and the left, to adopt increasingly anti-Islamic discourse strategies (Bunzl and Hafez 2009).

This chapter therefore presents the Austrian political parties and the competition between them as the main drivers of Islamic politics. Other important actors are the representative Muslim organizations. These political stakeholders operate in a political context that is largely characterized by a long-standing institutionalization of relations between the Austrian state, political elites, and the Muslim community. This setting of Austrian Islamic politics also provides important opportunities for political actors to advance its interests and advocate on behalf of its community. The Austrian state's long-standing policy of relative tolerance toward Islam is closely related to these opportunities in the form of periods when the Austrian government felt the need to present to the world an image of Austria as a liberal, tolerant, and cosmopolitan society, for the reasons discussed in this chapter.

Before we delve into the history of the institutionalization of Islam politics and explain the distinct aspects of the Austrian case, we need to briefly introduce the political parties that will be referenced throughout this chapter and provide some background on them. Austrian society was for a long time deeply divided between a Catholic bourgeois and traditionalist rural milieu on the one side and a secular, socialist working-class milieu on the other. Conflict and contestation between these two camps as well as some degree of cooperation after the Second World War were the principal determinants of Austrian politics, leaving little space for third parties and issues outside the concerns of the two mainstream parties. However, with the emergence of a new middle class in the context of economic modernization in the late 1960s and 1970s, Austrian politics began to change. The emergence of multiculturalism, neoliberalism, and environmentalism on the one hand, and of radical far-right nativist and nationalist ideas on the other, broadened the political contest beyond the classic socioeconomic left-right axis and introduced new political actors focused on sociocultural and post-materialist ideas such as environmentalism and cultural diversity.

The Greens and later the Liberals (LIF, now NEOS) emerged from these changes. This "silent revolution" (Inglehart 1997), in turn, created a "silent counter revolution" (Heinisch and Werner 2021) in the form of the already mentioned populist radical right FPÖ, which had been founded in 1956 but whose forebears represented radical anti-Catholic, anti-Semitic, pan-German nationalism. In the subsequent decades the FPÖ became more liberal, even joining the Social Democrats in government (1983–1986). However, under the leadership of the young and charismatic Jörg Haider, who took control of the party in 1986, the Freedom Party converted into radical populist party, campaigning at first on issues of public corruption and then increasingly on identity politics. This party is a major protagonist in our account of Austria's Islam politics and the reaction of the other parties to the FPÖ's agenda-setting thus represents our main focus. We will return to the issue of party competition toward the end of this chapter. First, however, we need to provide a brief introductory overview of the state of Austrian Islam politics.

Austria's official policy toward Islam has long been one of inclusion and recognition. Islam in Austria is currently one of sixteen legally recognized churches
and religious communities that date back to the Austro-Hungarian monarchy. As
early as 1912, "the followers of Islam" were legally recognized as a religious community in Cisleithania (the then Austrian half of the Habsburg Empire) as a result
of the annexation of Bosnia and Herzegovina to the greater empire. By that
time, the Jewish community had already been legally recognized. In 1867, there
was thus a need for the freedom of public religious practice for Bosnian Muslims
in the Austrian part of Austria-Hungary. As a consequence, the permanent status
of legally recognized churches and religious societies was introduced. During
World War I, Muslim Bosnia and Herzegovina was routinely depicted as one of
the territories in the Balkans that was most loyal to Austria, and Bosnian soldiers
serving in the Austro-Hungarian army were considered particularly brave. Thereafter, in 1921, the newspaper *Neues Wiener Journal* celebrated the construction of
a mosque in Vienna "as a clear sign of Austria's friendship with Turkey [which
would have] a mighty impact on the Muslim world far beyond Turkey" (Fürlinger 2013).

This legal recognition of Islam paved the way for the type of relationship the
Austrian state and its Muslim constituency developed over the years. When the
first prominent mosque was built in Vienna in 1979, the Austrian Press Agency
wrote, "If Allah wills, we will soon also have a muezzin in Vienna, who calls the
faithful to prayer."[1] *Arbeiter Zeitung* ran the following headline at the time: "Austria's First Mosque and Islamic Center Opened: A Symbol of Reconciliation and
a New Landmark for Vienna" (*Arbeiter Zeitung* 1979). This reflects the general
political discourse of elites in those years following the authorization in 1979 of
the IGGÖ, which was widely seen as a soft-power tool of Austrian foreign policy
(Hafez 2016). At the time, Austria enjoyed markedly cordial relations with much
of the Arab and Islamic world. Chancellor Bruno Kreisky had emerged as one of
the West's foremost champions of the Palestinian cause, and his close contacts,
even with internationally controversial Arab leaders from PLO leader Yasser
Arafat to Libya's strongman Muammar Gaddafi, were regarded in the public discourse as a sign of an independent foreign policy that was garnering global attention. Visits by Arab leaders and the transfer to Vienna of the headquarters of the
Organization of the Petroleum Exporting Countries (OPEC) were regarded
with pride. Saudi Arabia and the Gulf States, with which Austria maintained
very close relations, were considered lucrative export markets for Austria's still
largely nationalized and struggling heavy industry (Hafez 2016).

Although Austrian citizens and even members of the Austrian elite may have
lacked direct personal contacts with Islam, the public discourse about the religion and the Muslim community generally did not have a negative connotation.
Even after a Palestinian commando raided OPEC's headquarters in Vienna in 1975,
and after another attack by Arab militants at the Vienna International Airport in

1985, there were no noticeable attempts in Austria to frame these developments in sociocultural terms or to link national security to a particular ethnic or religious community in the country. Although these terrorist attacks were perpetrated by secular nationalist forces, the conflation of Arabs and Muslims, as suggested in studies at that time (Said 1978; K. Hafez 2002a, 2002b), was absent in Austrian political discourse.

Most importantly, the recognition of Islam as an official religion gives the Islamic Religious Society in Austria the status of a public corporation. This is unique in Western Europe. While many countries such as France, Germany, and the United Kingdom are trying to find ways to accommodate Islamic practices, Austria has an approach to regulating religions that is based on legal recognition. As public corporations, legally recognized churches and denominations are regarded as partners to the state with "shared interests." This means there are certain areas in which the state delegates tasks to these churches and denominations. One of these areas is religious education, meaning the IGGÖ has the right to teach Muslim students Islamic religion in classes in state schools, just as the Israelite Act and the Protestant Act guarantee the same rights to the Jewish and Protestant communities. The IGGÖ thus trains teachers, determines the educational curricula for schools in their respective religion, oversees the work of teachers, and hires staff, while the Austrian state finances these efforts. Religious education is just one of several areas where some degree of autonomy has been in place, while countries with a very similar state-church relationship are still searching for a way to grant their Muslim minorities equality before the law. This includes Germany, which has not recognized any Muslim institution as a corporatist body, with the recent exception of the recognition of the Ahmadiyya in Hesse in 2013.

The importance of the IGGÖ markedly increased after Islam became one of the most politicized issues in the Austrian public sphere. The politicization of Islam in the West surged following the 9/11 attacks (Hafez 2013). In response, the president of the IGGÖ and its media spokespersons have regularly discussed Islam and negotiated with the government on a number of political areas related to religion. This institutionalized communication has provided several advantages, most notably a basis for cooperation, especially in the period between 9/11 and 2005, as both sides benefited from this cooperative relationship.

The relationship between the IGGÖ and the state was first put to the test when a right-wing coalition government composed of the ÖVP and the populist radical right FPÖ was in office from 2000 to 2002 and from 2002 to 2005. The FPÖ was widely seen as anti-Semitic and xenophobic, which resulted in the Conservatives (ÖVP), the larger and more experienced partner, coming under severe international criticism. In fact, the Austrian government was even boycotted for a time by the (then fourteen) EU-member governments in 2000. However, the far-right coalition did not have a negative impact on the relationship between the IGGÖ and the state. On the contrary, the ÖVP tried to present itself in a better light and made considerable efforts to promote close cooperation with the IGGÖ by launching a number of initiatives. For example, in 2003, when Graz, the capital of Styria, was the European Capital of Culture, the Austrian Foreign Ministry initiated the first European Imam Conference, which was organized jointly with the IGGÖ and supported by various Austrian official organizations and government agencies. Cultural and scientific events like this conference helped Austria in its cultural diplomacy and in maintaining close relations with the Muslim world. The IGGÖ benefited from these initiatives both in Austria and internationally, as the first imam conference was followed by another Austrian and two European conferences. With the support of European Union institutions, the European Imam Conference was established as a supranational institution playing a leading role in the landscape of European Muslim organizations. Other European conferences were held in 2006 and 2010. These conferences proved to be invaluable opportunities to discuss issues that were of great importance at the time and are still relevant today. In a way, Austria thus became a forerunner in the establishment of Muslim institutions not only in Austria, but also at the European level.

Among the benefits enjoyed by legally recognized churches and religious communities in this system of secularism that is nonetheless favorably disposed toward religion—"inclusive secularism," as it is termed by legal scholars (Kalb, Potz, and Schinkele 2003 42–43)—is tolerance toward minority cultural practices that might otherwise prompt political actors to politicize certain issues. Contentious issues such as circumcision, which was banned in some European countries, were not politicized at all in Austria, while the Jewish and Muslim practice of kosher and halal slaughter of animals was explicitly exempted from the prohibitions based on the Animal Protection Act of 2004 (Tierschutzgesetz). When Austria started a constitutional overhaul and reform process (2003–2005), churches and religious denominations were invited by the Austrian Parliament to provide their perspectives on religious matters. The Islamic religious representatives proposed the exclusion of an invocation of (an ostensibly Christian) God from the constitution (Österreich Konvent 2003) and was also granted the opportunity to engage regularly in discussions about religion on Austria's public broadcaster (ORF) as part of its religious programming available to all legally recognized churches and denominations.

However, despite the public space afforded to the IGGÖ and the political efforts to achieve closer cooperation with this body, the IGGÖ remained less privileged than other churches, especially the dominant Catholic Church, which has more than five million members in a population of 8.6 million. Thus, while the IGGÖ represents one of the largest minorities, with around 364,000 Muslim members in 2001, it has never received significant financial support or obtained a corresponding number of chaplain positions in hospitals, prisons, and the military.

Moreover, from a legal standpoint, the Islam Act of 1912 had been designed for a comparatively small community and also failed to address a number of issues that have arisen since.

Nonetheless, the tolerant framework allowed for close cooperation between the state and Muslims. However, eventually it began to crumble, and the question is, why? Interestingly, it did not happen as an immediate response to the 9/11 attacks. Rather, the change came later, when the Freedom Party was in danger of imploding in the polls and returned to the opposition, moving sharply to the right again. Before we look at the reasons for the end of the tolerant framework, we need to better understand how the tolerant Islam policy came about and what sustained it for so long.

## WHY DID AUSTRIA CHOOSE A TOLERANT POLICY IN THE FIRST PLACE?

The history of tolerance toward Islam is not necessarily self-evident. In fact, Austria is a country with an ethnocultural citizenship regime. In contrast to societies with a multicultural or Republican orientation, which usually affords people easier access to citizenship and are thus less restrictive in drawing boundaries as to who belongs to the nation and who does not, Austria is restrictive with its citizenship laws and tends toward a homogeneous conception of national identity (Bauböck and Perchinig 2006). In Austria, the Catholic Church has played a dominant role, especially culturally, although it is not a state church (Hanisch 1977, 1994). Due to its historically hegemonic status in Austrian society and state, it still enjoys privileges beyond those afforded to other legally recognized denominations (Kalb, Potz, and Schinkele 2003, 446–540). Moreover, Austria has historically discriminated against ethnic minorities such as the Slovenes, and this has never been fully remedied by minority policies (Reiterer 1996; Knight 2017; Hafez 2021a). In addition, the country shares a history of anti-Semitism culminating in the Holocaust during the Nazi regime, in which many Austrians were willing accomplices. Austria's postwar record is also marred by anti-Semitic episodes such as former chancellor Bruno Kreisky's public attacks on Simon Wiesenthal (Pelinka, Sickinger, and Stögner 2008) in defense of the FPÖ party leader, Friedrich Peter, whose SS unit was implicated in massacres of civilians. Another such case was the affair surrounding former UN secretary general and Austrian federal president Kurt Waldheim, whose official biography had omitted crucial aspects of his war record and whose subsequent international denunciation prompted an anti-Semitic backlash in Austria, especially against the World Jewish Congress (Gruber 1991). In that context, coded language, such as references to "influential East Coast circles," meaning politically influential U.S. Jews, became common in public discussions. Likewise, more recently, the head of the Austrian Jewish community, Ariel Muzikant, was publicly mocked by the former leader of the Freedom Party, Jörg Haider, because of his Jewish background (Pelinka and Wodak 2002). Notwithstanding the commitment of Austrian governments to fight anti-Semitism and the adoption of a more pro-Israeli foreign policy position, Austria cannot be considered a particularly liberal or tolerant society. Nonetheless, violence against immigrants and ethnically motivated unrest have been extremely rare in Austria compared to Germany or other European countries.

Moreover, it is certainly also the case that in the imagination of Islam in Austria, a specific form of Orientalism (Said 1978) has always been evident, as identified by the anthropologist André Gingrich (Gingrich 2015). Austria's favorite traditional drink, coffee, is associated with an exoticized image of Osman Turkey, visually rendered in the logo of the national coffee brand and gourmet food store Meinl, which depicts a happy dark-skinned boy wearing a fez. "Meinl's Moor" is as iconic and universally recognized a symbol in Austria as Aunt Jemima and Uncle Ben's are to older Americans. The other side of the Orientalist coin is that even liberal and progressive Austrians ascribe to Islam as a threat narrative, in that it is seen as creating a problem for Austria's constructed identity as a postreligious and "enlightened" society. Despite these indications of cultural myopia and ethnic stereotyping, state authorities were clearly willing to pursue a "tolerant" approach to Islam. This was the case at least until the FPÖ actively pursued an Islamophobic political campaign strategy from 2005 onward (Hafez 2010a, 2015a; Hödl 2010), which it maintained until the adoption of a new Islam Act in 2015 (Dautović and Hafez 2015). This leads us first to the question of how a tolerant Islam policy can be explained against this less than culturally tolerant background.

If we compare Austria with various other European countries and consider the restrictive headscarf policies in countries such as Germany, Belgium, and France, and the nonrecognition of Islam in Germany, which, unlike Austria, did not allow the institutionalization of Islamic theology at universities (Hafez 2014a) or the establishment of Islamic religious education in public schools, then we may consider Austria comparatively "tolerant" in its Islam policy. This applies at least to certain policy areas, such as the issue of headscarves (Gresch et al. 2008, 2012).

This section explores how this "tolerant" Islam policy came about, by posing the following interrelated questions: What was the cause of the political incorporation of Islam that occurred in Austria's Second Republic? Is the establishment of the legal recognition of Islam in 1912 sufficient to explain Austria's initial postwar approach to Islam? If not, what other explanation may account for this development? For instance, Austrian authorities must have known that applying the Islam Act of 1912 in the contemporary republic would inevitably result in recognized religious communities that would eventually be able to establish autonomy, self-determination, and self-organization. Why were they willing to accept this?

Two possible explanatory approaches suggest answers. In their monograph on the accommodation of the Islamic religion in Britain, Germany, and France, the two political scientists Joel Fetzer and Christopher Soper (2004) argue that the historically developed state-church relations are of central importance in explaining how state authorities deal with Muslim religious affairs. This account fits well with our understanding of historical institutionalism (Hall and Taylor 1996), as it helps us understand the turn toward a "tolerant" Islam policy. Second, we will also investigate the opportunity structures present when progress can be observed in the relationship between the state and the Islamic Religious Association on behalf of the community, to see whether a given context provided political actors with strategic windows to move their agenda forward.

## OUR EXPLANATORY FRAMEWORKS: INSTITUTIONALISM AND OPPORTUNITY STRUCTURE

The theory of institutionalism assumes that institutions are central to political decision making (Weaver and Rockman 1993). Here we draw especially on historical institutionalism as the basis for explaining "tolerant" Islam policy and complement this framework with an analysis of political opportunity structures. Historical institutionalism by itself does not offer sufficient critical junctures in its focus on path dependence to explain path change.

Institutionalism assumes that conflicts over scarce resources are at the heart of politics and that certain institutional solutions improve the odds of political actors in securing a share of these resources relative to the absence of institutions. In their seminal account of institutionalism, Hall and Taylor distinguish rational choice institutionalism, historical institutionalism, and sociological institutionalism (Hall and Taylor 1996). Guy Peters discusses six variants (1999, 17–20). Common to all forms of institutionalism is that institutions are the primary determinants of collective action and political outcomes. They structure identities, create roles, define interests, and shape interactions. Although there are strong similarities with structuralism, institutionalism is not deterministic in the sense that actors do not necessarily always follow the prescribed institutional path or apply an institutional logic. Nonetheless, this happens often enough that institutionalism provides a powerful explanatory framework. It also accounts for why actors may deviate from instrumental rationalism in their behavior, since institutions shape behavioral incentives (Hall and Taylor 1996, 937). Given the longevity of the institution under consideration, which has survived multiple regime changes, we employ historical institutionalism, which is often used to explain persistent multigenerational policy regimes, such as welfare regimes. In particular, it has three central characteristics that matter. First, historical institutionalism captures the relationship between institutions and individual behavior very broadly. Second, it emphasizes power asymmetries in the emergence and development. Third, it emphasizes the importance of the ideational dimension in its analysis of institutions (941–942). According to Peters, historical institutionalism differs from other institutionalist theories in that it postulates "time matters," thus forming the historical dimension (Peters 1999, 63). As a consequence, decisions made by political actors at one time influence decisions in the same policy field taken at a later time (63–65). It is thus especially suited for analyzing continuities. However, whether it can also explain discontinuities or ruptures is a matter of debate in the literature (Peters, Pierre, and King 2005).

A central analytical category of historical institutionalism is the concept of "path dependence," which was adopted by Stephen Krasner (1984). It states that policy decisions have a lasting impact on the overall development in a policy field. Past policy practices are assumed to influence present policy practices and thus prescribe a development path in a corresponding policy area. Choosing the predetermined path offers fewer adversities to overcome and thus resource advantages for the actors. Any of these paths can be abandoned (Peters 1999, 19). Typically, however, such change requires stronger stimuli—Hall and Taylor cite an economic crisis or military conflict—that would legitimize deviation from an established path (Hall and Taylor 1996, 942). Since revolutions and other exogenous shocks are not part of everyday political life, the presence of institutional lock-in is the typical consequence, suggesting that path deviations or path changes tend to be the exception (for a critique of this, see Beyer 2006). This does not mean, however, that the path dependence thesis does not recognize change. On the contrary, the focus of historical institutionalism is on questions of change and continuity of institutions (Helms 2004, 28). Various concepts of path dependence assume "that those conditioning factors that originally emerged for the reproduction and change of institutions may be quite different from those due to which institutions originally emerged" (33).

In contrast to the rational choice approach, historical institutionalism analyzes institutions in the way that they order the preferences of actors. Institutions are defined by Hall and Taylor as "formal or informal procedures, routines, norms, and conventions embedded in the organizational structure of the polity or political economy" (Hall and Taylor 1996, 938). The concept of institutions, particularly in historical institutionalism, is broader than in the rational choice approach in its inclusion of cultural factors and its overlaps with sociological institutionalism (Hall and Taylor 1996; but see Pierson 2000).

Following on from this, Jürgen Beyer points out that with respect to the path-dependency thesis, the "spectrum of justifications for path-dependent developments . . . is quite large" (Beyer 2006, 27). Since the path-dependent development thesis—typically focused on functionality, complementarity, power, legitimacy, and conformity—is not unambiguous, it may require additional explanatory concepts to account for institutional changes. These may include the emergence of functional equivalents, change of constitutive elements and underlying arrangements, the buildup of countervailing forces, the infiltration of rival ideas, the encroachment on path dependency by other policy regimes, and mounting political pressures for change (23–25, 36–38). A central category by which the change of a path development is determined is that of critical decision points (critical junctures). Hall and Taylor mention economic or military conflicts, for example, without using this term explicitly. Critical junctures are able to explain the termination of or deviation from a path. Thus they analytically capture how institutions emerge and disappear, but not why they persist (Thelen 1999, 387). Others argue that path changes without critical turning points are associated with high transaction costs (North 1993). Various authors raise the objection that the central question of how institutions influence the actions of actors would not be answered unambiguously (Csigó 2006, 44). At the same time, some authors reinterpret concepts such as path dependency in such a way that it is no longer about reproducing the identical but rather about changing the gradual (North 1990). In contrast, Hall and Taylor (1996) have already pointed out that within the literature of historical institutionalism there is a rational as well as a cultural approach. The former emphasizes the strategic action of actors, while the latter assumes not only that utility maximization affects the actions of actors, but also that these actions are also shaped by norms and values. Accordingly, the latter provides answers to the three central questions—how actors behave, what institutions do, and why they persist for a certain period of time (Hall and Taylor 1996, 952).

When Fetzer and Soper (2004) suggested that Islam policies in Western Europe are primarily influenced by the existing state of church-state relations, this corresponds closely to our understanding of historical institutionalism. Accordingly, it can be hypothesized that Islam policy has been institutionally shaped in a path-dependent manner, since in Austria, relations between state and church are regulated by religious law (Kalb, Potz, and Schinkele 2003).

Similarly, it can be assumed that the institutionalization of Islam has followed the same causal pattern. Thus, on the one hand, there is the effect of historical structuring due to institutionalized state-church relations; on the other hand, there are opportunity structures that can be used by political actors to induce change that cannot be explained by historical processes. The institutional context, especially the 1912 law, also cannot explain the timing of certain events such as the institutionalization of the IGGÖ, which is the representative body of Austria's Islamic community, since this did not happen until 1979. In fact, the law had recognized the existence of an organized Islamic society de jure from the very beginning. An early decision of the Supreme Court of Justice (OGH) in 1960 also acknowledged this reality, ruling that a Muslim community as such did indeed exist, in the context of a case deciding the legality of the marriage of a Muslim couple in the province of Salzburg. The court based its decision on two facts: (1) the establishment of a Muslim community in Vienna in 1943; and

(2) the existence of a Muslim association in Salzburg that had fled the Red Army and later cared for 1,000 Muslims as displaced persons under U.S. troops (Dautović 2019c, 101–102).

While this decision built on a historical institutionalist reading of a legally recognized Muslim society, this pattern was not followed in the 1960s, when Muslims in Vienna attempted to establish a Muslim religious society based on the Islam Act of 1912. There were no political actors willing to push for the full implementation of the law, although efforts by Muslims to achieve this aim date back to the mid-1960s. While research assumes that Austria's "tolerant" Islam policy is a consequence of the early legal recognition of Islam (Gresch et al. 2008, 420), and while this is undoubtedly an important prerequisite, it presents tolerant Islam politics and institutionalization as an automatic and deterministic fait accompli that does not pay enough attention to context and agency.

To complement institutionalism—and to gain a more comprehensive understanding of why Austria was characterized by its early recognition of Islam as a religion, the nevertheless long delay in institutionalizing a corresponding religious society, but otherwise relatively tolerant government policies toward Islam in an overwhelmingly Catholic and conservative society—we turn to the concept of opportunity structures. This theoretical framework is often used very differently in the literature in terms of both how the concept is defined and how it operates (Goodwin and Jasper 1999, 31ff.). Jon Elster proposes viewing the opportunity set as the possibilities for action within a given context from which actors can choose according to their preferences (Elster 1992, 13). Doug McAdam and others who follow his approach have provided a conceptualization that counters the ambiguity of the concept. For example, McAdam considers the question of the openness or closedness of a political system as a central feature. In addition, the attitudes and coherence of elites, the question of the presence or absence of allies, and the ability of the state to take repressive measures shed light on the political opportunity structures within a political system (McAdam 1996, 26).

The notion of windows of opportunity speaks to the fact that due to structural triggers, certain events are placed on the political agenda, which in turn enables new policies at the structural level. John Kingdon referred to this as the "policy window": "The policy window is an opportunity for advocates of proposals to push their pet solutions, or to push attention to their special problems. . . . These policy windows, opportunities for action on given initiatives, present themselves and stay open for only short periods. If participants cannot or do not take advantage of these opportunities, they must bide their time until the next opportunity comes along" (Kingdon 1984, 173–174).

As quickly as issues can be placed on the agenda, they can also disappear. It is therefore crucial for actors to recognize these windows of opportunity in order to take advantage of them. Beyer echoes Lipset and Rokkan (1967) when he integrates the concept of window of opportunity into the concept of path dependency by identifying the point in time when a new path can be taken because different options are available (Beyer 2006, 26). In this respect, it seems appropriate to examine the relevance of opportunity structures to account for the institutionalization of the Islamic community in Austria. However, we must first turn to the foundation of Islam's institutional trajectory and the beginning of modern Austrian Islam politics: the creation of the Islam Act of 1912.

## THE ISLAM ACT: THE HISTORICAL INSTITUTIONAL DIMENSION

In their work on the accommodation of the Islamic religion in Europe, Fetzer and Soper (2004) show that the historically developed state-church relations are of central importance for explaining how state authorities deal with Muslim religious affairs. They present a persuasive framework explaining that how the state deals with (organized) religion determines how Islam is treated as a minority religion. Accordingly, we present a brief outline of the development of state-church relations in Austria. With the ex lege recognition of the IGGÖ in 1912, one may consider this the institutionalization of Islam, even in the sense of classical institutionalism, which defines the concept of institution more narrowly than new institutionalism.

The so-called Josephine Tolerance Patent of 1781 laid the foundation for the pluralization of religious life in Austria (Wandruszka 1985, xivf.). At the same time, freedom of religion for the state meant creating a means of control over social groups through a regulated relationship with religions (Furat 2012, 2019). The Josephine Patent of Tolerance first recognized the Evangelical Church as well as the Greek Orthodox Church and, via the so-called Jewish patents (Judenpatente), the Israelite Religious Society. In 1849, a patent granted full freedom of faith and conscience and the right to practice one's religion at home. Islam was thus recognized as a religious community lex generalis, but it was not constituted as such (Kalb, Potz, and Schinkele 2003, 93–102). However, due to the denunciations of the Concordat of 1855 in parts of society, which was an attempt to preserve the "Catholic character of the 'neoabsolutist' centralist unitary state," and the subsequent establishment of a constitutional monarchy in 1860 to 1861, along with the School Acts of 1868/69 and 1874, confessional pluralism became constitutionally secured (Wandruszka 1985, xvf.). From then on, the Recognition Act of 1874 formed the legal basis for the recognition of other churches and religious societies. After the Statute on the Autonomous Administration of Islamite Religious, Foundation and School Affairs in 1909, the legal recognition of Islam followed in 1912 with the Islam Act (Kalb, Potz, and Schinkele 2003, 625–627).[2] It therefore stands in the tradition of several other special laws governing churches and religious societies, such as the Protestant Act of 1867 and the Israelite Act of 1890, and therefore clearly embodies the tradition of path-dependent historical institutionalism. Accordingly, "historical coincidences" (small events) form a dependent chain of institutional decision making and resulting arrangements that led directly to the creation of a law recognizing Islam as a religious community, thereby laying the groundwork for the recognition of an Islamic religious association as its organizational and institutional basis.

This development must be seen in the context of great power politics in the late period of the Habsburg monarchy, whose expansion into the Balkans resembled an Austrian imperialist project in the age of imperialism. If Habsburg Austria was already too weak to acquire overseas colonies, it could still muster enough strength to colonize the near abroad in the Balkans and add "exotic" southern lands to the aging empire at the expense of the Ottomans, whose influence in the region was waning. It is therefore important to demystify the notion of a "selfless" and "tolerant" Austrian Islam policy (Sticker 2008; Rustemović 2019) by recalling more soberly the motives of Austrian decision-makers (Hafez 2014b).

For the Austrian state, a law on religion is always also meant to empower the religious subject, who is taken out of the private sphere into the domain of the public. This addresses the observable asymmetry of power between the state and, in this case, the Muslim religious society (Hafez 2014b, 64–69). Nonetheless, the foundation for the legal recognition of a minority religion in a multiconfessional, multiethnic state remained in place. In comparison with other European countries, not least Germany, which has a similar state-church relationship and in which Islam is not recognized ex lege (Spielhaus and Herzog 2015), the Austrian case must be regarded as distinctive. However, despite the legal recognition of Islam as a religion and the reasoning of the Supreme Court of Justice to see the establishment of an Islamic community in Vienna in 1943 and the organization of Muslim religious life of displaced persons in Salzburg as evidence of the legal recognition of a Muslim community in Austria, there was no recognized Islamic religious society in Austria that could have functioned as an institutional umbrella organization. This situation remained unchanged until 1979, despite repeated attempts to establish such a representative body (Dautović 2019b, 2019c). This prompts the question as to what accounts for this long delay and also what explains this institutional next step in 1979.

## POLITICAL OPPORTUNITY STRUCTURES: AUSTRIA ON AN INTERNATIONAL STAGE

World War I, the disintegration of the empire, and the subsequently small number of Muslims in Austria's First Republic meant that there was little opportunity to form a religious society, as the 1912 Islam Act had intended. In fact, with the end of World War I, not only did the Muslim Bosniaks disappear from Austria but also the Muslim population overall declined sharply to about 1,000 persons (in Vienna) in the interwar period (Strobl 2005, 522–523; Dautović 2019c). Fragile democracy was followed by two fascist regimes that sought to eliminate any political and cultural space beyond their control. Austrofascism, an authoritarian form of radical right Catholicism inspired by Italian Fascism after 1933 and Nazism following the German takeover in 1938, ensured that very few Muslims lived in what is now Austria.

When Austrian democracy was resurrected, the Second Republic reestablished its previous constitutional and legal framework. This was because Austria had to maintain the fiction that it had nothing to do with Nazism and Hitler's war of aggression but was in fact its first victim through a forced takeover called the Anschluss. To this end, Austria faithfully transferred and resurrected its entire prefascist constitutional and legal framework, parts of which, such as the fundamental rights and freedom, dated back to the Habsburg monarchy. In due course, Austria's postwar legal system, resurrected in 1945, recognized the Church of Jesus Christ of Latter-day Saints (Mormons) in 1955 (BGBl 1955); after all, the United States was an occupying power in Austria from 1945 to 1955. After a hiatus of seventeen years, Austria recognized the Armenian Apostolic Church in Austria in 1972 (BGBl 1973).

The Islam Act was taken up in the Second Republic only as a consequence of the influx of Muslim students and became relevant again, especially after the immigration of so-called guest workers. However, as already mentioned, whereas the Habsburg monarchy may have wanted to accommodate its new Bosnian Muslim subjects, the Austrian Republic lacked that motivation. Thus, these initial conditions and their functional rationale that mattered to the empire no longer applied to the diminished mostly Catholic Austrian Republic. When Bosnian migrant workers started arriving from then Yugoslavia and Turkey in the 1950s and 1960s, they were not perceived as immigrants with a different religious background but rather as temporary laborers whose beliefs would have no consequences for Austria and the Austrians. The government needed to maintain the notion that these workers were only "guests," people who came without their families, so there was no cause for new legal arrangements. Otherwise, this would have drawn unwelcome attention to the immigration of people that in the eyes of a population still largely socialized under Nazi rule were cultural strangers.

If applied strictly and consistently, institutionalist path dependency should have pushed the Austrian government to adopt a religious policy on Islam that mirrored the approach with regard to Mormons and Armenian Christians. However, compared to the latter two groups, whose communities were tiny, the emerging Muslim population was larger and growing, and the Austrian government hesitated. Since each step along the path confirms each further step, thereby reducing the likelihood of deviating from that path by choosing an alternative political course of action (Sorensen 2015, 21), it initially appeared that Austria was going to go in a different direction. This hesitation also calls into question the argument of sociological institutionalism (Thelen 1999, 386f.) that state authorities would prefer to follow an already established religious policy for reasons of political and administrative consistency, given that the legal basis already existed in the form of the Islam Act of 1912. It specifically provided the possibility for the recognition of a religious society under its first article, which states that "the followers of Islam [are given] recognition as a religious society." Missing was the creation of an Islamic religious body that was recognized to speak on behalf of a religious community that was already recognized. As such, recognition did not happen for fifteen years, and institutionalism does not suffice as an explanation (Thelen 1999). To this end, we need to take actors' perspectives into account and examine the preference structure and opportunities that emerged in the 1970s.

At the time, an existing organization in the Islamic community, the Muslim Social Service (MSD), included the goal of founding such a representative institution in its statutes as early as the 1960s and held several talks with the Ministry of Education in this regard (BMUK 1978). On 26 January 1971 it formally submitted for the first time an application for the establishment of an Islamic religious society to the Federal Ministry for Education and the Arts. However, this application was revised several times before it was finally approved on 2 May 1979. Between 1975 and 1978, four rounds of negotiations were held annually at that ministry's office, as it was legally responsible for officially recognized churches and religious societies, which was confirmed by one of the negotiators (Anas Schakfeh, interview with Farid Hafez, 7 July 2011).

This prolonged process was in part due to several objections on the part of the Austrian authorities. First, there were financial concerns; recognition as a religious society would entail various financial entitlements, which would have resulted in new expenditures for the government. The most contentious issue, however, was cultural. The Austrian authorities feared that male Muslims could claim a right to polygamy by invoking freedom of religion (BMUK 1978). This was surprising insofar as article 7 of the Islam Act of 1912 already expressly excluded this possibility. What is more, such a reservation vis-à-vis the applicants had already been invalidated in 1972 by an expert opinion rendered by DIYANET, the Turkish Directorate of Religious Affairs (Diyanet 1972), and again in 1976 by an expert from Al-Azhar University (Al-Azhar 1976). Nonetheless, the application did not receive any further consideration. No endogenous factors came into play and no critical issues arose that would have justified a departure from established religious policy (Sorensen 2015, 25–28). It seems clear that prevailing stereotypes about Islam and its supposed preference for a polygamous family model led to skepticism on the part of the authorities, or that the authorities feared a possible political backlash if the issue were widely discussed in public. Differently stated, the traditional prevalence of Austrian cultural conservatism was more influential than the uniform application of an already existing institutional framework, which for decision-makers meant that the status quo was preferable to all other options. Thus, we need to turn to political enabling structures that ultimately led to a change and the establishment of an Islamic religious society by 1979. The opportunity structure that eventually presented itself came in the form of a change in Austria's posture in international politics. A letter from the ministerial official responsible for religious policy at the time indicates that the MSD's request for a permit for external legal relations had stalled because a planned Islamic center in Vienna had not developed any activities since the project had been initially conceived. The Islamic Center Vienna, which was later established as a foundation in 1979 and whose board of directors included diplomats from Muslim countries, had not shown any activities after 1961, the year when the Egyptian ambassador, a major force behind the project, was recalled (BMUK 1978). This not only was the formal reason given for Austrian inaction but also connected the recognition of an Islamic society with foreign policy. Fortunately, by the 1970s, the Social Democratic government under Chancellor Bruno Kreisky had embarked on a globally oriented foreign policy that was meant to establish neutral Austria as an important international actor not only between West and East but also between the industrialized and the developing world. Kreisky was particularly eager to enhance Austria's reputation in Muslim-majority and Arab countries. To this end, the establishment of an Islamic center or an Islamic religious society would serve as an internationally recognizable symbol. A letter referring to the request by the Cultural Office for recognition of the IGGÖ from the then constitutional lawyer of the Federal Chancellery, Ludwig Adamovich, dated 6 April 1979, stated, "The Federal Chancellery-Constitutional Service is of the opinion that the aspect should also be included in the considerations that an amendment or new enactment of the Islam Act would be expedient given the increasing number of diplomats from Islamic countries employed in Vienna (e.g., UNO, OPEC)" (Adamovich 1979, 2).

This shows that the attempt to position Austria in the international arena as a country that is open to Islam was part of the strategy of the Federal Chancellery. Thus, the position taken by Kreisky and his officials is an important piece in the puzzle concerning the recognition of the Islamic Religious Association at the time. This also clearly illustrates the power asymmetry between the later partners, the government, and the Islamic Religious Association. Kreisky's "active neutrality policy" led him, as an envoy of the Socialist International in March 1974, to Sadat and Nasser as well as to Gaddafi and Arafat, who at that time was still widely regarded as a "terrorist." The Austrian chancellor, himself of Jewish heritage, was known for his pro-Palestinian stance and offered the Palestine Liberation Organization (PLO) a seat for an embassy-like representation in Vienna in 1980. This came at a time when the organization was still suffering from marginalization and exclusion by the international community (Kriechbaum 2004, 261–283). This allowed Kreisky to gain increased prestige for Austria in many

Muslim-majority countries. The shift in policy also ultimately yielded important economic benefits for Austria's (still partially nationalized heavy) industry,
which could export machine tools, trucks, and other durable goods to countries that were eager to develop and modernize. As the cost of raw materials
surged, especially crude oil, many of these countries could count on substantial
U.S.-dollar revenues, which they were eager to invest. Efforts to internationally
showcase Austria's changed relationship with Austrian Muslims became evident
in the repeated invitations to the leadership of the Islamic Religious Association
to accompany the Austrian delegation on state visits (Anas Schakfeh, interview
with Farid Hafez, 13 July 2011). Also, the Republic of Austria presented itself
internationally as a tolerant country by creating exhibitions on Muslims in Austria that were shown at Austrian embassies in major cities around the world
including Cairo, Istanbul, London, and Paris (BMEIA 2006a). Activities of the
Ministry of European and International Affairs (BMEIA), from the time of Minister Benita Ferrero-Waldner (2000–2004) to Minister Ursula Plassnik (2004–
2008) and Minister Michael Spindelegger (2008–2013), reveal how important it
was for Austria at the highest level to present itself as tolerant toward Muslims
and Islam (BMEIA 2003, 2006b, 2011). The Foreign Ministry sponsored and co-
organized activities with its embassies abroad to present its tolerant accommodation of Islam (BMEIA 2009) and celebrated the one hundredth anniversary of
the Islam Act (Potz 2012).

Soft power (Nye 2004) or cultural diplomacy is usually a corollary of hard
power—in this case, presumably economic power. While the sudden oil shock
in 1973 hit Austria unexpectedly, the challenges could still be absorbed by
Austro-Keynesian policies surprisingly well (Scharpf 1993). In response to the
economic challenges, Kreisky sought to align the economic interests of his small
country with policies that would be favored by oil-rich economies in the developing world, many of which were Arab-Muslim majority countries. Government expenditures rose from 1974 to 1978 by over 48 percent (Getzner and Neck
2001), and Austrian industry supported Kreisky's policies. It benefited significantly from exporting products that Austria could produce competitively to
industrially less developed countries in exchange for much-needed resources.

Yet, the second oil crisis in 1978 to 1979 hit Austria much harder. The Austrian
National Bank (ÖNB) lost almost one-third of its reserves and the interest rate
had to be raised significantly (Unger and Heitzmann 2003, 375f.). This policy of
deficit spending, dubbed "Austro-Keynesianism," contributed to Austria maintaining a growth advantage vis-à-vis all other European OECD countries until
the early 1980s (Volk and Wieser 1986, 27). Owing to this offensive positioning,
Austrian companies gained important recognition in the Arab world (Horvath
2009, 102). For example, Austrian Airlines became the first Western airline to fly to
certain Arab destinations, which shows how much Austria was a pioneer in building Western-Arab relations (Woditschka 2015). Adamovich's explicit reference to

diplomats from Muslim-majority countries employed by the UN and OPEC illustrates the level of importance that the Austrian government at the time attached to Austrian-Arab relations at the time. This was strengthened not least by the opening of the Vienna International Center in August 1979, which made Vienna the third seat of the United Nations (Petritsch 2010, 291f.). Soft power was clearly at play. Its relations with the Arab world and other developing countries in Latin America, Africa, and Asia also established Austria as a relatively independent Western actor, which also boosted its credentials with the respect to the Soviet bloc. The country could thus function as a more genuine mediator, which became evident when former U.S. president Jimmy Carter and former Soviet leader Leonid Brezhnev met in Vienna in 1979 to sign the SALT II agreement.

We may conclude that the government's decision to establish an Islamic religious society in 1979 based on the 1912 Islam Act was made possible and encouraged by Austria's role in international politics and by economic calculations made at the time, and thus by an arising increasingly favorable political opportunity structure. Officially recognizing Islam in Austria, as one of the few countries in Western Europe that took this step (Potz and Wieshaider 2004), was intended to demonstrate Austria's political openness. According to Adamovich, diplomats from Muslim-majority nations residing in Austria would take note of the recognition and thus help Austria gain even more prestige in their home countries. Austrian authorities had several options for dealing with the Muslims' application for reinstating the 1912 Islam Act. Hesitancy on the part of the authorities and especially the traditionally inculcated view of Islam as culturally "different" (Gingrich 2015), evidenced by the fears surrounding polygamy, would have signaled an end to the path development in Austrian religious policy. From the perspective of political opportunity structures, it can therefore be argued that the cultural diplomacy dimension of the Islam Act was an important opportunity that led to the de facto full recognition of Islam in the Second Republic. We can further conclude that it was not until the Second Republic that Islam was institutionalized in any depth. Austrian religious legal tradition achieved its full effect only after 1979, which brings us back to historical institutionalism.

While the legal framework of state-church relations explains the form of how Islam was legally recognized, it does not explain why the institutionalization of Islam took as long as it did. While the Islam Act of 1912 had bestowed a form of legal acknowledgment, a religious institution representing Islam never materialized at that time. Although the number of Muslims in Austria grew after the Second World War due to immigration, it took them more than a decade to establish an institutionalized community based on the precepts of the Islam Act of 1912.

When we talk of an opportunity structure, we also need to consider the bigger picture beyond foreign and economic policy. Bruno Kreisky's opening of Austria to the Arab world created a favorable environment in which such institutional development could take place and in which a more politically tolerant attitude toward "Islam" was possible. Domestically, Austria in the 1970s was gripped by ambitious political reforms that modernized everything from traditional gender roles to patriarchal legal structures, the education system, and the welfare state. In this spirit of change and societal liberalization, acceptance of religious ideas and cultural norms that were unfamiliar to the majority of Austrian society became possible, as religion was part of a range of established ideas and institutions undergoing reform. Politically, the 1960s arrived in Austria later than elsewhere, so the county's domestic political modernization and secularization in the 1970s formed an important corollary to Austria's shifts in external relations. Moreover, as a secular and at one point even atheist political party, the Social Democrats were not wedded to particular religious traditions and were clearly more open to the idea of community-based religious self-regulation. Social Democratic voters were least likely to perceive Islam through the prism of traditional Catholicism, which mitigated the risk of a voter backlash for the SPÖ. Moreover, the issue of Islam had an overall low salience and was not at the forefront of strategies employed by the opposition until much later.

## "TOLERANT" ISLAM POLICY: ONGOING INSTITUTIONALIZATION

Austrian religious law does provide that all churches and religious societies are treated equally. Yet, the Catholic Church, with the new Concordat signed after the end of World War II, as well as other historically stronger churches and religious communities still enjoy certain advantages over others (Kalb, Potz, and Schinkele 2003, 446–540). Nevertheless, the recognition of the IGGÖ has allowed it to become deeply institutionalized in particular policy areas.

Recognition under public law implies that the state presents an "offer for cooperation, for coordination in partnership" (Potz 2007, 170). From the state's point of view, this is a matter of not only "ecclesiastical" but also "public tasks," such as education, child-rearing, charitable work, and the like. Matters of the federal government are, for example, religious education in general, state assistance in collecting church taxes, making apportionments, protecting church officials, and organizing military and prison chaplaincy (Heine, Lohlker, and Potz 2012, 103–122). For example, the IGGÖ has offered denominational religious education in the schools since 1982. In 2021, according to the IGGÖ, there were approximately 60,000 students taught by 430 teachers. The IGGÖ fielded thirteen school inspectors responsible for supervising Islamic religious education (School Authority IGGÖ, personal communication with Farid Hafez, 3 June 2015). The IGGÖ also runs private Islamic schools, for which it receives state subsidies on favorable terms. The training of teachers of religion is also carried out within the framework of a privately operated study program for training educational professionals in Islamic religion at compulsory schools, which was founded in 1998 and is also funded by the state (Heine, Lohlker, and Potz 2012, 103–112; Shakir 2019, 191–198).

Anas Schakfeh revealed in an interview with Farid Hafez that the application to establish this teaching institution was approved by the government within two weeks and thus in an extremely expedited manner (7 July 2011). In pastoral care in the military and in prisons, by contrast, this took much longer. In those cases, there were often only informal or contractual agreements between the IGGÖ and the relevant ministries so that rites such as Friday prayers and holidays could be observed by inmates, ritually pure (halal) food would be provided, and certain related expenses would be covered (Heine, Lohlker, and Potz 2012, 111–120).

In addition, the IGGÖ, like other legally recognized churches and religious societies, has the right to offer expert opinions, which arises from article 14 of the Protestant Act, based on the principle of parity. Accordingly, the IGGÖ also has the right to review legislative initiatives that affect its interests. Conversely, federal authorities must consult in advance with the IGGÖ on new draft legislation that affects the religious society and its external relations (Kalb, Potz, and Schinkele 2003, 178). This became significant, for example, in the case of the Animal Protection Act over the issue of animal slaughter (Potz, Schinkele, and Wieshaider 2001). In addition, the IGGÖ was invited to the Austria Convention (on constitutional and state reform) together with other—at that time, twelve—recognized churches and religious societies (Parlament Österreich 2003). In this sense, the IGGÖ functioned as a religious interest group and, more broadly, was part of Austrian corporatism and consociationalism.

The official acceptance of the IGGÖ is also of symbolic importance in a culturalist way, as it challenges and shapes the perception of the Islamic community by Austrian political elites, as the following account indicates (Sturm 2004, 303, 311). In a private letter to the feminist journalist Elfriede Hammerl, who had previously criticized the hijab as an oppressive practice for women, the then second president of the Austrian Parliament and later federal president Heinz Fischer (2003) stated:

> Recently we held a hearing of representatives of religious communities for the Austrian Constitutional Convention in the National Council meeting room and the representative of the Muslim community was a woman . . . and I was actually quite proud of this sight and thought to myself, it is nice that Austria is a country where a woman with the headscarf (as an identification of her religious affiliation) can even sit in the National Council meeting room undisturbed and without anyone taking offense. (Fischer, quoted in Gresch and Hadj-Abdou 2009, 78)

This example shows not least how much the recognition and institutionalization of Islam on the part of government representatives is interpreted in terms of a political culture of inclusion. Recognition of the IGGÖ not only confers rights, it also entails protection. For example, Austria stands for a "tolerant" hijab policy. A reverse example may be instructive here: in 1995, when the first president of the IGGÖ demanded that headscarves be worn in denominational Islamic religious education, the Social Democrats publicly opposed this move. In turn, the minister of education, Erhard Busek (ÖVP), backed the president of the IGGÖ and countered the critics:

> He has drawn attention to a provision of the Koran and to the custom that is customary in his faith community and has urged his religious teachers to insist on this during religious instruction. This has nothing at all to do with the curriculum. It's not a decree, it's not a regulation. Therefore, nothing can be taken back. If you always talk about the multicultural society, and that's what the critics who are now criticizing this order by the President of the Islamic Religious Association are doing, you have to accept everything. Even the way someone dresses according to his religion. This has nothing at all to do with a discussion of feminism. (Busek, quoted in Hafez 2012a, 71)

Here, the minister of education refers to a central principle resulting from legal recognition: internal autonomy. Once a church or religious society is recognized as such, its internal autonomy allows it to define what constitutes its religion and what does not (article 15 StGG). With this form of institutionalization, Muslims are not subject to any external determination but are empowered to determine the content of their religion. In contrast to several federal states in Germany, where bans on wearing a headscarf were introduced in the 2000s on the basis that it was a political symbol and not a religious requirement, in Austria a ban by a state parliament would only be possible with an expert opinion from a recognized Islamic religious society. This is in line with Austria's corporatist political model, in which interest groups are autonomous up to a point in matters in which they are involved in decisions that affect them. In this respect, the IGGÖ can be described as a (religious) interest group representing Muslims.

Unlike in other countries, there were no hijab-related public debates in Austria until 2017 (Gresch and Hadj-Abdou 2009). There have been disputes in the classroom when school administrators spoke out against wearing the hijab, but there was also a corresponding intervention by the state in those instances. In 2004, for example, a decree was published by the Ministry of Education that established the right to wear the hijab on the basis of the free exercise of religion (BMBWK 2004). This was drafted in consultation with the IGGÖ (Anas Schakfeh, interview with Farid Hafez, 7 July 2011). In summary, this results in a "nuanced" understanding of the term "tolerant" as applied to Islam policy. On the one hand, there is a recognized Islamic religious society with its rights, powers (e.g., religious instruction in public schools), and freedoms, such as self-determination.

On the other hand, it does not have equal rights in comparison with other religious actors in various policy areas, as the matter of pastoral care shows. "Tolerance" is thus an expression of power asymmetry in the relationship between the state and churches and religious societies.

## POLITICAL OPPORTUNITY STRUCTURES: THE LOW SALIENCE OF ISLAM

With the "Islamic Revolution" in Iran in 1979, the issue of Islam became more relevant again in German-language political discourse (K. Hafez 2002a, 2002b). At the party-political level, however, this hardly played a role in Austrian domestic politics. In general, the literature notes that populist radical right parties such as the FPÖ had started to mobilize voters through racist election campaigns since at least the late 1980s, calling for policies aimed at the exclusion and discrimination of ethnic minorities (Geden 2005, 11–13). However, while other far-right parties in Europe had already discovered the issue of Islam as especially suitable to achieving these ends in the 1980s and 1990s (Skenderovic 2006, 90–91), the FPÖ did not fully embrace it until after 9/11. This does not mean that the FPÖ was not tempted. In his book *Die Freiheit, die ich meine* (*The Freedom I Mean*), Jörg Haider stated that the "social order of Islam . . . is opposed to our Western values" (Haider 1993, 93). Nonetheless, the low salience of the issue seemed to have prevented the FPÖ from taking up the Islam issue as an agenda for mobilization. Matters that garner little public attention in the electorate are less suited for mobilization (Wlezien 2005), thus the FPÖ seemed motivated to focus more on the "ethnic other" and the competitor for jobs than on the "religious other."

Moreover, as Wlezien points out, the salience of an issue does not mean that it is perceived as a problem and that political action is necessary to overcome it (for a more detailed discussion on salience, see Bromley-Trujillo and Poe 2020). As several studies have shown, political elites respond to the importance of issues based on whether they are brought into play by the media or identified based on surveys and popular opinion. The key fact here is that the FPÖ initially did not frame the issue as being about Muslims but rather about unwanted laborers who took jobs away from native Austrians. As a result, Austrian policymakers had to respond not to an alleged religious and cultural threat but rather to a labor market issue, which extended beyond Muslims. This, in turn, allowed Austrian governments to continue a "tolerant" Islam policy that closely follows the institutionalist path-dependent trajectory, even as the governments started taking a harder line on immigration.

Even 9/11, which would have allowed political actors to defect from this established trajectory and entertain a policy shift, did not lead to a change in political attitudes toward Islam among Austrian political elites. Although the

FPÖ joined the ÖVP in government in 2000, this did not have a significant influence on how Islam was debated in public circles. Although the FPÖ initially tried to take political advantage of the controversial nature of the Islam issue, which was a consequence of the media coverage of 9/11, the Conservative coalition partner rejected the attempt at marginalizing Muslims in Austria. This was borne out in 2003 when a Freedom Party MP, Helene Partik-Pablé, called for a ban on hijabs after a similar ban had been introduced in various institutional contexts in Germany and France. Yet, as we already mentioned earlier, the response of then chancellor Wolfgang Schüssel (ÖVP) was unequivocal: "We do not have to import every discussion from Germany" (*Profil* 2003). The fact that the FPÖ, as part of the Austrian government, was boycotted until September 2000 by the governments of the other fourteen EU member countries may have prompted the ÖVP to take the least racist and cultural myopic position possible. Indeed, the first FPÖ-ÖVP government was under such political scrutiny internationally that the federal president at the time, Thomas Klestil, felt compelled to insist that the government adopt a preamble to its program that contained an explicit commitment to fighting xenophobia, anti-Semitism, and racism (Fallend 2012, 122).

Initially, the government did not want to give international observers any reason for concern. Later, when the shock of the FPÖ in government had worn off, the Freedom Party was increasingly weakened by internal conflict. Its leadership faced a grassroots revolt, which led to new elections in 2002. In these, the FPÖ lost nearly two-thirds of its electorate and was subsequently forced to rejoin the coalition with the Conservatives as a much-diminished partner (Fallend 2012, 114). As a result, the FPÖ's influence on migration policy was generally not very strong and the extremism of the party base had little impact on government policy (Heinisch 2003, 106; 2008, 50f.; Fallend 2012, 134f.). This is consistent with findings in other European countries where far-right parties in office have had difficulty adapting to their new roles (Akkerman 2012; Heinisch 2003), although the opposite is also possible (Albertazzi and McDonnell 2010). The president of the IGGÖ who was in office between 1997 and 2011 even called the governments under Wolfgang Schüssel "the golden era of the Islamic Religious Association" (Anas Schakfeh, interview with Farid Hafez, 13 July 2011). The Norwegian Islamic scholar Jørgen Nielsen still remembers Schakfeh saying, at the presentation of a report on Islamophobia that he co-authored with the European Monitoring Centre on Racism and Xenophobia (now the Fundamental Rights Agency) (Allen and Nielsen 2002; EUMC 2006), "I do not recognize this term. I don't see myself in the victim role" (Jørgen Nielsen, interview with Farid Hafez, June 2012). This can be explained by the not insignificant involvement of the IGGÖ in the political system. While elsewhere in Europe, especially after 9/11 and after the 7/7 attacks in London in 2005, there were complaints about attacks on Muslims and a tightening of political conditions, the Austrian Islamic representative body saw itself in good shape.

One could even say that due to the attack on the World Trade Center in 2001, an institutionalized form of Islam was presented by the political elites as a necessary ally against terror and radicalization. For example, the anthropologist Maja Sticker points out that even after the inclusion of the Haider-FPÖ in government, the "special model Austria," which was also praised by Austrian officials as a "showcase model" and as an "export model," can be seen as an attempt to present Austria positively, as an open rather than racist country (Sticker 2008, 160). After the attacks on the Twin Towers, Klestil invited religious leaders to a meeting in the Vienna Hofburg under the banner of "Interreligious Commemoration." To send a signal of unity and dialogue, representatives of the IGGÖ were invited and the meeting was broadcast live by Austrian state television. Shortly thereafter, Schüssel and Foreign Minister Benita Ferrero-Waldner (ÖVP) invited representatives of the IGGÖ and the Jewish Community (IKG) to a meeting to issue a joint statement against the interpretation of the Israeli-Palestinian conflict as being a conflict between Muslims and Jews (Hafez 2012a, 102ff.). In 2003, the Foreign Ministry, together with the IGGÖ, convened the first European Imam Conference, where representatives of Islam from all over Europe met to position themselves on European values and against terror. The "special model of Austria," it seemed, was to be presented as an idea to be exported by the Austrian ÖVP-FPÖ government.

In contrast to the far-right populists, who mobilized against Islam as the new enemy, the political elite at that time saw Islam as part of the narrative of Austrian identity. The growing rejection of Islam was regarded by the political elite as an opportunity to present a "tolerant" Islam policy as an antidote to "extremism." For example, the former federal president Thomas Klestil said on the occasion of the second Islamic book fair on the OPEC premises in Vienna in 2002: "Austria is not only proud to be the permanent host of OPEC, but also to have special relations with the Arab region and Islamic culture. This is probably historically related to the fact that the great Danube monarchy formed a geographical bridge to the Eastern Mediterranean and the Middle East" (Klestil 2005, 345).

In this narrative, Austria is imagined as a unifying place that still echoes the multiconfessional and multinational character of the past empire. In connection with the legal recognition of Islam, the "special Austrian model" is praised for setting an example for other nations in Europe. This view was presented by both state officials and Muslim representatives (Sticker 2008; Hafez 2014b). Until 2006, for example, even the Conservatives were still claiming that Islam was part of Austrian society. This can be gleaned from a quote by the then president of the Austrian Parliament, Andreas Khol. At the opening of the second European Imam Conference in Vienna, to which the IGGÖ, among others, were invited, he said, "Austria knows no clash of civilizations. . . . Our Muslim citizens are an important part of our society. . . . Let us continue the good Austrian tradition of peaceful coexistence of different cultures and religions. Austria is a model for many states in this respect—we can be proud of that" (Khol 2006).

It was only then when the FPÖ went into opposition after the party underwent a split that the populist radical right drastically changed its rhetoric on Islam. This allowed the FPÖ under new leadership to boost its credentials with its voter base following its exodus from the government. From then on, it was locked in an intense battle for leadership of the radical right with the more economically liberal BZÖ, which had broken away from the Freedom Party and remained in government. The rump FPÖ embarked on a voter-seeking strategy, moved sharply to the right, and embraced extremely polarizing and radical rhetoric on Islam. As a result, anti-Islamic mobilization became increasingly acceptable in the party-political discourse, but it was pushed chiefly by the new FPÖ leader Heinz Christian Strache (Hafez 2010b). This set a dynamic process in motion whereby Islamophobic ideas and images began to infiltrate the discourses of other parties. It is important to note, however, that until 2005, the government was able to pursue a "tolerant" Islam policy due to the FPÖ's inattention to the issue of Islam. This was largely a consequence of favorable political opportunity structures. Even after 9/11, political elites saw Islam politics as a means to position Austria internationally as a tolerant and open society that had nothing in common with the frequent portrayals of Austria, especially in Anglo-American media, depicting the country as still haunted by the long shadow of Nazism.

## PARTY COMPETITION IN AUSTRIA AND THE ROLE OF RELIGION

In 1970, the emergence of a new middle-class society changed Austrian party politics. The rise of multiculturalism, neoliberalism, and environmentalism on the one hand, and of radical right nativist and nationalist ideas on the other, broadened political contestation and infused a new dynamic beyond the classical socioeconomic left-right axis (Heinisch and Werner 2021). The political competition centered increasingly also on sociocultural and postmaterialist ideas, such as environmental protection and cultural diversity.

As political contestation shifted away from economics, new political actors placed a growing emphasis on identity and tradition. The radical right was poised to occupy the illiberal end of the sociocultural spectrum by exploiting and stoking concerns that Austrian identity and traditions were now under threat from "foreign" influences. Political contestation over sociocultural issues created new space for the politicization of religion, especially in the case of Islam. While these developments were also occurring in other Western democracies (Inglehart 1997), Austria is distinctive in that this development emerged later and at a time when the avowedly secular Social Democratic Party was politically dominant.

Before the 2000 election, the SPÖ had achieved three absolute majorities in succession (1971, 1975, and 1979) and majorities on seven more occasions (1970, 1983, 1986, 1990, 1994, 1995, 1999). All except the 1999 elections left the SPÖ in control of the coveted chancellorship.

As already mentioned, Austrian society had long been divided between a Catholic milieu and a secular, socialist milieu. Conflict and contestation between these two camps, as well as some degree of cooperation, were for decades the principal determinants of Austrian politics, leaving little space for third parties and their issues. Only with the growth of the new middle class in the late 1960s and 1970s did Austrian politics begin to change. As certain voter segments gravitated toward the liberal and cosmopolitan part of the emerging new political spectrum, the radical right was poised to occupy the illiberal and socioculturally right-wing political space by exploiting and stoking concerns that Austrian identity and traditions were now under threat from foreign influences. Political contestation over sociocultural issues created a new space for the politicization of religion, especially Islam.

The Austrian Social Democrats thus avoided the fate of their sister parties elsewhere when political power shifted to the right in much of Western Europe in a rising tide of neoliberalism and neoconservatism in the 1980s and 1990s. Nonetheless, the power of the SPÖ, and indeed of both mainstream parties, was increasingly undercut by massive voter defections beginning in the 1980s. Thus, despite the late arrival of postmaterialist political contestation in Austria, the initially delayed effects were subsequently felt dramatically when the two major parties, SPÖ and ÖVP, lost nearly half of their voters between 1986 and 2000. This period saw a series of electoral successes by the FPÖ, which increased its support from 4.9 percent of the votes in 1983 to 26.9 percent in 1999. In the process, the FPÖ established itself as the third major force, nearly equal to the two mainstream parties in terms of electoral success. While the FPÖ made increasing inroads into the SPÖ's blue-collar supporters, eventually becoming the dominant blue-collar party, the leftist environmentalist Greens began siphoning off other parts of the Social Democratic electorate, leaving the SPÖ weakened among young and urban voters.

These developments created conditions in which religion became an issue of concern, either positively or negatively, primarily for the right. With its Marxist roots and a strong commitment to enlightenment, the SPÖ had a highly secular tradition, strengthened by its historical contestation with political Catholicism as embodied by the ÖVP and its predecessors. Thus, from the Social Democratic perspective, religion was seen as, at best, a cultural holdover from premodern times—something to be ignored or, ideally, to be overcome entirely (Walter 1999). The emancipation of women and the destruction of patriarchal structures of exploitation both in the family and in society required the rollback of religion, and the hope was that contemporary education and the modern welfare state would be vehicles through which religion would be rendered largely obsolete and irrelevant. Promoting female participation in the workforce and providing women with economic independence were important political goals.

The Greens, in comparison, shared similar convictions but were less focused on economic questions and more on individual emancipation and self-realization. Their supporters were relatively more likely to be female, middle-class, and better educated, which meant that the Greens and their voters were more favorably disposed toward multiculturalism and thus naturally more skeptical of Austrian traditionalism, including political Catholicism. The Greens also shared a universalist understanding of people and cultures as being fundamentally equal and thus regarded immigration as in many ways a vehicle for cultural enrichment of society rather than a threat.

The SPÖ shared this commitment to internationalism and universalism, emphasizing the fundamental equality of all people and, implicitly, all cultures. As a result, both parties had no problem in principle with Muslim immigration from a cultural and ethnic standpoint, and they repeatedly called for religious tolerance, although their secular orientation meant they were never explicit advocates of Muslim religious and cultural demands. However, egged on by their labor wing and in response to the party's unrelenting loss of blue-collar voters to the populist radical right, the Social Democrats continually changed their platform to become more restrictive on immigration. While this especially affected Muslim immigrants from Turkey and later, Bosnians fleeing the war in Yugoslavia, religion remained largely a nonissue for the SPÖ. This eventually allowed the ÖVP, the coalition partner of the Social Democrats for most of these years, to appropriate the issue of religion.

Competing with the FPÖ on the sociocultural dimension after the Freedom Party had changed its platform in favor of identity politics, the ÖVP began reacting to the perceived growing cultural influence of Muslims on Austrian society. The fear was that Catholicism and Austrian Catholic culture were under siege on two fronts, by secularism and Islam. Yet, it was the Freedom Party that set the agenda on immigration and religion and had the most consistent policy approach. The Social Democrats opposed intolerance but also wanted to restrict immigration. Whereas the business wing of the Conservatives favored labor immigration, the party's cultural traditionalists opposed it if it came from non-Christian and non-European societies because such migrants would have difficulties "integrating"—a term denoting Muslim and non-European immigration in particular. The Greens, meanwhile, were committed to multiculturalism but were not especially sympathetic to religious ideas and practices that seemed suspect from an "enlightened" perspective. In short, the Muslim community had no real political advocates, even before the discourses on terrorism and securitization after 9/11 and the large influx of refugees that followed from the wars in Syria in 2015.

## CHALLENGING THE CONSENSUS: THE FPÖ

The political party most opposed to Islam in Austria today is the Freedom Party. Descended from both liberal and nationalist currents of the nineteenth century that favored a politically and culturally unified Germany, the Freedom Party was founded in 1956 and attracted many former Nazi sympathizers. From the start, the FPÖ vehemently opposed the political hegemony of both the Social Democrats and the Conservatives. For many years, the Freedom Party remained a marginal opposition party shut out from the levers of power at the federal and state levels. As already mentioned, the FPÖ was historically rather anticlerical and particularly anti-Catholic and certainly never regarded itself as a defender of Christian or Catholic traditions. This stance on religion remained essentially consistent until 1986, when Jörg Haider took over the leadership of the party (Heinisch 2002).

The FPÖ formed a coalition with the Social Democrats in 1983, after the latter party's three successive terms of absolute majorities in Parliament had come to an end. The FPÖ's inexperience in government and its subordinate role as the junior coalition partner threw the Freedom Party into turmoil. In particular, a long-simmering conflict between the party's far-right nationalist wing and the more moderate liberal faction now intensified. This situation came to a head when the young and charismatic leader of a regional party faction, Jörg Haider, deposed the liberal party leader Norbert Steger in 1986. When the Social Democrats terminated the coalition, Haider transformed the FPÖ from a libertarian-nationalist formation into a populist radical right protest party (Hauser and Heinisch 2016, 4). As a result, the party shifted its electoral focus and support base away from both libertarians and anti-Catholic German nationalists—a group typically comprising small business owners, professionals, and civil servants in more rural regions—to urban and blue-collar voters (McGann and Kitschelt 2005).

As a consequence, the "new" FPÖ increased its electoral share from 9.7 percent in 1986 to 26.9 percent by 1999 (as shown in table 2.1) and its number of seats in Parliament grew from five to fifty-two. By the end of the 1990s, the Freedom Party had also greatly expanded its power at regional and local levels, emerging as the second biggest party in five of Austria's nine provinces (including Vienna) and the dominant party in one province. It had achieved this success by adopting a programmatic mix of Austrian cultural parochialism, welfare chauvinism, and anti-internationalism, as well as by expanding into areas where it had hitherto been weak, such as industrial centers and rural Catholic areas (Heinisch 2002; see also Luther 2008). The FPÖ gained international notoriety by engaging in xenophobic and identity-oriented rhetoric, launching an antiforeigner referendum drive and introducing racist terminology such as *Überfremdung* ("over-foreignization" of the Austrian people) into public discourse in state, national, and European elections from the early 1990s onward (Heinisch 2002).

TABLE 2.1    Elections to the National Parliament (Lower House)

| Year of election[b] | Greens | Social Democrats (SPÖ) | People's Party (ÖVP) | Freedom Party (FPÖ) | Alliance (BZÖ) | Team Stronach | Liberals/ NEOS |
|---|---|---|---|---|---|---|---|
| | | | Political parties[a] | | | | |
| 1983 | — | 47.7 | 43.2 | 5.0 | — | — | — |
| 1986 | 4.8 | 43.1 | 41.3 | 9.7 | — | — | — |
| 1990 | 4.8 | 42.8 | 32.1 | 16.1 | — | — | — |
| 1994 | 7.3 | 34.9 | 27.7 | 22.5 | — | — | 6.0 |
| 1995 | 4.8 | 38.1 | 28.3 | 21.9 | — | — | 5.5 |
| 1999 | 7.4 | 33.2 | 26.9 | 26.9 | — | — | — |
| 2002 | 9.5 | 36.5 | 42.3 | 10.0[c] | — | — | — |
| 2006 | 11.1 | 35.3 | 34.3 | 11.0 | 4.1 | — | — |
| 2008 | 10.4 | 29.3 | 26.0 | 17.5 | 10.7 | — | — |
| 2013 | 12.4 | 26.8 | 24.0 | 20.5 | — | 5.7 | 5.0 |
| 2017 | 3.8 | 26.8 | 31.4 | 25.9 | — | — | 5.3 |

SOURCES: BMI (Bundesministerium Inneres) n.d. "National Council Elections," Federal Ministry of the Interior, https://www.bmi.gv.at/412/Nationalratswahlen/.
[a] Cells in gray indicate the parties that formed governments after the respective elections.
[b] Legislative and government periods do not always correspond exactly. Most new governments take office at the beginning of the following year (e.g., in 1987, 1996, 2000, 2003, and 2007).
[c] The second ÖVP–FPÖ cabinet lasted only until April 2005, when the BZÖ formally replaced the FPÖ as the ÖVP's coalition partner without new elections being called.

The Freedom Party subsequently moved closer to conservative groups in the Catholic Church (Hauser and Heinisch 2016) and began advocating a social policy agenda centered on motherhood and the traditional family that was popular among religious Conservatives in the ÖVP (Heinisch 2002). Increasingly, the FPÖ described itself as a defender of the Christian "Occident" by depicting Islam as a cultural threat. In a radical departure from its long-standing anticlerical tradition, the new Freedom Party program of 1997 (FPÖ 2005) devoted extensive attention to Christianity as the "foundation of Europe" and the traditions of the *Abendland* (Christian civilization), which required a "Christianity that defends its values" (*wehrhaftes Christentum*).[3]

Following the national elections of 1999, the Conservatives and the Freedom Party seemed to be in a position to form a coalition (Heinisch 2002). However, the switch to the unfamiliar role of governing party proved a political fiasco for the FPÖ (Luther 2003). Following massive losses in the national elections in 2002, the party renewed its coalition with the Conservatives, only to fall apart in 2005 when Haider led a group of relative moderates out of the party to continue the coalition with the ÖVP under a new guise as the BZÖ. While the FPÖ was in government, it faced intense international and national scrutiny and thus had to present itself as a responsible actor. As a consequence, its radicalism on display during the 1990s was toned down. Also, whereas the FPÖ had made Islam and the defense of European Christian culture an issue, other topics such as immigration, EU membership, and public corruption were far more salient. Moreover, since 9/11 occurred during the period when the FPÖ was in government and thus under scrutiny, it was reluctant to exploit the issue as it might have done in opposition.

It was only after the party reconstituted itself under the leadership of Heinz-Christian Strache as a populist radical right opposition party that it markedly radicalized once again. Fearing an existential threat and facing dramatic losses according to the polls, the FPÖ wanted to rebuild its hardcore base by projecting sharply polarizing messages and pushing identity politics in ways that had not been possible while the party was serving in government (Hauser and Heinisch 2016).

The 2006 parliamentary elections were the first in which Haider's BZÖ and the "new" FPÖ led by Strache competed directly against each other. Both groups fought hard to appeal to voters concerned about immigration and European integration (Hafez 2010a). Both the BZÖ and the FPÖ were claiming to be the "real deal." Thus, Strache wanted to position his party as the most far-right and antiestablishment in the Austrian political landscape. The BZÖ was less effective in this respect, as Haider tried to position himself as committed to combining a culturally right-wing agenda with responsible government politics. As a politician who wanted to protect Austria from Islam, he also faced various structural challenges. Haider was a provincial governor in his home province and a member of a coalition government, which imposed political limits on how far he could go in competing with an unhinged FPÖ in radical opposition mode. Unable to outdo the FPÖ in terms of cultural radicalism, the BZÖ began focusing more on market liberalism. In consequence, the Freedom Party emerged as the principal advocate of cultural identity politics. This in turn forced the ÖVP to respond, since it no longer had an exclusive lock on conservative and religious voters concerned about multiculturalism and Islam.

The FPÖ was also in the best position to take ownership of the immigration issue and, by extension, opposition to Turkish accession to the EU. This meant that the FPÖ focused almost exclusively on patriotism, defending Austrian culture and tradition, security, and welfare (taking the position that immigrants should be denied social benefits). Seeing this strategy prove successful after gaining votes and momentum in the 2008 national elections, the FPÖ continued its radical sociocultural message to boost its support in two state elections (Luther 2008). In the state of Styria, the party demanded a ban on the construction of mosques and minarets, while in Vienna the FPÖ ran on an anti-immigration and anti-Muslim platform, reminding voters of the Ottoman siege of Vienna. There, it more than doubled its vote share, from 10.9 percent to 25.8 percent (Jenny 2011), suggesting that this was a key issue for the electoral success. Examples of major FPÖ campaign slogans at the time include "Vienna must not become Istanbul" (Viennese elections 2005); "No home for Islam" (national parliamentary elections 2006); "No home for radical Islam" (Graz local elections 2008); and "The sound of church bells instead of muezzin call" (Tyrol regional elections 2008) (Hafez 2009a).

In terms of party competition after the elections of 2006, the center-right ÖVP entered once again into a coalition with the center-left SPÖ. This meant that the Conservatives were facing the challenge of needing to distinguish themselves from their Social Democratic senior coalition partner. Not only was it harder for the ÖVP as the lesser partner to communicate political successes of the coalition to the voters, since the SPÖ held the chancellorship, but the Conservatives shared equally in the blame when it came to unpopular policies. Moreover, the context of the global financial crisis and the crisis of the European currency required joint economic management of Austria's economic affairs. This constrained any opportunity the Conservatives may have had to show off a socioeconomic policy profile that was markedly distinct from that of the Social Democrats. The shoring up of the Austrian banking system, massive investments in job-protection programs, and opposition to more generous bailout conditions for crisis-prone EU member states such as Greece were supported by the SPÖ and the ÖVP alike and thus hardly a way of underscoring a Conservative political profile.

Its role in a coalition government constrained the ÖVP from moving further to the right on most issues precisely at a time when it was facing a persistent challenge from the populist radical right in the form of the FPÖ and the BZÖ. Taking up the Islam issue fairly publicly and stridently allowed the Conservatives to raise their profile vis-à-vis their unloved coalition partner in an area that was not of core interest to the Social Democrats, while appealing to a wider cross section of voters on the right. Unlike other social issues that were dear and near to the left, Islam and religion was not an issue over which the SPÖ would escalate a political conflict. In fact, the ÖVP could count on the eventual acquiescence of the SPÖ, given the latter's relative disinterest in all matters of religion.

In 2006 the ÖVP-dominated Ministry of the Interior published a study on the basis of which the Conservative interior minister Liese Prokop argued that 45 percent of all Austrian Muslims were "opposed to integration." Later in 2008, the ÖVP, which was in coalition with the FPÖ at the provincial level in Vorarlberg, implemented a ban in that locality on the construction of mosques and minarets. In 2009 the state of Carinthia, which at the time was governed by the BZÖ in coalition with the ÖVP, followed suit (Hafez 2010a). These developments were preceded by a shift in the public debate on Islam and represented the first time that concrete policy changes toward the Muslim minority population manifested themselves. Taking advantage of the political space that had opened up, the Conservatives were in a position to take the lead in this issue area by appropriating an agenda that the populist radical right had introduced.

In response, the Social Democrats maintained an ambivalent position, struggling to reconcile their tradition of secularism and distance from all things religious with their stance on cosmopolitanism and sociocultural tolerance. Unable to overcome this dilemma and recognizing the potentially divisive nature of the Islam issue, party members watched as the issue increasingly pitted secularists against multiculturalists and specifically the Vienna branch of the party against more conservative party factions in the provinces. As a result, the SPÖ resorted to a strategy that political scientists call "blurring" (Rovny 2013). The situation was made even more acute by the fact that the SPÖ had been hemorrhaging blue-collar voters to the FPÖ. As a result, defending the Islamic community or openly advocating the acceptance of Islam in Austria were not seen as winning strategies by the Social Democrats, and the party thus refrained from forcefully countering populist messages.

Within the government coalition, the Conservatives took control of this issue. As a co-governing party with the Social Democrats from 2007 to 2017, they were able to implement several of their policy demands and thus had an advantage over the FPÖ, which was in opposition and could do little more than "talk" about issues. As such, the ÖVP under the influence of its later chancellor, Sebastian Kurz, became the primary driving force behind the creation and implementation of acts such as the Burqa Ban Act in 2017 and the Islam Act of 2015, which were widely seen as discriminatory toward Muslims.

The combination of factors discussed in this chapter explain the continuation of "tolerant" Islam policies by governments even between 11 September 2001 and 2005, when Austria had a right-wing government, as well as the later policy changes. In the next chapters, we will discuss changes in four different areas: the elite discourse on Islam, the legal status of Islam, the regulation of the Muslim headscarf, and the state's security politics.

The Islam Act and Austrian corporatism in managing societal cleavages had created a path-dependent institutional trajectory that facilitated tolerant Islam politics, which was fully realized in 1979 as a consequence of political actors availing themselves of a favorable opportunity structure. As mentioned above, a reform-minded Social Democratic government and Chancellor Kreisky, who had won an absolute majority in the 1971, 1975, and 1979 elections, pursued a deliberate policy of rapprochement with the Arab world. They most likely cared little personally about religious particularities, but they provided the context within which the political actors of the Muslim community and government officials could successfully push for institutionalization.

# 3 · THE DISCOURSE ABOUT ISLAM

As mentioned in chapter 1, Islamophobia was not even an issue in Austrian political discourse after the September 11 attacks. It was only when the populist radical right Freedom Party discovered Islam as a salient topic that political parties chose to react to the increasing anti-Muslim mobilization by the far right. After 2000, sociocultural and postmaterialist ideas increasingly became a defining cleavage in party competition. This opened up space for the politicization of religion, especially with regard to the role of Muslims as members of a religious minority. In this way, the situation in Austria mirrored developments that were happening on a global scale (Bail 2014).

The SPÖ, with its Marxist roots, had a strongly secular tradition, reinforced by its historical confrontation with political Catholicism, as embodied by the ÖVP and its predecessors. For the SPÖ, religion was at best a cultural relic of premodern times—something to be ignored or, ideally, overcome altogether. While it advocated for a multicultural society to some degree, religion was still largely seen as an obstacle to enlightenment and societal progress. The second party on the left of the political spectrum, the Greens, more explicitly endorsed the idea of multiculturalism by regarding the immigration of refugees as a basic human right and framing the influx of migrants as cultural enrichment of society. Both the SPÖ and the Greens advocated internationalism and universalism by emphasizing the fundamental equality of all people and, implicitly, of all cultures. Consequently, both parties had no fundamental problem with the immigration of people of different cultural and ethnic origins and repeatedly called for religious tolerance, though their secular orientation meant that they never advocated explicitly on behalf on the religious and cultural demands of Muslims.

In contrast, the populist radical right FPÖ, which had increasingly made inroads into the working-class base of the SPÖ, took the view that foreigners and specifically Muslims represented a cultural and social threat to Austria's national identity. The Conservative ÖVP was most affected by this discourse, since it saw Austrian Catholic identity threatened—first, by the secularism espoused by the leftist parties, and second, by an "otherized" culture and religion.

This was the context in which the governing parties portrayed Islam as an integral part of Austria, defending the privileged position of Muslims as a legally recognized religious community against calls for Islam to be regulated in a completely new way, unlike any other church or religious community before.

## THE GOOD AND LOYAL AUSTRO-BOSNIAN MUSLIM

Muslims have long been included in the national organizations of the Austrian political elite. Public discourse has historically been characterized by inclusion and recognition, reflecting the legal status of the Islamic Religious Society in Austria from 1912 to 2015, based on its earlier recognition during the Habsburg monarchy. Even after the collapse of the monarchy, the remaining, much smaller country of Austria continued this relatively tolerant attitude toward its tiny Muslim population of a few thousand people. As early as 1921, the newspaper *Neues Wiener Journal* celebrated the construction of a mosque in Vienna "as a visible sign of Austria's friendship with Turkey, which will have a powerful effect in the Muslim world far beyond Turkey" (Fürlinger 2013, 170). Similarly, Muslim Bosnia and Herzegovina was routinely portrayed as one of the areas in the Balkans most loyal to Austria. Bosnian soldiers serving in the Austro-Hungarian army were considered particularly brave.

Also later, as we have already described, good relations with Muslims and finally recognizing the Islamic Religious Society in 1979 was welcomed by Austrian elites as a soft-power tool for foreign policymaking (Hafez 2016). At the time, Austria enjoyed excellent relations with the Arab and Islamic world. Chancellor Bruno Kreisky was one of the West's foremost advocates of the Palestinian cause and had close contacts with controversial Arab leaders such as Yasser Arafat and Muammar Gaddafi. In the public discourse, this was seen as a sign of an independent foreign policy that was garnering global attention.

Despite lacking personal contact with Islam, most Austrians and especially the political elites considered neither the community of Muslims nor the religion as such in especially unfavorable terms.

The view that Austrian elites had a rather sympathetic attitude toward the presence of Islam in Austria was also widely shared by the leaders of the Muslim community themselves. Even after 9/11, representatives of the Islamic Religious Association, as well as those of the Foreign Ministry, praised the "Austrian model" of good relations between the state and Islam (Sticker 2008). During the first Austrian Imam Conference, the stalwart conservative president of the Austrian parliament, Andreas Kohl, praised the excellent relationship with the Muslim community and touted the virtues of the Austrian model as exemplary.

This position is exemplified by a commemoration of 100 years of the Islam Act of 1912 in 2012. The rich entangled history of Austria with the Ottomans and with Bosnia and Herzegovina allowed for a somewhat more complex image of the Muslim "Other." In contrast to the British and French Empires, whose scholars and literati are discussed in Edward Said's *Orientalism*, the Austro-Hungarian Empire, as one of the major players in World War I, had a much more diverse relationship with Muslim culture. Hence, the anthropologist Andre Gingrich adds to the enlightening work of Edward Said a specific characteristic that applied especially to Austria: the frontier dimension. This finally creates a dual image of the Muslim, the "Good and Bad Muslim Orientals: either the loyal ally or the dangerous enemy, on either side or the other side of a nearby frontier" (Gingrich 1998, 109), referring to the Muslim Bosnians within the territories of the monarchy and the Ottomans outside the borders.

The creation of the Islamic Law of 1912 is seen not only as the result of a process of pluralization of religious law in the monarchy, which it is in a sense, but as a comprehensive instrument of rule and power of the Habsburg monarchy. As such, it must also be seen in the context of the annexation of Bosnia and Herzegovina and the resulting military challenges, the existing nationalisms in the Balkans, and the political confrontation with the Ottoman Empire.

The incorporation of Bosnia and Herzegovina into the Austro-Hungarian Empire was thus part of great power politics. This process aimed at separating the Bosnian Muslims from the Ottoman Empire with the caliph as the symbolic head of the religious authority of the time. When Austria-Hungary began to occupy the lands of the Bosnians in 1878, which at that time were still part of the Ottoman Empire, the first reaction was for Bosnian troops to fight the invaders. After the annexation, a lively debate began among scholars about whether life under Austro-Hungarian rule was even legal under Islamic law. In fact, 150,000 Bosniaks fled to the heart of the Ottoman Empire (Karčić 1999, 109–118). Soon after, the mufti, who had previously been elected by the regional muftis from Bosnia and Herzegovina and appointed by the Shaikh al-Islam, was reinstated and appointed by the Austro-Hungarian state. The highest religious authority at this point was the *reis-ul-ulema* (president of the religious scholars), who was initially critical of the Monarchy (Hauptmann 1985, 686–690) but became an extension of the empire, serving it with loyal fatawa (118–123). Thus, Austria-Hungary managed to stabilize and extend its power to the religious sphere by constructing its own Austro-Hungarian Islam, cut off from the center of Muslim power. Bosnia and Herzegovina were formally annexed in 1908, when the Ottoman Empire was preoccupied with domestic issues (Vocelka 1993, 268–270). The annexation was consolidated by strengthening the loyalty of Muslim soldiers, who were deployed to counter the more nationalistically oriented Slavic population. Four years later, the Islam Act guaranteed Muslims living in the empire at that time the right to practice their religion privately and publicly. The

legal recognition of churches and religious communities was not only a legal recognition of de facto religious pluralism but also an attempt to control the religious communities and their leadership by including them in the state system;
this not only gave them rights, but also set limits (Vrankić 1998; Wandruszka
1985, xvf.).

Even after 9/11, the discourse of inclusion was taken up by Austria's political
elite. To this day, Austria is one of the very few countries to recognize the Muslim community as a religious community in the legal sense, and this provided
the political elite with a unique position to present itself as particularly tolerant
even after the al-Qaeda attack in 2001. When the then president of the Austrian
Parliament said, "Austria does not know a clash of civilizations. . . . Our Muslim
fellow citizens are an important part of our society," he referred to this legal position, which is unique in Western Europe. The legal recognition of Islam in Austria
is therefore often referred to as a symbol of Austrian openness and tolerance.
Moreover, it was used as a means of soft power, especially by representatives of
Austrian foreign policy, when Muslim delegates accompanied representatives
of the state to Muslim countries in order to gain their sympathy by pointing out
Austria's state relations with the Muslim community.

## WHEN THE FPÖ DISCOVERED ISLAM AS A SALIENT ISSUE

After the 1999 parliamentary elections, the Conservatives and the FPÖ were able
to form a coalition (Heinisch 2002). The change to the unfamiliar role of governing party proved to be a political disaster for the FPÖ (Luther 2003). After losing
many deputies in the provincial and national elections (2002), the party renewed
its coalition with the Conservatives, only to fall apart in 2005 , and was then
forced to compete with a populist radical right rival formation that had broken
away from the FPÖ. Meanwhile, the remaining FPÖ, led by Heinz-Christian
Strache, formed itself into a radical, far-right and populist opposition party. Fearing an existential threat and facing dramatic losses in the polls, the FPÖ had to
rebuild its core support base by spreading polarizing messages and pushing identity politics in a way that had not been possible during its time in government
(Hauser and Heinisch 2016).

The 2006 parliamentary elections were the first in which Haider's Bündnis
Zukunft Österreich (BZÖ, Alliance for the Future of Austria) and the "new"
FPÖ led by Strache competed directly against each other. As a result, the FPÖ
and BZÖ made intensive efforts to appeal to voters concerned about immigration and European integration (Hafez 2010a). As long as the FPÖ was in government as a minor coalition partner of the Conservative ÖVP, the FPÖ had no
reason to combine its anti-elite discourse with an Islamophobic ideology. This
changed, however, when the FPÖ was forced into opposition in 2005 and, faced

with an existential political crisis, had to turn to its radical political base to avoid going under. The breakaway of the BZÖ, led by the former FPÖ chairman and main political brain Haider, posed an unprecedented threat to the rest of the Freedom Party, as both Haider's BZÖ and the Strache-led FPÖ claimed to be the "true party." Given Haider's crucial role in engineering the Freedom Party's meteoric rise after 1986, Strache had to present himself as the true heir to Haider while also accusing the former leader of being a traitor as well as mentally unbalanced.

However, because it was no longer constrained by its role in government and had greater leeway to move further to the right, the rump FPÖ was better able to exploit popular grievances and thus tie down the traditional far-right grass-roots support of the "old" Freedom Party. Strache wanted to position his party as the most far-right, antiestablishment party in the Austrian political landscape at the time. The BZÖ was less successful in this regard. For one thing, it was composed of more moderate elected officials; for another, Haider himself was a provincial governor presiding over a coalition government in his home province. This placed natural limits on the extent to which he and his party could compete with the FPÖ by pandering to far-right voters. As the BZÖ began to focus more on market liberalism, the FPÖ was able to distinguish itself as the main proponent of cultural identity politics. This in turn forced the ÖVP to react, as it could no longer rely exclusively on conservative and religious voters who were concerned about multiculturalism and Islam. The FPÖ was in the best position to embrace the immigration issue and, by extension, opposition to Turkey's EU accession. This meant that the FPÖ focused almost exclusively on nationalism, defense of Austrian culture and tradition, security, and welfare (namely, that immigrants should be denied social benefits). The FPÖ saw its strategy vindicated after gaining votes and momentum in the 2008 parliamentary elections, and it continued its radical sociocultural message in two state elections (Luther 2008). The FPÖ succeeded both in Styria and in Vienna and more than doubled its electoral support. In the election campaigns, it called for a prohibition on the building of mosques and minarets, campaigned on an anti-immigration and anti-Muslim agenda, invoking memories of the Ottoman siege of Vienna.

Viewed from the point of competitive logic, the center-right Conservatives faced the challenge of differentiating themselves from their senior Social Democratic coalition partner after 2006. As the smaller partner, not only was it more difficult to communicate their political success to voters because their coalition partner held the chancellorship, but the Conservatives also shared the blame for unpopular policies the government had jointly adopted. Their role in this arrangement prevented the ÖVP from moving further to the right on most issues at the very time when it faced a sustained challenge from the far right. As a result, by publicly raising the Islam issue, the Conservatives were able to raise their profile vis-à-vis the Social Democrats.

While the FPÖ had been practicing an increasingly Islamophobic discourse in Austrian society by 2012 and was represented in the national parliament with around 20 percent of the vote, the other parties had not yet moved. The political elites of the two governing parties, the SPÖ and the ÖVP, continued to invoke the established discourse of relative inclusion, although this had already begun to change at the regional level, as demonstrated by anti-Islamic legislation in the provinces of Carinthia and Vorarlberg.

## AMBIVALENT TOLERANCE: COMMEMORATING 100 YEARS OF THE ISLAM ACT OF 1912

On 29 June 2012, senior political leaders and representatives of churches and religious communities gathered at Vienna's City Hall to commemorate the one hundredth anniversary of the 1912 Islamic Act. This was a unique event that signified several developments. First, the 1912 Islam Act, and with it, the institutionalization of Islam, had become important cornerstones of Austrian religious policy. Second, the commemoration represented an increased public awareness of the role of Islam. Third, this occasion also symbolized the still existing ambivalence in the public discourse in terms of the degree to which Islam and Muslims were actually understood as an integral part of the collective Austrian identity and community. Moreover, this event provided a stark contrast to the growing anti-Muslim agitation of the populist radical right FPÖ.

This section will show how government officials and representatives of public and religious institutions used the 2012 "Islamic Year of Remembrance" politically in their own ways. We look at which processes of inclusion and exclusion were observed and require an explanation. We discuss the parallels and differences between the Islamic Year of Remembrance and other commemorative events of the Second Republic (De Cillia and Wodak 2009), against the background of a growing Islamophobic public discourse. Next, we analyze the speeches given by high-level representatives of the Austrian political system at a ceremony held in Vienna's City Hall to mark the one hundredth anniversary of the Islam Act. Speakers included the president of the Islamic Religious Society in Austria, the federal president, the vice chancellor and party leader of the ÖVP, the minister of education from the Social Democratic Party, and the state secretary for integration affairs, Sebastian Kurz. In addition, two representatives from abroad were invited, the mufti of Bosnia and Herzegovina and the president of the Turkish Ministry of Religious Affairs.

The discourse of the representatives of the Austrian political leadership aimed to position Austria as a tolerant and inclusive nation by referring to Muslims in terms of "we" and "us." The statements also attempted to broaden the historical perspective beyond the founding of the Second Republic in 1945 by linking it to the Austro-Hungarian monarchy while omitting the period of Nazi rule. This narrative of a tolerant Austria was also used by Muslim representatives from Austria and abroad. It is worth mentioning that the conflictual aspects of the creation of the Islam Act were completely omitted. The Turkish minister of religious affairs stated, similarly to the Austrian representatives, that the Austrian Islam Act was an internationally unique model. At the commemoration ceremony, he said, "This . . . celebration . . . is the official recognition of the religion of Islam for the first time by a European country in which Islam is not the faith of the majority. Today, this celebration is held in Vienna in a period in which even many democratic countries are still hesitant [to recognize] Muslim existence within their borders" (IGGÖ 2012, 7–8).

The discourse reveals a selective reading of history, referring to the loyalty of Bosnian troops to the monarchy but omitting the armed resistance and the bitter divisions in viewpoints about Austria's role in Bosnia. For the religious dignitary, the sole explanation for the creation of the Islam Act is Austria's pluralistic legal tradition concerning religion, which is a result of particular historical developments in the Habsburg monarchy (Kalb, Potz, and Schinkele 2003). However, remaining silent about the conflictual aspects is tantamount to remaining silent about the imperial dimension of the colonial-type conquest of Muslim lands. It also ignores the legacy of the Islamic Religious Association, which was built essentially on an invented institution that was itself rooted in an imperial policy of *divide et impera*, divide and rule. In relation to this silence, the following quote from an Interior Ministry press release is instructive: "The Islam Act of 1912 did not only serve the better incorporation of Muslim soldiers from Bosnia and Herzegovina into the Austro-Hungarian Empire but ought to give a legal basis for the integration of Muslim peoples as a minority and Bosnia and Herzegovina into the multi-confessional federation" (IGGÖ 2012, 7–8).

This shows how the Islam Act served as a valuable tool both to facilitate the expansion of the imperial military and to provide a legal basis for a segment of the population and its relationship to the state. As enlightened as this may seem to have been in the heyday of colonialism at the time, we must not lose sight of the fact that the 1912 Islam Act was also an expression of power and power relations, created under postconquest top-down conditions. By now reaffirming these old institutional arrangements without further reflection and contextualization, especially without interpreting them in light of contemporary integration policies, these discourses perpetuate several myths about Austria that do not stand up to scrutiny. First, they suggest that the motives of decision-makers in both the Habsburg monarchy and contemporary Austria were guided by comparable concerns for integration and political inclusion. However, Austria the colonizing imperial state engaged in great power competition on the eve of World War I operated in a different context than Austria the small neutral democratic member state of the European Union, which has a growing Muslim population and faces political divisions over immigration that includes significant numbers of non-Muslims.

Second, the 1912 Islam Act deals with a conquered people who had offered military resistance to the conquest. The Habsburg monarch had mobilized some 150,000 soldiers to overcome sporadically fierce resistance from both Muslim and Orthodox defenders. Muslims in particular feared that they would lose the privileged status they had enjoyed under Ottoman rule. At that time, this population was largely outside the existing empire and its evolved political structure. Ignoring this fact without further contextualization is problematic at best and would likely be frowned on in other historical remembrances. Third, the conquest of Bosnian territory and thus the demonstration of strength by the ailing monarchy was a boost for Austrian nationalism, and the expansion into exoticized Muslim lands lent an air of colonial luster at a time when colonies were seen as conferring great power status. The addition of a Muslim population that remained outside traditional Austrian society is thus different from a growing Muslim population within that society, and nationalists react to it quite differently.

A comparison of this commemoration with other political remembrances, as analyzed by De Cillia, Wodak, and Reisigl (1999), is striking for invoking a potential or imagined conflict between Islam and Muslims. While the IGGÖ as the beneficiary of the Islam Act is presented as the "good Islam," other manifestations of Islam are criticized. The Conservative secretary of state for integration speaks of everyday "challenges" between "Muslims" and the "majority society." The Social Democratic minister speaks very openly of latent Islamophobia when she says, "Especially the teachings of Islam, as they are interpreted by some Muslim scholars today, can lead to a relationship of tension, can lead to conflicts. . . . It is a sign of the good relationship between Austria and the Muslims in our country that these tensions have never led to serious conflicts" (IGGÖ 2012, 7–8).

Both the Social Democratic and the Conservative ministers point to a core conception of Islam and Muslims as carriers of fundamentally contradictory and different meanings to Austria. Even the Austrian federal president emphasized that the commitment to the democratic state had already presented the IGGÖ with "challenges" in recent years. Reminding the representatives of the IGGÖ of this in a commemorative year highlights the obligations that are also imposed on them in public discourse, since the federal president has great moral and symbolic significance in a parliamentary republic such as Austria and, by virtue of his office, must as a rule be particularly careful not to exclude certain groups in the interest of social harmony (De Cillia, Distelberger, and Wodak 2009, 31). This not only solidifies the prevailing Islamophobic themes but also reinforces latent Islamophobia by portraying Islam as the opposite, the ultimate "Other." But it also suggests that this Other can be "civilized" or "cultivated," and here the IGGÖ is a welcome ally. In this process, the economic and social causes of political radicalization or radicalization of non-Muslims, especially on the extreme right, have been left out of the public discourse. This construction of a good and a bad Muslim is reminiscent of anthropologist Andre Gingrich's theory of "border Orientalism":

> Along a central structural device of a nearby territorial frontier . . . the repertoire locates the Oriental, a dualistic metaphoric figure. The "bad Oriental" is a dangerous rival, a threat to local selves; the "good Oriental" is our reliable ally and submissive supporter. The Turk as a bad Muslim and the Bosnian as a good Muslim constitute the standard of the primary register. . . . A mythological pairing of "good" and "bad" frontier Orientals (Turkish wars and Bosniaks in Habsburg Monarchy, F. H., R. H.) alludes to a broader narrative and provides a standard and widely understood option for interpreting current national issues using key symbols of the past. (Gingrich 1998, 117)

As a result, what could be called the submissive Muslim subject—formerly the Bosnian Muslim and now the IGGÖ representatives—are presented as good and civilized Muslims. Not surprisingly, IGGÖ representatives praise the Austrian model of legal recognition of Islam, in which Muslims are seen as equals.

Nonetheless, the elite discourse began to change significantly after 2006, when the FPÖ began to run anti-Muslim populist campaigns (Hödl 2010) to compete with the BZÖ and win back their grassroots support. As already mentioned earlier, examples of key FPÖ campaign slogans from this period include "Vienna will not become Istanbul" (Vienna elections 2005), "No home for Islam" (parliamentary elections 2006), "No home for radical Islam" (Graz city council elections 2008), and "Sound of church bells instead of muezzin singing" (Tyrolean state elections 2008; Hafez 2009a).

Despite the sharp tone of the Freedom Party rhetoric, its fundamental themes (security, identity, cultural compatibility) seeped into the public discourse and into the programs of other parties. The impact of the changing discourse can be seen in the ambivalence expressed during the commemoration. While almost all government representatives praised the Islam Act, many also referred to current problems with Muslims or challenges for Muslims trying to fit into contemporary society. Prior to 2006, the elite discourse was far less ambivalent, as evidenced by the increasing prominence of the FPÖ's Islamophobic discourse, which demonizes Islam and Muslims. This discourse had undergone a major shift, as evidenced by the debate over a new Islam Act that was introduced in late 2014 and implemented in early 2015. The following section examines how the new Islam Act was legitimized in public and parliamentary debates.

## DEBATING THE 2015 ISLAM ACT

After the 2013 parliamentary elections, when the coalition of Social Democrats and Conservatives returned to power, the intention to amend the 1912 Islam Act became part of the new government's agenda. According to the deputy state secretary of the Ministry of Culture, this issue was largely accepted without objections or partisan differences (Brian Schmidt, interview with Farid Hafez, 17 March 2015). The government's officially published working paper states that the 1912 Islam Act will be updated and amended "according to the principles of parity, state neutrality, autonomy, and cost neutrality" (BR 2013, 28). Although the IGGÖ—represented by its president—initiated this process and was part of the negotiations, the first presentation of the new law on 2 October 2014 was followed by a strong protest from Muslim organizations, civil society, legal scholars, and others (Hafez 2017b). The draft legislation received more than 160 review comments, the majority of which were highly critical, especially those from legal scholars (Potz and Schinkele 2010; Schima 2014). The IGGÖ itself made a critical assessment, due to the growing protest.

Following a few months of public debate, the law was accepted on 25 February 2015 by the Austrian Parliament with a few amendments, and on 12 March by the Federal Council (Bundesrat). These two chambers constitute the bicameral Austrian parliamentary system as the legislative organs of the republic and thus we will primarily analyze debates in these two chambers. The more powerful of the two chambers is the directly elected National Council, while the Federal Council is indirectly elected by the nine provincial assemblies (Altwanger and Zögernitz 2006). (Note: Since this terminology can lead to confusion, we will refer to the National Council as often as possible as the Austrian Parliament, which it is de facto.) They constitute the core institutions of Austria's democracy, since "parliaments are democratically constituted fora for a political deliberation, legislation, problem solving and decision making" (Ilie 2010, 1).

While the SPÖ minister of culture, whose portfolio includes religion, was virtually absent from the political stage, Sebastian Kurz, then minister of foreign affairs and integration (ÖVP), dominated the public debate on the Islam Act. The ÖVP was more likely than the SPÖ to address the issue of religion because it plays a more important role ideologically for a Christian Democratic party. At the same time, this initiative can be interpreted as a shift in the ÖVP's general strategy to set the agenda on emotionally charged issues such as "integration," as the ÖVP took the lead from the FPÖ, while the SPÖ remained fairly silent on these issues

(Rosenberger 2013, 64–65). Acting in this manner can therefore also be understood as seeking to maintain issue leadership.

The next section focuses on the arguments used to defend, amend, or support the legislative proposal that was enacted in early 2015. As Van Dijk has demonstrated, in parliamentary debates, racism involves the "reproduction of . . . prejudices or ideologies" (Van Dijk 2000, 88) and can thus contribute to marginalization and exclusion. The analysis provides an insight about (1) how politicians speak about "the Other," (2) their social representation of "the Other," (3) the possible effect on recipients, and (4) the "socio-political context of legislation and public opinion formation" (88).[1]

The FPÖ's constant thematization of Islam in the election campaign made a lasting impression on other parties, especially the ÖVP and the SPÖ. Among other things, the FPÖ called for a reconsideration of the legal status of Islam as early as 2008. The argument is that "immigrant Islam cannot be given the same rights as autochthonous Bosnian Muslims in the days of the Habsburg monarchy" (Hafez 2009a), and thus it questions the political culture of inclusion of Muslims in the present. For the FPÖ, legal recognition as a religious community should be reserved for Bosnian Muslims, who were part of the monarchy. The Christian Democratic ÖVP relied on a narrow image of Austrian culture that at the same time includes Muslims in an ambivalent way. The effects of Islamophobic discourse strategies were increasingly evident in party election manifestos. Terminology such as "parallel society" (Parallelgesellschaft) and "hate preachers" (Hassprediger), which originated in the FPÖ's discourses on Islam, found its way into the ÖVP's election program as early as 2008 (ÖVP 2008, 19). Sebastian Kurz, then head of the Young Conservatives (JVP) and later a central figure in drafting the new 2015 Islam Act, demanded that the German language should be the standard in the community to ensure that the Islamic faith becomes more transparent and open. He also stressed that the IGGÖ should consider stopping the construction of mosques with minarets in every capital city. He also proposed that imams should speak German and try to fit in, and that integration should be promoted (JVP 2010). All these demands that singled out Islam in a way unheard of in connection with other religions had been voiced openly by the FPÖ before (Hafez 2009a).

Programmatically, the SPÖ seems to vacillate between its antireligious tradition on the one hand and its desire to protect minorities on the other (Hafez 2010a). In contrast to the ÖVP, the SPÖ has no Islamophobic agenda in any of its election programs. Antiracist positions condemning Islamophobia can be found alongside Islam-critical positions, which corresponds to the party's historically critical attitude toward religion in general. In 2007, the president of the SPÖ women's caucus, Barbara Prammer, described the headscarf as a "symbol of the subordination of women" (Dannhauser 2007). At the same time, she pleaded in the same interview for the acceptance of mosques with minarets in public spaces. Similarly, a Social Democratic member of the European Parliament from Austria, Hannes Swoboda, spoke out against a headscarf ban in Turkey but also argued that state employees in Austria and Turkey should not wear religious symbols, including headscarves (APA 2008). In 2010, the executive secretary of the SPÖ, Laura Rudas, publicly stated that the headscarf was a "symbol of oppression" and that while it could not be banned, "it must be a goal to drop the headscarf" (Nowak 2010). This clearly shows how difficult it is for Social Democrats to include Islam in the public sphere, against the backdrop of a conflict between secularism on the one hand and antiracist positions on the other. The party's secular traditions call for abolishing religion, while their antiracist positions urge them to protect marginalized minorities.

After a draft of the Islam Act was submitted by two ministers from the ruling SPÖ and ÖVP on 2 October 2014, the legislation was referred to the Constitutional Committee by the Ministerial Conference on 3 December 2014. The Islam Act was debated in Parliament on 25 February 2015 and in the Bundesrat on 12 March 2015. The transcripts of the two debates (stenographic transcripts) serve as our primary data. In addition to the two coalition parties (SPÖ and ÖVP), the opposition parties with seats in both chambers were the (left-leaning) Greens, the far-right FPÖ, and the short-lived Team Stronach. The more socioeconomically liberal party, the New Austria and Liberal Forum (NEOS), was represented only in the National Council. While only the two governing parties supported the law, the opposition parties had different reasons for voting against it, depending on their strategic and programmatic orientations, but this had no influence on passing the legislation. Thus, parliamentary debates in Austria generally serve to project messages beyond the confines of the chamber to the general public, rather than to directly influence the decision at hand (Ilie 2010, 8–9). The legislation was eventually signed into law on 30 March 2015.

Parliamentary discourse "displays particular institutionalized discursive features and complies with a number of specific rules and conventions" (Ilie 2010, 8). According to the rules of operation in the National and Federal Councils, the strongest opposition party by number of seats is entitled to open the debate with a request for the floor (Altwanger and Zögernitz 2006). Hence, the populist radical right FPÖ started the debates in both parliamentary chambers. This is important in that the FPÖ introduced a number of issues with the Islam Act and nearly all MPs responded to them in their statements and paid attention to them throughout their contributions to the discussion. Hence, the FPÖ clearly set the agenda in both debates. This observation supports findings of earlier studies that show that the FPÖ has thematic leadership in immigrant and asylum policy (Sedlak 2000). But more importantly, it also shows us how the structure of Austrian parliamentarianism impacts parliamentary practices (Ilie

2010, 3) and how this confrontation affects the dynamics of parliamentary agenda-setting (10).

According to the FPÖ leader, Heinz-Christian Strache, the Islam Act should have been an "Anti-Islamism Act" to counter "radical Islam" and "Islamic Fundamentalism" (NR 2015, 144). He regrets that although there are "threatening developments" in Islamism, the Islam Act fails to provide an answer to these "radicalisms" (NR 2015, 144). "Dangerous radicalisms" and "dangerous Islamization" (NR 2015, 145) are two phrases repeatedly used by Strache. While he stated that "not all Muslims are to be put under general suspicion, . . . when radical Islamism refers to Islam, then it has something to do with Islam" (NR 2015, 145). Compounds like these have the effect of transferring the meaning of one term (radical) to the other (Islam), and vice versa. This vagueness of meaning occludes the real relationship between the two terms and keeps the reader in a state of uncertainty as to whether the problem lies with Islam or with a political and radical interpretation of it (Schiffer 2005). This was apparent when another MP (ÖVP) referred to "500,000 Islamists living in Austria," clearly meaning Muslims, not "Islamists" (NR 170). Using similar language, Strache tried to avoid the appearance of generalizing about all Muslims but still essentialized Islam by referring to its core in terms of "Islamic radicalism."

For Strache, it was important to stress what the Islam Act was not. Importantly for him, it lacked a ban on minarets and a ban on burqas (NR 2015, 145). He argued, "The Islam Act is half-hearted, incomplete, and cements privileges that unfortunately play into the hands of radical Islam and prevent the integration of Muslims into society" (NR 2015, 145). Because of this, Strache concluded that the Islam Act would "promote the Islamization of Austria" (NR 2015, 146). Since Muslims are allowed to teach their religious rites to children, this was interpreted by Strache as "carte blanche for radical Islamists to pass on culturally alien patterns of behavior with the help of the state" (NR 2015, 146). This goes hand in hand with earlier claims, in which the FPÖ saw a conspiracy between Marxist elites and the SPÖ as proponents of Islamization (Hafez 2019d).

While the FPÖ shaped the debate overall, more socioculturally progressive arguments were generally rare. These included the statements by members of the governing and opposition parties from the left and more progressive spectrum, who argued that the law needed to be renewed to meet today's challenges (NR 2015, 150, 165; BR 2015, 35). They targeted not so much the law as the exclusionary demands of the FPÖ discourse. Thus, the governing parties initially succeeded in presenting their new Islam Act as a progressive and tolerant initiative vis-à-vis the Islamophobic discourse of the FPÖ. For example, the parliamentary party leader Reinhold Lopatka (ÖVP) argued that all churches and religious societies should have the opportunity to develop, as he advocated, a "liberal, open state, an open society" (NR 2015, 153). Similarly, a Conservative Muslim MP argued for the Islam Act as an outgrowth of religious freedom (NR 2015, 199). In short, by qualifying the law as part of a liberal and fundamental rights agenda, Conservative MPs sought to portray the Islam Act as wholly positive.

During the debate on the Islam Act, politicians from the FPÖ took the opportunity to fundamentally question the place of Islam and Muslims in Austria. The issue of belonging was at the center of this parliamentary debate. The question was raised whether Islam should be considered as belonging to Austria or not—a question that produced very heated public discourse in Germany as well (Adam 2015, 447). This symbolized the central question of including or excluding Islam and Muslims in the course of the discursive construction of national identity. Strache criticized the ÖVP leadership for tacitly affirming the inclusionary perspective and negating the clear dichotomy that presented itself: "I say: no! [Islam] does not belong to Austria, neither culturally, nor historically" (NR 2015, 144). This coincides with the FPÖ's programmatic distinction between "immigrant Islam" and historical "autochthonous Bosnian Islam" and the resulting position that "the legal status of Islam in Austria should be reconsidered" (Hafez 2009a). An FPÖ deputy quoted a liberal philosopher who criticized German chancellor Angela Merkel for claiming that Islam belongs to Germany. The MP argued that it was correct to say that Muslims were part of Austria as citizens, but stressed that this was due to the government's misguided immigration policy (NR 2015, 196f.), implying that if the FPÖ had been in power, Muslims would not have become Austrian citizens in the first place and thus would not have been given the same rights as other citizens.

Another MP from the FPÖ[2] went a step further, arguing, "Why have I said at the beginning that Islam does not belong to Austria? This is because Islam is not a religion like other religions . . . but a political system" (BR 2015, 29). She uses a rhetorical move typical of far-right politicians by presenting her claim as a fact, when in reality it is only her own perception (Van Dijk 2011). With this statement, she reformulates the religion of Islam in a way that would make any discrimination against Muslims acceptable and not a violation of human rights and, in particular, not a violation of a person's religious freedom. If Islam is no longer considered a religion but rather a (dangerous) political ideology, then any action could conceivably be taken to combat this threat in the interest of societal freedom. This argument also creates an antagonism between Islam on the one hand and the Austrian political system on the other. This exclusion of Islam from the Austria tapestry was strongly rejected by members of the ÖVP. In line with his own party, Integration Minister Kurz argued, "In my opinion, Islam belongs to Austria. We were the first country in Europe to recognize Islam in 1912. . . . We have to be cautious not to deny reality. . . . It doesn't help us to act as if there were no Islam in Austria, given that we have 500,000 Muslims" (NR 2015, 164).

The reactions of Social Democratic MPs differed. Some argued that Muslims had been living here as citizens for three generations (NR 2015, 149f.) and thus were part of Austria. Josef Cap (SPÖ) disagreed with the German chancellor that Islam was part of Germany (or in this case, Austria; NR 2015, 157). For a Green MP, Muslims are "part of Austrian society as much as Jews . . . atheists . . . Buddhists . . . and Christians" (NR 2015, 150). Hence, the more left-leaning deputies generally tended to accept Muslims as people with a different religion and felt that religion was not a reason for mistreatment and discrimination.

Another theme was "radical Islam." While FPÖ leader Strache complained that there was no ban on minaret or burqas in the Islam Act, MPs from the ÖVP defended the omission on the basis that the Islam Act was never intended to regulate construction work or clothing (NR 2015, 148). Many MPs from the government parties as well as from the non–radical right opposition argued that the Islam Act was not meant to serve as a security law or antiterrorism legislation, but rather as a law of religion, although with different goals in mind (NR 2015, 148, 161, 162, 165, 169, 172, 199; BR 2015, 36). In apparent contradiction to this, numerous MPs from the governing parties argued that the Islam Act was also "a means of exerting pressure against radical preachers," who would have to subordinate themselves to the Islamic Religious Society or the Alevis (NR 2015, 149). For example, an ÖVP deputy argued that the Ministry of the Interior would now have the possibility "to intervene in associations that provide space to hate preachers" (NR 2015, 149). The FPÖ deputy chairman did not question this statement per se, but only its practicality, since in his opinion, state officials were not religious scholars (NR 2015, 166). His Conservative counterpart asserted in response, "We will do everything to move against radicals, we will do everything, I tell you, we will not allow anything" (NR 2015, 153). "Radical Islamism" was thus openly recognized by coalition MPs as a challenge to be addressed by the Islam Act, although the law was not presented primarily as a security law. Again, the issue of security was used to argue both for and against the Islam Act, depending on whether MPs viewed it in part as a law to address security issues, as advocated by the center-right ÖVP and the populist radical right FPÖ, or as a nonsecurity issue, as advocated by the socioculturally liberal parties, namely the SPÖ, the Greens, and NEOS.

The topos of "the people" as an amorphous and unified whole without differences of class or interest is the quintessential populist concept (Reisigl 2014, 78). Accordingly, politicians have to do something if they perceive that "the people" want them to do something. In our case, this is acting upon the people's imagined fears. One Conservative MP from the ruling parties (ÖVP)[3] argued that "we have to quell the fears of the people. We want to suppress the radicals' influence" (NR 2015, 153). MPs from the ÖVP agreed with the FPÖ that the people's fears must not be ignored (NR 2015, 144, 146, 152, 199). While opposition MPs (FPÖ) argued that the law "would not help to solve these problems" (BR 2015, 43) and Conservative MPs contended that this law would help to dispel fears, both shared the assumption that reducing fears among the population is an essential part of the Islam Act.

One of the most central arguments actively advanced by the two ministers was the theme of the primacy of national law over religious law, reminiscent of the frequent references to law and order in populist discourse (Reisigl 2014, 79). The theme of the primacy of national law is based on the assumption that Muslims follow a Sharia law that is contrary to national law, another familiar discourse of the far right (Yazdiha 2014; Hummel 2021). This notion was strongly challenged in the public debate on the law. Many stakeholders protested that no other religious law would contain such an article. The fact that a statement on the primacy of national law occurs more than once in the draft legislation implies that Muslims are people who should not be trusted (Schinkele and Potz 2014). An ÖVP deputy explained why the retention of this article was necessary: "If we had not kept it, this may have increased people's fear. Why? Because there are people on the street who fan fear. They would have taken this as an opportunity and said: Now that the law no longer invokes national law's precedence, Islam has essentially gained the upper hands. Some may have said that sharia was now at center stage" (NR 2015, 153–154).

This issue was particularly hotly debated after many legal scholars and Muslim organizations criticized the first draft of the legislation. This approach meant that the governing parties had linked this law to concerns about law and order. The idea of the supremacy of national law was regularly emphasized by deputies from the coalition parties (BR 2015, 30) and criticized by the non–radical right opposition, which accused the governing parties of spreading a general suspicion of Muslims (see discussion below). A similar theme frequently emphasized by deputies of the coalition (NR 2015, 148, 172; BR 2015, 36) and Minister Kurz (NR 2015, 163) was that the law entailed "rights and obligations," meaning that Muslims would now have to comply with the law and fulfill certain obligations that did not exist before this law would come into force.

Another important theme was the German language. The FPÖ chairman demanded that use of the German language be obligatory in mosques, Islam classes at public schools (which was already the case), and prisons; he criticized the fact that this would not be the case under the new Islam Act (NR 2015, 145). The centrality of the German language in the FPÖ's discourse is strongly linked to the party's nativist ideology, which imagines Austria as an ethnically German nation and not as a civic nation. The focus on the German language as an indicator of Austrian identity has also become central to the ÖVP (Hafez 2010a, 101), even after the issue of "integration" became part of its political agenda and institutionalized in the form of a government ministry (Rosenberger 2013, 62–63). An implication of this argument is that Muslims might have a hidden agenda that could be uncovered if they were forced to use German as their language of communication. When "sermons and religious instructions are not given in German ... hate-preachers can hardly ever be convicted" (NR 2015, 146), said FPÖ chairman Strache; for this reason, "public authorities have to be able to understand what is being preached" (NR 2015, 147). Strache justified his aim of the surveillance of Muslims by using emotive terms such as "holy warriors" and "devil warriors" to brand the Muslim preachers collectively as potential threats (NR 2015, 146). An MP from the far-right opposition party Team Stronach supported Strache's arguments and called on the Islamic Religious Association to "openly declare their articles of faith, traditions and rituals ... in German, because only then are they verifiable" (NR 2015, 154). This harks back to the FPÖ's call in 2007 for Muslims to be transparent by confessing their basic beliefs in the German language (Hafez 2010a, 23). And according to Strache, the law would even hinder integration, because use of the German language was not enforced in Muslim religious life (NR 2015, 145).

Government deputies reacted to these argumentations in different ways. An MP from the SPÖ argued that Christian denominations also preached in other languages (NR 2015, 149), which for him represented "the diversity of our state ... living integration" (NR 2015, 149). An MP from the ÖVP claimed that in the future, imams would teach and themselves be taught in German (NR 2015, 197), thus affirming Strache's view on the importance of German. The ÖVP deputy replied that religious instructions already had to be given in German anyway, and therefore "one can hear and see what is taught" (NR 2015, 197). This was strongly countered by Minister Josef Ostermayer (SPÖ), who argued that the only reason the articles of faith had to be published in German was formal (BR 2015, 40). So, while some MPs—from the governing and the opposition parties—stressed the importance of the German language in order to appeal to nativists and traditionalist sentiments and suggested the need for securitizing Islam, the minister formally in charge of this law refuted their claims.

An important rhetorical device closely linked to the issue of language is the idea of an Austrian Islam (*Islam österreichischer Prägung*). Minister Kurz published brief comments on this topic (Kurz 2015) and organized a conference on 15 June 2015 to promote the concept. It is an Austrian version of a Europe-wide trend to create institutional conditions for the creation of a national Islam to "gradually take ownership of the Muslim population" (Laurence 2012, 12–13). The new Islam Act was presented as an initiative to give Islam a home in Austria, as if there had not been a national Islam Act for 103 years. The law would resolve the constructed "contradiction" of being a devout Muslim and an avowed Austrian at the same time, a concept repeated by other Conservative MPs (NR 2015, 197). This idea was also repeated in parliamentary debates. Kurz argued that the Islam Act is "an opportunity for Islam to develop in Austria on its own, without dictates and pressure from abroad" (NR 2015, 162). This was supported by the

Conservative MPs (BR 2015, 36). Only one Green MP, who later switched to the ÖVP, supported this argument (BR 2015, 34). According to the MP Stefan Schennach (SPÖ), the 1912 Islam Act had already "laid the foundation for a modern European Islam" (BR 2015, 37), while for MPs of the FPÖ, a "European Islam" was impossible. Using the strategy of perspectivization with reference to Henryk Broder, who is considered clearly Islamophobic by some (Schneiders 2009), the FPÖ MP claimed that Islam and Islamism could not be separated (BR 2015, 42). The SPÖ deputy argued that Muslims would now have a place in university where they could be trained academically "in Austria . . . within the framework of Austrian traditions and the Austrian legal system" (NR 2015, 148), thus appreciating "Austria as a place for shaping the understanding of Islam in a positive way in the future. Interestingly, Katharina Kucharowits (SPÖ) was the only member of the coalition to question this formulation—"a distinctive Austrian manifestation of Islam"—although she did not specify why (NR 2015, 172). The phrase "Austrian manifestation of Islam" was not used by the opposition parties either, although the institutionalization of Islamic theology at an Austrian university was welcomed by some opposition MPs and even more so by the governing parties (NR 2015, 172). MPs from both the governing SPÖ (NR 2015, 173) and the Greens welcomed the "high-quality, transparent training for the education of Austrian imams" (NR 2015, 150). According to these statements, Islam was to be "civilized" by being "Austrianized," an argument that harks back to the colonial era (Hafez 2014b).

Another theme was the "prevention of foreign funding." According to an MP from the SPÖ, the law would prevent foreign financing (NR 2015, 148), which was one of the dominant arguments in the public debate for supporting the law. Minister Kurz stressed that continuous foreign funding not only would allow foreign interests to have an impact on religion but would also enable them to have "socio-political influence in Austria" (NR 2015, 163). The opposition (the Greens, the FPÖ, and Team Stronach) pointed out that the law would not really make such a ban possible, because foreign funding could be maintained through other institutions (NR 2015, 154; BR 2015, 29). From another perspective, a Green Party MP quoted two legal experts to justify her general criticism that all churches and religious communities should make their international money flows transparent so the government could measure possible influence from abroad (NR 2015, 151). Kurz defended the ban by arguing that it was "legitimate to say that we do not want imams from other governments abroad to preach and work in Austria" (NR 2015, 163). This was supported by the argument of MP Stefan Schennach, who identified Turkey as the country in focus: "Yes, we want a religious society to develop in a European way, far away from orders coming from Turkey" (BR 2015, 39). Thus he formulated a superior "European way" as opposed to a devalued "Turkish way." The only voice explicitly challenging this argument was the Green MP Wolfgang Zinggl, who argued, "We do not think that 500,000 Muslims can do without their places of worship, mosques and imams. The question must be asked, who should pay for this" (NR 2015, 198). He also mentioned that the Mormons and the Greek Orthodox are also funded by foreign donors, and if they did not get money from abroad they would have to stop offering religious services.

Closely related to the idea of the superiority of the German language was the idea of being able to control and discipline the Muslim subject. The theme of "law and order" is central to populist discourse (Reisigl 2014, 79) and could also be found in the argument of Josef Cap (SPÖ), who held a special position in his party as one of the longest-serving Social Democratic members of Parliament. He repeatedly problematized organized Muslims, which was unusual in his own party. MP Cap said, "We want this order and this transparency so that no material is disseminated in individual mosques resembling the material of the Islamic State. . . . We have to be attentive and we have to look closely at how things develop. And that is what the law does. That is exactly followed by the law when it comes to the exercise of religion" (NR 2015, 157–158).

This idea of legitimate surveillance is propagated through a variety of means, such as the allusion to dangerous "Islamic State materials," which would enable surveillance on the basis of a general suspicion that Muslims are not to be trusted. The general distrust feeds on the theme of national security. This is followed in the public discourse by repeatedly stressing the importance of fostering a civilized European Islam ("an Austrian manifestation of Islam"). Thus, the idea of surveillance based on general suspicion of Muslims reveals the core concern for law and order. According to the Green MP Harald Walser, one of his main reasons for not supporting the law was that it did not regulate religious education in public schools, an area over which he wanted to have more control (NR 2015, 169). A Conservative MP responded by arguing that in religious education classes, "you can listen and see what is being taught" (NR 2015, 197) (since, according to the law, they must be taught in German anyway, which is not the case).

Another Green Party MP, Wolfgang Zinggl, made the criticism that this debate was more about a "police security law" (NR 2015, 198) than about a religion law, as the government and representatives of the SPÖ had repeatedly claimed. This argument was rejected by Minister Ostermayer (SPÖ), who said, "It is not the task of the Cultural Office to be a religious police. A religious police . . . exists only in absolutist dictatorships, in dictatorial states" (BR 2015, 40). Yet, this is precisely what legal experts such as Richard Potz later claimed (Potz 2017). Other legal scholars also see the 2015 Islam Act as a law at the intersection of religion and security (Scheu 2021). Minister Ostermayer also stated that while he thought it was "important" to "train preachers in Austria," it was a "radical intrusion into a democratic constitutional state" to "listen to what a pastor says to his community" (BR 2015, 40–41). However, apparently the Conservative MPs were more supportive of the idea of law and order. Only one Green

Party MP and the minister responsible questioned the state's intrusion in principle, calling it an argument fit for an authoritarian political system. Later, as part
of the antiterror package, the Islam Act was amended in July 2021 to include a list of
imams (Amnesty International Austria 2021), which made the law-enforcement
character of the Islam Act more explicit. The then interior minister clearly linked
the Islam Act to the issue of security, saying that "a strong Islam Act is necessary"
(Parlament Österreich 2021).

The law was challenged by the far-right opposition, who claimed, among
other things, that it had not been sufficiently involved in the drafting process. For
the FPÖ leader Strache, the law dealt with the wrong institutions. He criticized
the IGGÖ for not submitting its articles of faith and therefore not being transparent, and he described it as a small organization without members or legitimacy (NR 2015, 147). An FPÖ MP backed his party leader, arguing that "the
Islamic Religious Association in truth represents organized political Islam" (NR
2015, 196) and referring to the participation of various Islamic movements and
institutions—including the ATIB (connected to the Turkish Ministry of Religious Affairs), the Turkish Islamist Millî Görüş, and the Muslim Brotherhood—
in the highest body of the Islamic Religious Association, which in his opinion
represent the "interests of Saudi Arabia and Turkey" (NR 2015, 196). He was supported in this by fellow MPs from the FPÖ, who also tried to delegitimize the
IGGÖ (BR 2015, 27). It is interesting that the first Social Democratic speaker in
the plenary also defended the law on the same grounds, stating that "moderate
forces of the Islamic Religious Association had been involved substantially in
this law—substantially! . . . The fact that there are radical and more moderate
forces within the Islamic Religious Association must be noted because the more
radical forces also disapproved of the law" (NR 2015, 148).

Hence, MPs from both the government party and the opposition used what
may be considered a strategy of predication by using modifiers like "moderate"
versus "radical" to make their arguments. Strache delegitimized an institution
that had had legal recognition since 1912 by tarnishing it as "radical." A Social
Democratic MP[4] agreed in part with the argument that the law was directed
against the radicals in the Islamic Religious Association and therefore countered
claims by Strache that the Islam Act would ostensibly benefit "radical Islamists."
Similarly, MP Schennach argued, "If the Alevis have no problems with the law,
then we are all ok, too" (BR 2015, 39). Similar to the discourse strategies previously
introduced by the radical right political figurehead Jörg Haider, these populist
claims relied on an image of the bad versus the good Muslim, in which the con-
struct of the good Muslim is used to justify discriminatory legal practices (Hafez
2015b, 42). Another MP from the left-Green opposition portrayed the IGGÖ's
internal disputes as a struggle between Arab- and Turkish-dominated groups.
He even argued that opposing the law would constitute creating a "state within a

state" (BR 2015, 33), which is reminiscent of old anti-Semitic conspiracy theories, here applied to an Islamophobic discourse (Schiffer and Wagner 2009;
Langer 2020). Minister Ostermayer also defended the Islam Act by arguing that
it was supported by Muslims themselves. Since both legally recognized Muslim
institutions—the IGGÖ and the Alevis—had (finally) accepted the law, it had
to be good (NR 2015, 160f.). Conservative MPs (BR 2015, 36; NR 2015, 197)
shared this perspective. However, this view did not take into account that the
original draft had triggered a wave of protests after it became public, which initially forced even the IGGÖ to come out against the law (Hafez 2017b). NEOS as
well as Green MPs criticized the bill for communicating a "general suspicion"
of Muslims. A Green MP argued: "Stefan Schima [a professor of law and
religion]—I think a recognized person in this context—criticized (the Islam
Act) saying: 'The explicit mention that Muslims must adhere to the Austrian
legal regulations is . . . a sign of an expectation of the state that there are more
legal violations among Muslims than with other religious communities'" (NR
2015, 170). Minister Kurz and Conservative MPs rejected the accusation that the
law would reflect a general suspicion against Muslims (NR 2015, 163, 200).

Another central aspect of critique of the Islam Act was the idea of unequal
treatment. One liberal MP from the NEOS[5] argued that the law was unequal:
"There is also a very fundamental reason to reject this law, and this is indeed the
unequal treatment of a recognized religious society" (NR 2015, 171). He referred
to the French principle of laïcité, according to which the state must be neutral
with respect to all religions and hence may not discriminate or privilege one
above another. Alm also criticized Lopatka (ÖVP) for positioning the Islam Act as
the best way to counter the Islamic State. In his argument he framed the Islam
Act as "domesticating a religion and at the same time isolating it from abroad.
This is contrary to the constitutional principle of equal treatment" (NR 2015, 172).
A fellow liberal MP from the NEOS[6] argued that there was no ban on foreign
funding for any other church or religious society. He argued that "different religious societies are treated differently" (NR 2015, 159); for him, "Islam is treated
differently, that is to say more strictly, than other religions" (NR 2015, 160). For
Minister Kurz, there was "no unequal treatment" (NR 2015, 163). Rather, the ban
on foreign funding was, first, in line with the separation of state and religion, and
second, consistent with religious societies' capacity for self-preservation (Selb-
sterhaltungsfähigkeit; NR 2015, 163). A Green MP[7] questioned this reasoning by
arguing that other churches and religious societies were also funded by foreign
entities (NR 2015, 198). Likewise, another Green MP[8] criticized the law as
unconstitutional and a violation of the principle of laïcité (BR 2015, 34). On the
other side, a Social Democratic MP[9] defended the new restriction in order to
underscore the consequence that imams would now have to be trained in Austria (BR 2015, 30).

A traditional theme used by political elites in the past and developed during the years of the center-right coalition (2000–2007) is the idea of Austria as a model for Europe. Indeed, the 1912 Islam Act was conceived by state officials and representatives of the IGGÖ as a unique prototype to be exported to other European countries (Sticker 2008). This idea was introduced into parliamentary debates by many ruling-party MPs (NR 2015, 197f.; BR 2015, 37, 39). A Conservative deputy (ÖVP) stated, "We can go out with pride because we have succeeded, thanks to the initiative of our foreign minister . . . Sebastian Kurz. . . . We have arrived at a law that is truly recognized in Europe" (NR 2015, 164). Although the new law had not been recognized in any way outside Austria's borders, this implied that the legal regulation of Islam was in itself a success story that would continue regardless of de facto challenges from legal scholars and Muslim civil society. What was good in the past would surely be good in the future. Minister Ostermayer (SPÖ) was the only one from the government parties to openly question this argument (BR 2015, 40).

The formal structure of parliamentary debate (opposition deputies speak first) had a major impact on the dynamics of the debates. The centrist coalition government tried to distance itself from the far right, which clearly dominated both debates. A vivid example was the classification of the Islam Act as a law on religion rather than a law on terrorism, security, or the like. This radical right narrative was partly countered but also implicitly confirmed by declaring that the law was an instrument against preachers of hate, which led to the ambivalent reactions by MPs from the coalition parties. The adaptation of many Islamophobic populist arguments is instructive when looking at the FPÖ deputies who argued that "the intention [of the law] is sound, but the implementation is unfortunately imperfect" (BR 2015, 29). This is also true of the leftist parties. The concept of order, for example, was also embraced by some members of the Green Party and the ruling SPÖ.

The idea of the centrality of the German language revealed the greatest divide between the coalition parties. The Social Democratic deputies defended the right to preach in any language, while for the Conservative deputies, speaking German was central to the clergy's adaptation to Austria, which went hand in hand with the ÖVP's general integration policy. This clearly reflected the ÖVP s more identitarian ideas when compared with those of the left, which was more comfortable with a multicultural society. As for the idea of an Austrian variant of Islam, it is also interesting to see the diversity of positions represented. While this notion, which is clearly culturalist and identitarian, was central to the Conservatives, it was openly challenged by their coalition partner.

Opposition MPs from all political camps pointed to the problems of "general suspicion" and "unequal treatment." Moreover, even within the opposition and in the government party SPÖ there were sharp differences. While positions were generally taken along ideological or party lines (Ilie 2010, 9), some left-wing

MPs, such as Efgani Dönmez (Greens) and Josef Cap (SPÖ), echoed certain arguments of the far right to justify the law. Cap was subsequently rebutted by his own minister. This may be explained by the fact that the leftist parties had not developed a sufficient programmatic stance on dealing with issues of integration in general and "Islam" in particular. It is also the case that these two MPs generally held sociocultural positions that were to the right of their own parties (Hafez 2009b). In addition, we may assume that the minister felt compelled to correct MPs from both coalition parties who questioned the government's official position of not wanting to discriminate against Muslims.

## CONCLUSION

The analysis of the discourse on Islam and Muslims in Austria shows that they were no longer seen as mythological objects linked to the Habsburg past that were tolerated and thought to enrich the cosmopolitan city of Vienna. The idea of the good Bosnian Muslim, loyal to political authority, corresponded to the idea of the good Austrian Muslim for some time. When the FPÖ discovered Islam as a salient issue in 2005 and began to mobilize against Muslims, this had an obvious impact on the debate about Islam and Muslims in Austria. As we can see from the commemoration of the 1912 Islam Act, political elites presented ideas about the place of Islam and Muslims in Austria that were rather ambivalent, despite the fact that Islam had been legally recognized and Austria had a fairly tolerant and long-established legal regime for Islam. Only three years later, the parliamentary debates on the new Islam Act of 2015 showed the extent to which the FPÖ's position, which the party had first comprehensively formulated in 2008, had become mainstream and supported by both center-right and center-left governing parties.

While references to human rights, tolerance, and the right as "a model for Europe" were rarely used to defend the 2015 Islam Act, restrictive arguments that called for defending "the people," protecting the "supremacy of national law," enforcing "law and order," and banning foreign financing, as well as culturalist themes that referenced the "creation of an Austrian Islamic variant," "cultivating the German language," and "belonging" served as justifications for a new restrictive Islam Act. While the radical opposition parties (the FPÖ and Team Stronach) used these same ideas to argue that the law was incapable of implementing these intentions (and also questioned the representativeness of the IGGÖ), the liberal and left-wing opposition criticized the law, arguing that it spreads "general suspicion" and represents "unequal treatment" before the law.

The parliamentary debate on the Islam Act is the first comprehensive elite discussion to highlight this major shift. A law-and-order approach to governing Muslims, the framing of the IGGÖ as a partner that might actually be a breeding ground for extremists, the framing of the Religion Law as a security law, and the

# 4 · LEGAL STATUS OF ISLAM

As already noted, the Islam Act of 1912 was the result of great power politics and the development of the law of religion that started in the Habsburg monarchy. The liberalization of religious freedom came with the Josephine Tolerance Patent of 1781 and the Recognition Act of 1874. The latter formed the legal basis for the recognition of other churches and religious societies besides the dominant Catholic Church. After the Statute on the Autonomous Administration of Islamite Religious, Foundation and School Affairs in 1909 in Muslim-dominated Bosnia and Herzegovina, which was legally occupied by the Habsburg monarchy, the legal recognition of Islam followed with the Islam Act of 1912 (Kalb, Potz, and Schinkele 2003, 625–627). This Islam Act thus follows a traditional path with several other special laws for churches and religious societies, such as the Protestant Act of 1867 that governed the Protestant Church and the Israelite Act of 1890 that governed the Jewish community. While the Islam Act of 1912 represented a version of "tolerance" toward Muslims as a religious minority only in the sense of toleration by the powerful, it nevertheless granted Muslims some legal recognition (Abuzahra 2022, 92–93), something unheard-of in other Western European countries. Hence, representatives of the Austrian government as well as representatives of the IGGÖ had praised this unique legal position of Austrian Muslims within the legal framework of the Austrian polity (Sticker 2008).

## THE LEGACY OF THE 1912 ACT:
## A SYMBOL OF TOLERANCE

But while many of these special laws for churches and religious societies have been amended to better serve new circumstances of the respective churches or religious communities, the Islam Act of 1912 remained unchanged for more than one hundred years. A new Islam Act had long been in the interest of the IGGÖ, which until 2013 was the only legally recognized Muslim denomination and until 2015 was the only institution regulated by the Islam Act of 1912. However, while the IGGÖ had pushed for an amended Islam Act that would give Muslims more privileges and had even presented an amended version of the act in 2005 that reflected the amended Protestant Act of 1961, the leadership of the IGGÖ had no positive response from the Cultural Affairs Office (Kultusamt). Indeed, there are many arguments for such an amendment. Whereas in 1979 fewer than 77,000 Muslims were living in Austria, the number had increased to more than half a million by 2009 (Mohr 2016). Also, the number of Muslim institutional foundations had grown, from kindergartens to schools and even higher educational institutions that trained Muslim teachers for public education, and they had their own needs. Hence, an amended act—like the Protestant Act amended in 1961 and the Israelite Act amended in 2012—seemed to be a useful necessity. Unfortunately, according to the then president, the draft "ended up in the drawer" (Anas Schakfeh, interview with Farid Hafez, 13 October 2014). One reason for this was the changing political climate in which the IGGÖ found itself.

## Questioning the Islam Act of 1912

The idea to restructure the relationship between the state authorities and the IGGÖ was initiated by an unexpected source—the FPÖ, a political player that had not been part of this debate before. The FPÖ started claiming the issue of Islam as early as 2005, when its former chairman, Jörg Haider, established his new party, the BZÖ, to continue in coalition with the Conservative ÖVP. In 2008, following a statement by the regional FPÖ leader Susanne Winter claiming the last prophet of Islam was a child abuser—for which she was prosecuted and convicted in 2009 (*Der Standard* 2014)—the FPÖ felt under pressure to make a comprehensive statement on its positions on Islam and Muslims. In the same year, the FPÖ presented its platform, "We and Islam" (Hafez 2009b). It included several restrictive provisions, such as surveillance of Muslim private schools, a requirement that religious education be in the German language only, a ban on minarets by way of an amendment of the federal constitution, surveillance of mosques, and a hijab ban, among other things. For our discussion here, another objective is central. In the very last sentence of this party platform, where the FPÖ presented four policy recommendations, it said, "The legal status of Islam in Austria shall be reconsidered." The argument goes that "immigration-Islam cannot receive the same rights as autochthonous Bosnian Muslims during the times of the Habsburg Monarchy" (FPÖ 2008c, 5). This is interesting in several ways. On the one hand, the FPÖ positions itself as a political party that recognizes the historical position of Muslims in the history of Austria and the Habsburg monarchy, while at the same time, it draws on the notion of the good Bosnian Muslim, thereby reproducing this one-sided mystification of Muslims in the days of the monarchy. On the other hand, it breaks with this discourse by creating the notion of "immigration Islam," which the FPÖ construes as an opposing idea to the good "autochthonous Muslim"—a rather antiquated terminology that frames Muslims as domesticated subjects. The essential recommendation of the FPÖ is that Muslims that have immigrated to Austria and are not considered the heirs of the "autochthonous" Bosnian Muslims should not "receive the same rights" (5). Thus the party questions the Islam Act of 1912 and, more precisely, the IGGÖ, which represents the enactment of the Islam Act of 1912. In other words, the FPÖ tried to find a way to strip the vast majority of Muslims of their equally recognized legal status that is similar to that of adherents of other churches and religious communities in Austria.

However, it was not only the FPÖ that questioned the equality of the legal status of Muslims in Austria. The Wiener Akademikerbund (Viennese Association of Academics), an association affiliated with the Conservative ÖVP (Bridge Initiative Team 2020d) which forms part of the Counter-Jihad Movement, "a network of European and North American anti-Muslim movements, institutions, political parties, authors, bloggers, and activists who claim that 'Western civilization' is 'under attack' by Islam" (Bridge Initiative Team 2020a), attempted to organize its second conference in Europe in Vienna in 2008—more specifically, in the halls of the Political Academy (Politische Akademie), which is the ÖVP's educational institution. As we will see later, some of the Islam policy claims of the Viennese Association of Academics were successfully implemented many years later.

## A Changing Paradigm: The New Islam Act of 2015

In 2011, a year that saw the election of the new IGGÖ president and the establishment of the position of integration state secretary in the Ministry of Interior Affairs, the renewal of the Islam Act seemed to become a viable option, but it happened under different circumstances than in the early 2000s. When Anas Schakfeh served as president of the IGGÖ from 1997 to 2011, he approached the Cultural Affairs Office (Kultusamt) to amend the Islam Act. The Kultusamt is formally in charge of regulating the relationship of the state authorities with the legally recognized churches and denominations. However, in 2011, with the installation of the integration state secretary in the Ministry of Interior Affairs, another pattern became dominant in the relationship between the IGGÖ and state authorities. This pattern followed a European trend that placed Muslims under scrutiny by the ministries in charge of domestic security issues (Laurence 2012). Especially since the violent attacks of 9/11, governments of European countries have seemed to be more interested in shaping the relationship between state authorities and Muslim institutions rather than leaving this responsibility to Muslims themselves. In most European countries, such initiatives have come from ministries of the interior, which have institutionalized "dialogue platforms" with Muslim actors to discuss issues of Islam, society, inclusion, and the perceived growing threat posed by radicalization.

Similarly, the first and only integration state secretary in Austria's Ministry of Interior Affairs, Sebastian Kurz (ÖVP), initiated a process called the Dialogue

Forum Islam (*Dialogforum Islam*) in January 2012. Kurz presented the Dialogue Forum Islam as a means to "improve coexistence and increase the sense of belonging of Muslims" (Dialogforum Islam 2012). His seemingly inclusive mode of speech, which rhetorically opposed discrimination and called for improving the lives of Muslims, was used to support this new institution. When the Dialogue Forum Islam attempted to introduce a new form of governance over Islam, it soon became clear that this initiative differed from the state's usual approach to other legally recognized religious societies and churches. On the one hand, the initiative engaged in ambivalent discourse that invoked stereotypical generalizations about Muslims, while on the other hand, it co-opted populist radical right concepts such as countersociety (*Gegengesellschaft*), a theory developed from that of a parallel society (*Parallelgesellschaft*), which insinuates that Muslims would create their own legislation in a territory that was dominated by them (Ronneberger and Tsianos 2015). These discourses are not based in reality, but they prove very effective for populist radical right political actors attempting to stir fear (Bracke and Hernández Aguilar 2021).

As a first step of the Dialogue Forum Islam, seven working groups were established to discuss seven issues: (1) education of imams in Austria, (2) integration and identity, (3) questions regarding values and society, (4) Islamism and Islamophobia, (5) gender roles, (6) the state and Islam, and (7) Islam and the media (BMI 2012c). The state and Islam working group discussed seven themes, one of which was the "Modernization of the Islam Act" (BMI 2012c, 42). Headed by a leading legal scholar, Richard Potz, the group framed the need for a new Islam Act very much along the lines of why the IGGÖ had wanted to amend the law: "Since the Islam Act is already 100 years old, many of its regulations are not timely anymore" (42). However, the details on what such a modernization should look like were kept ambiguous. The paper stated that "it has to be decided which orientation of Islam is to be regulated under the 'new' Islam Act" (42), since the Islam Act of 1912 dealt solely with the IGGÖ, which was established in 1979. The main argument was that according to the European Court of Human Rights, the state should remain in the position of a "neutral organizer" (42). The paper rightly described the role of the IGGÖ as connecting different Muslim associations that are organized based on the Law of Association (Vereinsgesetz) and serving as an important contact to the state. It validates the idea that the autonomy of these associations is important. In the conclusion, this last aspect is reiterated alongside the statement that the state has to be a neutral organizer (43). These were the results of one year of deliberations in working groups headed mainly by non-Muslim experts (BMI 2012b). For a long time, there were no further public announcements about this process.

However, in 2013, the SPÖ-ÖVP coalition government included a note on Islam in the "integration" section of its government program, specifically in the subsection titled "Societal Integration: Values and Engagement for Austria." This was the first time in the history of Austria that Islam was mentioned in a coalition program that defines the work for the upcoming legislative session. The program says, "The 1912 Islam Act will be updated and amended. The principles of parity, state neutrality, self-administration and self-financing are to be applied. In order to better embed imams and Islamic theologians in the linguistic and social context of Austria, they are to be trained in Austria in the long term. The bachelor's degree program in Islamic theology, which is currently in the process of being established, must therefore receive further support" (Coalition Program 2013, 29).

While the main emphasis was on the linguistic and possibly the cultural integration of imams in the Austrian education system, a pursuit that reflects the populist radical right perception of Austria as a German nation, it is still important to note that the government declared its intention to amend the existing Islam Act based on the constitutional framework of the Republic of Austria's secular system. This is expressed when the program refers to the principles of parity and state neutrality. Still, with its notions such as self-administration and self-financing, which were more of an invention at this point, the plan suggested that a new era was in the making. These new terminologies foreshadowed a new type of governance of Islam in Austria that was unknown to other churches and religious societies.

## INTRODUCING THE NEW ISLAM ACT OF 2015

It came as a surprise to most observers when the first draft of a new Islam Act was presented on 2 October 2014 by lawmakers of SPÖ and ÖVP, who comprised the coalition government. This proposal was harshly criticized for the way it was drafted. The IGGÖ was criticized for not including many Muslim institutions in this process (Hafez 2017b). Criticism was directed toward the government for presenting a bill that discriminated against Muslims. The Israelite Act of 1890, which concerned the legal recognition of the Jewish community and had been recently amended in 2012 (it was substantively an entirely new law), seems to have been used as a model, as twenty-two of its twenty-six paragraphs are nearly identical, although the two acts do include major differences. In general, the state is obliged not to interfere in the internal affairs of churches and religious societies, which in turn are obliged to avoid interfering in political affairs. The state must be neutral and hence treat churches and religious societies equally ("principle of parity"). In looking closely at the law, it is clear that these constitutional principles were not met. Rather, the Islam Act evidences massively unequal treatment and thus discrimination against Austrian Muslims as members of a legally recognized religious society. Broadly speaking, the principle of equality (*Gleichheitssatz*) and the principle of parity (*Paritätsprinzip*) (Potz 1996, 235), which require that all churches and religious societies are treated equally, were not upheld (Dautović and Hafez 2019).[1]

Although the Austrian constitution calls for the equal treatment of all legally recognized churches and denominations as prescribed by *Gleichheitssatz* according to article 7 of the Austrian Federal Constitutional Act (Prainsack 2006), the Islam Act became controversial for its discriminatory treatment of the IGGÖ. This was highlighted by leading legal scholars (especially in the law of religion, such as Richard Potz, Brigitte Schinkele, and Stefan Schima), social scientists (Dautović and Hafez 2015), and Islamic studies scholars (Skowron-Nalborczyk 2015), as well as the IGGÖ itself (IGGÖ 2014) and members of (Muslim) civil society (Hafez 2017b). This was a remarkable turn of events, because consociationalist rulemaking usually occurs not in opposition to but rather in consensus with the community and the interest groups representing it.

The Islam Act of 2015 starkly diverged from this consociationalist pattern and was widely regarded as violating the principle of parity, which is in itself derived from the broader constitutional principle of equality. In 2010, the draft legislation for the Israelite Act of 2012 had received only ten statements during the formal review process that is open to the public, whereas the draft of the Islam Act received more than 150. During the assessment procedure of the Israelite Act, which began on 18 October 2010, the draft elicited nineteen formal statements, primarily from government and different state institutions, including some very extensive critiques from the leading experts on Austrian religion laws at the University of Vienna, Richard Potz and Brigitte Schinkele (Potz and Schinkele 2010), and the constitution service of the Federal Chancellery (Hesse 2010). A critical assessment came even from the Organization for Security and Cooperation in Europe (OSCE 2015). The criticism resulted in changes to the text and renegotiation with the Israelite Religious Society, resulting in a delay of the submission of the draft to Parliament until 13 March 2012, when the government processed its revised version. Some significant changes were made, and some passages were removed—though some of them later reappeared in the new Israelite Act—but at least as many of the paragraphs that were criticized remained unchanged. The removal of one particular part (section 4 number 6 of the draft) concerning the pluralism of the Israelite Religious Society, in which Orthodox Judaism is quite dominant, was objected to by a small association of liberal Jews (or Chadasch, the Progressive Jewish Community Vienna) who felt they were discriminated against. This led to highly emotional debates in the media and Parliament. A consensus emerged among all parties that were relatively in favor of Or Chadasch, with the nationalist FPÖ being the most enthusiastic advocate of the liberal Jewish position; it had voted against amending the Israelite Act because from its point of view, the act did not meet the needs of liberal Jews sufficiently. As a result, the parliamentary procedure took almost another three months (from the beginning of the assessment procedure, the entire process was nearly twenty months) and resulted in the reintroduction of section 4 number 6 of the draft (Israelitengesetz 1890) (which then became section 3 number 11 of the Israelite Act). The amendment was passed with the consent of the Israelite Religious Society and its strongest group, the Vienna Israelite Community. In contrast, with the Islam Act, the progression from the draft's issuance to its implementation took only about half a year (Parlament Österreich 2014a), and no friction between the ministry officials and the Jewish community was reported. Whereas only one of the ten statements on the draft of the Jewish Act criticized it, the vast majority of the statements on the draft of the Islam Act—more than 130 of 150 statements—were critical (Parlament Österreich 2014a). Most importantly, the IGGÖ's criticism was not taken into account when lawmakers arrived at the final wording of the law, and the IGGÖ even objected to the final text (IGGÖ 2015).[2] A central principle of the cooperative model is that a law concerning a church or denomination must be approved by the respective church or denomination. The Supreme Council, the leading board of the IGGÖ, stated that it was not even informed about the draft before it was presented to the public (IGGÖ 2014). There were frictions within the IGGÖ in terms of how the draft came into existence. It was only after the president of the IGGÖ sent a letter to the ministers that entailed a "clear basis to recommend approval" of the law (Völker 2015)—although the official bodies of the Islamic Religious Association were not asked—that the law was formally adopted by the national parliament on this premise (Parlament Österreich 2015).

## Differential Treatment

Dautović and Hafez (2019) have shown in their detailed comparative study of the Austrian Islam Act of 2015 and Austrian religion laws with special emphasis on the Israelite Act of 2012 and the Protestant Act of 1961 that the principle of cooperation has been put in jeopardy. This principle is a defining characteristic of the institutionalized framework that regulates the relationship between churches and the state, as it views religious actors as partners of the secular state. The idea of Austria having a "cooperation model" (Brünner 2002) between the state and the church is an example of consociationalist rulemaking, a political science concept where the relevant stakeholders are part of the negotiation process.

The Islam Act of 2015 was, in many respects, a copy of the act recognizing the Jewish community, the Israelite Act of 2012, but it differed substantially in certain crucial ways. One major difference is the shift to an older pattern of state-church sovereignty. Compared to the laws pertaining the Roman Catholic Church and the Protestant Church, the Islam Act of 2015 gives the state extensive powers to intervene in internal affairs. During the age of the Austro-Hungarian monarchy—more specifically, in the late nineteenth and the early twentieth centuries—churches and denominations were treated as if they were state institutions, subordinated to the will of the Austrian emperor. However, this kind of state-church relation, called *Staatskirchenhoheit* (state-church sovereignty), in which the state unilaterally defines the limits of the internal affairs of churches and religious societies (Schima 2014), supervises and controls them, and may even appoint their (national) spiritual heads, is not compatible with the post-monarchic order of liberal democracies. The Austrian secular constitution as well as the European Convention on Human Rights (ECHR) clearly define religious freedom not only as an individual right, but also as a communal one.[3] The oldest and, by legal decree since 1920, highest state-church provision in the Austrian constitution states that "every legally recognised church and religious society has the right of mutual religious practice, organizes and manages its internal affairs autonomously . . . but is, like every society, subordinated to the general state laws" (Article 15 Basic Law). Nevertheless, Austrian law on religion has moved in another direction for years. Therefore, the legal scholars Potz and Schinkele felt compelled to state, with respect to the amended Israelite Act, that "the law in its entirety is breathing the spirit of the state-church sovereignty of that time. . . . Unfortunately, even in the present draft one can find some state-church sovereignty elements" (Potz and Schinkele 2010). Several provisions in both the Islam Act and the Israelite Act, there are manifestations of this reorientation. On the one hand, particular religious societies are strengthened in relation to lower entities, private initiatives, and associations of the respective religious society; on the other hand, the religious society is subordinated to state control.

There is critical wording in paragraph 1 of the Islam Act that seems to indicate a certain approach taken by the government in relation to this act.[4] The paragraph states that Islamic religious societies "are a public corporation." Public corporations are state institutions and entities, like the Austrian Federation, the nine federal states of Austria, municipalities, and state universities, among other bodies. In the Protestant Act of 1961, for example, the wording in the paragraph is "The Protestant Church enjoys the position of a public corporation," which emphasizes that a church or religious society is not a state institution but a unique public corporation.[5] Wording that states that a religious society actually *is* a public corporation probably has no differing juridical consequence, but it is misleading since it implies that the religious society is not independent of the state and its interests and that they are not equal, but rather that the religious society is subservient to the bodies governing the state.[6]

Dautović and Hafez (2019) emphasized that there is a general shift in the reintroduction of older patterns in more recent religion laws, such as the Oriental Church Act of 2003 (BGBl 2003), the Israelite Act of 2012, and the Islam Act of 2015. The latter explicitly states that the religious society's constitution is not valid until it is permitted by the state authority, a restriction that applies to no other law regulating a church or religious society. According to the new Islam Act, changes to regulations as well as appointments of bodies entitled to external representation become effective only on the day of approval by the federal chancellor. Not just the constitutions of the religious societies in question need approval from the state authority—even the organs of external representation (mostly, heads of religious societies) require this approval. The act also includes several other elements of state supervision that are obviously unconstitutional and demonstrate extensive intervention in internal affairs by state authorities: the appointment of custodians by the state;[7] the ability of the minister or chancellor to reverse the decisions of religious societies;[8] the ability to restrict freedom of assembly in a religious context—which conflicts not only with freedom of religion but also with freedom of assembly and the principle of equality.[9] These regulations are all unique to the Islam Act. The law explicitly regulates Islamic religious societies in the plural, already interfering in the process of recognition, as there can be various laws for different Islamic denominations. It includes the Alevi Islamic Religious Association, even though it was the smallest segment of the Alevi communities, and the larger ones were denied recognition (Çakır 2011). The Alevi Islamic Religious Association was originally recognized in 2013 under the Recognition Act of 1874 (RGBl 1874), but it gained many new privileges under the Islam Act in 2015, such as a faculty member of Islamic Alevi theology at the University of Vienna. Once it became governed under the Islam Act, it dropped the word "Islamic" from its name. While there is no one law governing all Christians, all Muslims were put under one Islam Act, thus weakening the dominant position of the IGGÖ as the sole representative of Muslims.

Another discriminatory invention was the creation of special religion law (*lex specialis*) specifically for Islamic religious societies, which established a system for the recognition of future Islamic religious societies that does not exist for any other church or religious society (paragraphs 3 to 5). It makes it easier for Muslim religious societies to be established, thus creating incentives to pluralize the landscape of religious societies—or in other words, to weaken the existing institutions by allowing increasing sectarianism to institutionalize. But most importantly, the unequal treatment of Muslim and non-Muslim applicants is not compatible with the principles of equality and parity.

The state has also given itself the power of revocation of an Islamic religious society that is recognized on the basis of the Islam Act of 2015, which is not the case with any other church or religious society that is recognized based on a special law of religion (*Religionssondergesetz*); this constitutes another violation of the principle of equal treatment and parity. Paragraph 5 allows the government to revoke the legal recognition of an existing Islamic religious society in many situations and gives the federal chancellor the power to dissolve cultus communities (which are the sum unities of a religious society) under many vague circumstances, even without the consent of the Islamic religious society of which they are part.

A rather symbolic article stating the obvious—namely, that state law takes precedence over internal religious law—is found only in the Islam Act, not in any other comparable legislation in Austria. This corresponds strikingly to the FPÖ's discourse that depicts Muslims as being loyal only to Sharia law and not the national constitution (Hafez 2015a). The legal scholar Stefan Schima points out that the wording of the earlier law, "not in contradiction to state laws" (Islam Act of 1912), compared to "not in contradiction to legal regulations" (Islam Act of 2015), implies that "the lawmaker of the year 1912 was willing to grant Muslims more rights than is the case in the present draft" (Schima 2014, 7). The background of the historic provision was the attempt to exclude the possibility of polygamy, since state matrimonial law in the Austro-Hungarian Empire depended on a person's religious status and the matrimonial laws of their particular religion (Potz 2010, 398). This justification is obviously irrelevant for the present legal situation, since Austria has had a civil matrimonial law for all its citizens only since 1938, so there is no justification for such a regulation from a legal policy viewpoint.

Paragraph 6 includes the demand for a "description of the teachings, including a text of the essential faith sources (Koran), which must differ from existing legally recognized religious societies, confessional communities or religious societies" to receive recognition. The significance of the requirement to provide a description of the teachings of a religious society as part of its constitution, including a translation of (or at least parts of) the Koran, cannot be underestimated. There is no similar requirement for any other legally recognized religious society, and this makes it incompatible with the principles of equal treatment and parity (Potz and Schinkele 2010, 13). In combination with another part of the Islam Act of 2015 (article 23, subparagraphs 1 and 3), which makes the validity of the constitution dependent on the permission of the federal chancellor, it gives the chancellor a de facto veto on questions of Islamic religious teachings and even on the Koran, since the translations must be displayed within the constitution of the Islamic religious society.[10] It is obvious that such a provision clearly contradicts the autonomy of legally recognized religious societies according to basic ideas of religious freedom guaranteed by the Austrian constitution and the European Convention on Human Rights (Potz and Schinkele 2016, 118–119).[11] The use of a state-sanctioned and exclusive translation of the Koran in religious instruction had been a demand from the populist radical right camp. In fact, this demand dates back to the conservative Wiener Akademikerbund's 2008 fifteen-point program that calls for the "disclosure of the foundations of Islamic faith" and "a certified translation of the Qur'an to be deposited" (Euro News 2008). The desire for transparency in the 2008 declaration was added to force Muslims to "display verses of the Qur'an which violate constitutional principles" (Alkan 2017). Although the Wiener Akademikerbund was formally banned from the ÖVP in 2011 for questioning the 1947 Prohibition Act that prohibits Holocaust denial and belittlement of Nazi atrocities (Bridge Initiative Team 2020d), its policy claims seem to have had a lasting impact within the power circles of the ÖVP.

The part of paragraph 6 most discussed publicly amounted to a ban on foreign funding for regular activities for the satisfaction of religious needs, which again has no counterpart in any other Austrian law on religion. This is another aspect that the Islam Act of 2015 is in conflict with the constitutional principle of equality and parity. Indeed, almost the opposite is stated in paragraph 2 of the Protestant Act of 1961: "The Protestant Church is granted the freedom to cooperate with domestic or foreign churches and religious societies." Richard Potz and Brigitte Schinkele have pointed out that "from all this no obligation can be deduced that the raising of funds for usual activities for the satisfaction of religious needs of their members has to happen domestically," and they state that "this provision contradicts established law in addition to constant judicature, according to which the acquisition of funds needed for covering material and human resources requirements is a precondition for churches and religious societies organizing and administering their internal affairs in every case" (Potz and Schinkele 2010, 15).

Potz and Schinkele rightly reminded Austrian lawmakers that the last time a law forced churches and religious societies to present their budget plans, share expected contribution amounts, render accounts, and give authorities access to church property administration, it was under Nazi rule. These measures were once sanctioned under paragraph 4 of the Church Rates Act (Kirchenbeitragsgesetz), which has been considered obsolete since 1945 for its incompatibility with Austrian basic law (Potz and Schinkele 2010, 16).[12]

The interference in the most internal religious affairs and religious teachings of Muslim religious societies can also be seen in paragraph 11, which concerns the right to religious care in special facilities (army bases, prisons, hospitals, etc.), as it requires the chaplains and caretakers to have three years of professional experience, German language skills at matriculation level, and a degree in theological studies from the University of Vienna or an equivalent according to paragraph 24 of the Islam Act of 2015. No similar regulation exists for any other church or religious society, although many of them are also locally led by non–German-speaking clergy and representatives of immigrant communities, be it Catholics from Latin America or Evangelical denominations or even the many Orthodox churches that exist in Austria.

Article (paragraph) 3 section (subparagraph) 4 states that "associations, which have the purpose of propagating religious teachings of a religious society according to this federal law and which exist at the time of this federal law coming into effect, are to be dissolved on 1 March 2016 by the administrative decision of the Federal Ministry of the Interior, if the purpose of the association is not adapted to the necessities of this Act." Article (paragraph) 31 section (subparagraph) 3, which regulates this further, represents one of the clearest basic human rights violations in the Islam Act of 2015, contradicting several articles of the Austrian constitution, especially in regard to freedom of association, freedom of religion (especially freedom of religious association, religiöse Vereinigungsfreiheit), and the principle of equality, since there is no similar regulation of the dissolution of already permitted and existing associations for any other church or religious society.[13]

## In the Footsteps of the Populist Radical Right

During the debates of 2014 and 2015, politicians and the media often said that the conception of the new Islam Act was very similar to that of the Israelite Act of 2012 (*Kurier* 2014b) and used this to justify it in the face of criticism. However, the broad, superficial, formal similarities disappear on detailed analysis of the content of the laws' texts.[14] While the new Islam Act was eventually passed with centrist party support (SPÖ in coalition with the ÖVP), the shift from the old to the new Islam Act reflects a larger move to the right in Parliament's discourse on Islam. A policy frame analysis strongly suggests that many of the regulations in the new act reflected claims made by populist radical right political actors in the decade leading up to the legislation, such as the implied general skepticism that Muslims abide by Austrian law.

For the then emerging leader of the ÖVP, Sebastian Kurz, the Islam Act of 2015 would become a cornerstone of his integration policy. As integration minister, Kurz met the FPÖ leader, Heinz-Christian Strache, for a public debate on the new Islam Act:

STRACHE: Concerning the Islam Act . . . there are positive elements like the ban on foreign funding that prevents foreign states from having an influence on our politics. But this also needs to allow for the possibility of control and sanctions. Until now, I have lacked the possibility to revoke the status of a corporatist public body [from an Islamic organization] and remove their legal status.

KURZ: Mr. Strache, it seems you haven't read the bill.

. . .

KURZ: The Act contains fines and the possibility for the chancellor to dissolve a religious denomination.

. . .

STRACHE: That's not enough. Another problem with the Act is that it has to specify that sermons and lectures have to be given in German. Also, the Qur'an must be translated into German.

KURZ: The translation of the Qur'an is in the Act too. I want to point out four aspects: First of all, the Act stipulates the priority of the Austrian legal system over faith. Second, the declaration of faith, which means the Qur'an, is part of the Act. Third, that German is the language of education is self-evident. And fourth, I was the first politician who urged that mosques should preach in German.

STRACHE: Mr. Kurz, I called for this even before you went into politics. (Metzger 2014)

This passage shows that the populist radical right demands, which the Freedom Party had been voicing for a long time, were partly implemented by a Conservative minister through the new Islam Act. In contrast to the ÖVP, the minister responsible for cultural affairs, the Social Democrat Josef Ostermayer, as shown in chapter 3, muddled his position by defending the Islam Act, suggesting that it had little to do with security issues but rather aimed to protect Muslims from foreign interference. In contrast, Kurz framed the Islam Act as a security measure. The pressure from the FPÖ on the policy formulations of the Conservatives was also evidenced by the head of the ÖVP's parliamentary faction, Reinhold Lopatka, who said during a parliamentary debate on the violent military organization Islamic State that the Islam Act was an "appropriate response to Islamism" (Neuhold 2014). It should be noted that the Conservatives were able to play this dominant role because the Social Democrats had largely ceded this policy area to the ÖVP. Hence, the ÖVP was now able to emphasize the issue of Islam as a core competency, while the FPÖ, which has an even more radical stance on this issue, was not able to demonstrate competence because it had been in opposition since 2005.

## CONCLUSION

On one level, the approach to Islam-related politics and the ambivalence in the debate on the new Islam Act apparent in both centrist parties, especially the SPÖ and the Greens, demonstrated the shift in the national debate on Islam. The ÖVP has co-opted many of the policy claims of the FPÖ, as shown by Sebastian Kurz's ability to take ownership of the issue from the other mainstream parties and stake out a position between the center and the populist radical right, leaning more toward the latter. This course of action was designed to appeal to voters who, like many in the ÖVP, were dedicated Catholics who felt apprehensive about the growth of Islam. Kurz's approach was designed to appeal to an electorate concerned about immigration but for whom the FPÖ was too radical and controversial. Lastly, taking a tougher stance on integration, as well as on the monitoring of the Muslim community, also allowed the ÖVP to shore up its reputation as the law-and-order party in uncertain times.

This led to substantial changes in the legal regulation of Islam. In the past, the IGGÖ had been regarded as one among several communities that had unique interests and concerns that the state and politics customarily handled through consensualism and organized interest representation. Now, the tradition of pluralist inclusion of different religions had given way to a view of Islam through the prism of securitization and its cultural compatibility with Austrian values. The IGGÖ was treated differently than other churches and denominations, and the principle of equality of all churches and denominations as well as the principle of cooperation have been jeopardized. The new Islam Act stands for two new tendencies: the IGGÖ is strengthened above lower entities, private initiatives, and associations of the respective religious society, but all the Muslim religious societies, including the IGGÖ, are subordinated to state control.

# 5 · MUSLIM HEADSCARF— AUSTRIAN CULTURE WAR

In comparison to the restrictive policies on the headscarf in other European countries, including Germany, Belgium, and France (Berghahn and Rostock 2009), Austria's policies have for a long time been described as "tolerant" (Gresch et al. 2008, 2012). As Permoser and Rosenberger have rightly argued, the corporatist inclusion of Islam with legal recognition in Austria in 1912, after the Habsburg monarchy had annexed Bosnia and Herzegovina in 1909, "is not the product of a multicultural perception of politics concerning ethnic and religious diversity, but rather the result of historic-political path dependency" (Permoser and Rosenberger 2012, 74). Empirically, they base their claims on legal studies.

Several years after this analysis, the situation changed completely. After the new Islam Act of 2015 was implemented, several new initiatives and laws made the tolerant Austrian policy a thing of the past. Any one of the very few controversies in connection with the Islamic Religious Association throughout the 1980s and 1990s would have given the state ample pretext to adopt more restrictive policies toward Islam, but this did not happen; this shows, yet again, that during that time the government's entire approach to Islam-related policies was very different. In the late 1990s, controversy arose from the fact that the IGGÖ made female students wear headscarves during Muslim religious classes in public schools. A female Social Democratic MP argued that this amounted to repression of Muslim women, while the then minister for education, Erhard Busek (ÖVP), pointed out that multiculturalism means the acceptance of others, along with all their differences (Hafez 2012a, 70–71), which confirmed the autonomy of the IGGÖ in these matters. After 2005, the debate about Islam started to shift and the institutional pattern vis-à-vis churches and religious societies began to change. The new Islam Act of 2015 was a manifestation of the increased contestation around Islam in general and the IGGÖ more specifically. This general mood could also be observed among some politicians on the left. In 2010, , as we already mentioned, the then executive secretary of the SPÖ, Laura Rudas, stated publicly that the headscarf was a "symbol of oppression" and that although it could not be outlawed, "it must be a goal to drop the headscarf" (Nowak 2010). Most of these claims had been made by the FPÖ in previous years. We can thus conclude that following a period of incendiary anti-Islamic rhetoric by the populist radical right FPÖ, the discourse also shifted among the centrist parties, including centrist-left parties such as the SPÖ.

The parties of the political left—the Social Democrats and the Greens—have strong secular streaks and view certain religious practices (such as the wearing of headscarves and traditional methods of slaughtering animals) as problematic. Consequently, they are ill equipped to combat anti-Muslim populist rhetoric and policy initiatives. Moreover, in a fragmented and contested political marketplace, defending Islam is generally not viewed as winning strategy. As long as Islam remained a cultural issue, consociationalism was well able to handle state-community relations. Once Islam had become politicized, it was introduced as an issue in party-political contestation, which in turn shifted state-community relations. The Islam Act of 2015 was the culmination of this shift and represents the first evidence of this change. While the ÖVP was able to monopolize the issue of Islam within the coalition, and thus exhibit its competence in this regard, the SPÖ muddled its position due to different divergent approaches among its leading members, leaving space for rivalry between the established Conservative Party and the populist radical right. The 2017 national elections campaign saw the Conservatives under Kurz and the FPÖ under Strache competed to see who would take tougher action on immigrants and refugees. The Conservatives' positions aligned with those of the FPÖ to such an extent that the latter felt compelled to launch a campaign titled "Vordenker-Spätzünder" (thought leader—latecomer), reminding voters that they had been the first to shape anti-Islam populist discourse in Austria. However, before the ÖVP and the FPÖ formed a coalition in late 2017, one more anti-Muslim policy was implemented by the SPÖ-headed government, with the ÖVP again as the main driver behind the law.

## BANNING THE FULL-FACE VEIL

Following the Islam Act of 2015, the other anti-Muslim legislation, which found little opposition, was the ban on the full-face veil. In March 2017, the Federal Law on the Prohibition of the Concealment of the Face in Public (Anti-Facial Disposal Act, *Anti-Gesichtsverhüllungsgesetz*) was introduced via the so-called Integration Act of 2017, which included the law.[1] Originally, Sebastian Kurz in his capacity as minister of foreign and integration affairs (ÖVP) also wanted to include a hijab ban for policewomen, attorneys, and court lawyers. However, the SPÖ countered these attempts not by silencing them, but by arguing that the dress codes for these professions did not allow women to wear a hijab in the first place. At that time, the position of the integration state secretary—then part of the Chancellor's Office—was in the hands of the SPÖ. Debate established a consensus that the hijab was implicitly not allowed in public offices in these three professions. This marked a stark shift in the regulation of the Muslim headscarf.

Few opinions that criticized the legislation were published, but those who contested it, did so in a fundamental way. According to the Association of Austrian Female Lawyers (Verein österreichischer Juristinnen), the legislation targeted "Muslim women who wear the niqab or burqa" (Association of Austrian Female Lawyers 2017, 2), although it was formulated neutrally. The association argued that "the planned ban can therefore be seen as a restriction of the liberties of a group that is already particularly vulnerable within Austrian society because it is often affected by multiple forms of discrimination" (2). It also criticized the legislation on the grounds that not more than an estimated 150 women were wearing a full-face veil in Austria.

However, the then minister of foreign and integration affairs, Sebastian Kurz, used this legislation to further position himself such that he sounded like the populist radical right. He argued that "total veiling" was "a symbol of antagonism and political Islamism and we resolutely fight it." He further said, "We stand by our European values, such as equality between men and women. We will continue to defend them unperturbed" (*Kurier* 2017). The Austrian Integration Fund (Österreichischer Integrationsfonds, ÖIF), formally in charge of implementing integration (social integration of minorities) at both the national and provincial levels, as well as an informal central mouthpiece of the ÖVP's integration policies, praised the law as enabling "the exchange between all people living in the public space" (Österreichischer Integrations Fonds 2017). Although the IGGÖ considered the Anti-Facial Disposal Act violations of privacy, religious freedom, and freedom of expression (IGGÖ 2017), it seemed that because of the Islam Act of 2015, the representative body of Muslims in Austria did not have the power it once had. It was no longer the only representation of Muslims, as had been the case before 2015, nor was it consulted whether such a ban would contradict its interpretation of some tenets of Islam. In a nutshell, the Islam Act of 2015 sidelined the IGGÖ and weakened its political status. Two years later, the first legislation to allow state authorities to regulate Muslim religious dress was implemented. The dam was broken, and other legislative measures soon followed.

## BANNING THE HIJAB IN PRESCHOOL

Shortly after the Integration Act of 2017 was implemented, the coalition between Social Democrats and Conservatives fell apart and the following elections were won decisively by the ÖVP under the leadership of Sebastian Kurz, who had fully rebranded his party. The "New ÖVP—List Kurz" won more than 30 percent of the votes, followed by the SPÖ with 26.9 percent and the FPÖ with 26.0 percent (BMI 2017). Kurz formed a coalition with the Freedom Party and presented a government program that dealt extensively with issues related to national culture and identity and included several policies regarding Muslims, including a ban on the hijab in preschools.

The ban was presented by the Austrian government at an early stage in 2018 and was especially promoted by Vice Chancellor Heinz-Christian Strache (FPÖ). According to him, this measure was to assure integration. For Strache, the hijab "plays into the hands of political Islam, which has already created dangerous parallel societies in diverse structures of associations" (Pándi 2018). This initiative found little opposition, even among journalists from liberal newspapers, which was explicitly welcomed by Strache. On 4 April 2018, a hijab ban in kindergartens was commissioned to "allow all girls equal chances to develop," which Kurz described as a way to protect them from "political Islam" (Hafez 2019b, 106). While the minister of education had declared that the IGGÖ would be included in drafting the law, this did not happen. Originally, the government urged the opposition parties to support the act, since legislation on school affairs needs a majority of two-thirds to be amended, but ultimately, a different path was taken to assure a hijab ban. In the meantime, both Strache and Chancellor Kurz publicly argued on TV that a hijab ban should be extended finally to all levels of public schools, universities, and public offices (106–107). While several public figures embraced the idea of banning the hijab, and some even called for the ban to be extended immediately to children in schools, several legal scholars argued that a law that bans the hijab but allows other religious garments such as the kippah could not be legally implemented. Supporting this view was the president of the Constitutional Court, who argued that all religious communities have to be treated equally. The IGGÖ, which was not included in the drafting of the law, announced that it would go to court against such a regulation (107).

Since the opposition parties did not support the envisioned Child Protection Act, the federal government enacted a so-called 15a agreement. Such an agreement allows the federal government to draw up contracts with the nine provinces and gives the responsibility for the implementation to the state (provincial) level. However, the federal government approached the provincial governments only after making its plans public, safe in the knowledge that the majority of these governments were in the hands of the ÖVP, a party that generally represents more traditional and rural population groups than urban voters. The government's main argument was that the legislation would protect girls from "early sexualization" (Hafez 2019b, 108). The opposition parties—the SPÖ and the NEOS—argued that the hijab ban was nothing but a symbolic act to distract from other policies. Even ÖVP-leaning states initially argued that the hijab ban did not make sense, since at that age girls in preschool and kindergarten typically do not wear the hijab. At the same time, government officials stated that they had reason to fear that the ban would be litigated at the Constitutional Court. Following the public objections, the federal government declared that the hijab ban would be a condition for federal funding of kindergartens. The 15a agreement would "prohibit children from wearing ideological or religious clothing that aims at the early sexualization of children and thus sexual segregation, and therefore was incompatible with the constitutional values and educational goals of Austrian law, especially gender equality" (108). While the hijab ban paved the way for an extension of this law and its underlying reasoning to other spheres, as Kurz and Strache had already announced, many journalists criticized the ban for being only a symbolic measure; they nonetheless failed to see the dangerous precedent it set, which is exactly what happened. Finally, all states, including those led by the SPÖ (Burgenland, Vienna, and Carinthia), agreed with the federal government to implement this regulation.

The hijab ban was also a carefully orchestrated obfuscation strategy to help launch the new ÖVP-FPÖ coalition government, which had formed in December 2017. Serious cuts to the social welfare services, which had been slowly declining over the previous thirty years,[2] as well as the "flexibilization of working hours," a euphemism for increasing workdays to up to twelve hours were economic reforms which suited ÖVP interest groups, especially business owners, but posed a problem for the more protectionist-minded electorate of the populist radical right FPÖ. This is because the FPÖ generally relies on the electoral support of working-class voters who have left the Social Democrats to vote for the FPÖ. The government also faced constant criticism from the public and the media because of these policy plans. The Freedom Party, which had vowed to protect Jews against the alleged new anti-Semitism stemming from Muslims, was confronted with numerous incidents of anti-Semitic and racist statements from their rank-and-file functionaries (Macq 2018). In addition, the new government planned a severe cut in social services in the health sector, which would primarily affect the working poor. The populist radical right minister of the interior in particular was facing criticism after the opposition parties launched an investigation into his finally illegal dismissal of the head of the Austrian intelligence service (BVT, Office for the Protection of the Constitution and Combating Counterterrorism). He had even ordered raids on several high-profile BVT staff members. The minister of the interior was also criticized for allowing the BVT to be infiltrated by staff with neo-Nazi backgrounds (Die Presse 2018a). Amid these numerous accusations and the unpopular economic policy, engaging in diversionary tactics appeared promising as it shifted the focus from the government's problems to an imagined scapegoat, an exercise the FPÖ had mastered over the previous three decades (and which the New ÖVP under the leadership of Sebastian Kurz willingly co-opted).

## BANNING THE HIJAB IN ELEMENTARY SCHOOL

The ban on the hijab in preschools met nearly no opposition. One reason for this is that there simply are almost no children under the age of seven wearing a hijab. The next step of the ÖVP-FPÖ government coalition was to ban the hijab in elementary schools. The Constitutional Committee of the Austrian Parliament, which consists of members of each party represented in Parliament, interposed that a regulation to ban the hijab would be constitutional and respect religious freedom only if it affected all religious communities. Implicitly, it warned that the kippah, worn by young Jewish boys, could also be affected. Immediately, the government was cornered and hastened to emphasize that Jews would not be affected. This was especially important for Chancellor Sebastian Kurz, who had established a strong relationship with Benjamin Netanyahu that he could not afford to lose (Liphshiz 2020). Minister of Education Heinz Faßmann (ÖVP) said that he would need to formulate a hijab ban in a "more diplomatic way," arguing that civil servants must represent secularity and implying that secularity means neutrality. This strategy of hiding discriminatory legislation behind a seemingly inclusive and neutral policy is exactly what came to the fore with the new initiative to ban the headscarf for young Muslim girls. The ÖVP and FPÖ presented an amended version of the School Education Act of 1986 to include an additional passage in article 43, which said:

> In order to ensure the best possible development of all pupils, they are not permitted to wear clothing of a religious or ideological nature until the end of the school year when they reach the age of 10. The wearing of ideological or religious clothing that involves covering the head is prohibited. This serves the social integration of children in accordance with the local customs and traditions, the preservation of the fundamental constitutional values and educational objectives of the Federal Constitution, and the equality of men and women. (Rosenkranz et al. 2018, 1)

Hence, the hijab ban was conceptualized as being against "ideological or religious clothing," to promote "social integration" and "the equality of men and women." In the explanation of the amended legislative text, the proponents of the ban argued that "the state must exercise its special protective function to prevent social pressure on girls and ensure their free self-determination" (Rosenkranz et al. 2018, 2). The text also makes explicit that only attire that covers the "entire head of hair or large parts thereof" (2) is affected, thus ensuring that Jewish boys wearing the kippah are not affected by the new law. The explanation continues,

> The present regulation is also intended to protect Muslims who do not practice the veil out of personal conviction and those followers of branches of Islam in which the veil is not a practice and thus ensure a free decision about the practice of religion, as well as to enable successful integration. Integration is a two-way process that requires the participation of the respective target group. Wearing the Islamic headscarf until the age of 10 can lead to early segregation, especially gender segregation, which is not compatible with Austrian fundamental values and social norms. (2)

This argument draws on racist assumptions of a hypersexual male Muslim body, an image that holds up white Christian men as the ones to set women free from the oppression of Muslim patriarchy. This is reminiscent of the colonial idea of "saving brown women from brown men" (Spivak 2010, 268). The lawmakers position themselves as rescuers of Muslims, clearly framing one segment of the Muslim population as living lives in contradiction to the rest of the society, indicting them for gender segregation and framing the hijab as belonging outside of the sphere of self-determination.

Including a hijab ban in the School Act was thinkable only because of a general discourse that frames Muslim men as hypersexual, oppressive, deviant males prone to violence, while Muslim women are seen as having to be rescued by non-Muslim, nonbrown men (Abu-Lughod 2013). At the same time, debates about Muslim women and the hijab were overrepresented in Austrian media. As Maria Pernegger has shown in her study on the coverage of women's issues in Austrian media, 37 percent of all media coverage in Austria was on the hijab of Muslim women, while other policy issues about women made up only 63 percent:

> With the headscarf/burka, the coalition partners succeed in firmly anchoring an issue in the media discourse for years. Something like this is only possible if a topic has the corresponding polarization potential. The same (marginal) topic can be debated for years if it is transported in small bites with different emphases—from the burqa ban to the headscarf ban for policewomen and teachers, to the headscarf ban for girls in kindergartens. Thus, the topic remains a fixed point in the media debate and, at 37 percent, takes up by far the largest share of women's political reporting in print. (Pernegger 2019, 26)

In the following section, the debate about the hijab in the Austrian Parliament from 2013 to 2019 is analyzed, including the hijab ban in elementary schools that was implemented in early 2019.

## DEBATING THE HIJAB BAN IN PARLIAMENT

In an analysis of press releases and parliamentary debates from 2013 to 2019, Alen Hocko shows us why most parties represented in the national parliament generally supported a hijab ban. As Hocko has demonstrated, the FPÖ had been the primary supporter of anti-Muslim mobilization in regard to the debate to ban the hijab. Hocko's analysis shows that the argumentation during the era before the "refugee crisis" of 2015 was less restrictive than after the "refugee crisis," when people fled war-torn Syria and Iraq and arrived in Austria in late summer 2015. After the so-called crisis, the FPÖ dominated the debate. It published more than half—82 out of 148—of the press releases on this issue. Many conceptualizations of the topic as well as debate strategies for the headscarf ban were initiated by the FPÖ and found their way into other parties' discourses to varying degrees.

The theme of protecting Muslim women from oppression, which had been originally introduced in Austrian daily politics by Jörg Haider when he was the leader of the BZÖ (Hafez 2012b), had long been used not by the FPÖ but rather the ÖVP. Later, when the FPÖ started to become stronger and entered a coalition government with the ÖVP, both the ÖVP and the FPÖ argued for a hijab ban on similar grounds, such as protecting Muslim women from oppression and sexualization, or simply representing Muslim women. Both parties also point to hijab bans in Muslim-majority countries to legitimize Austria's ban. Muslim women are portrayed as passive actors with "typical" female characteristics, and as victims in need of liberation. Both parties used this theme extensively and related it to the construction of a societal divide between "us" and "them." The theme of protecting women was also used by the SPÖ and the liberal NEOS. While both populist radical right parties, the populist radical right FPÖ and the centrist-right ÖVP, competed for issue leadership in regard to Islam, they did not have a similarly consistent position in regard to the hijab ban. The SPÖ, as a propagator of white feminism, also used the theme of patriarchy. Even the SPÖ's 2018 party platform is quite inconsistent with regard to these issues. While the party platform does not specifically mention Islam and Muslims but speaks of religion in a general manner, it discusses patriarchy thrice. One paragraph brings together both concepts and discusses the tension between them:

> We are committed to the full freedom of thought and belief. We respect the commitment to religious faith and a non-religious worldview as the innermost personal decision of each individual. The full freedom of belief and thought may not be restricted by the state or in any other way. Social Democracy opposes all old and new attempts to misuse religion for political purposes and to impose values and ways of life on others. We clearly oppose the use of religion to promote patriarchal and outdated role models in the name of religion. Patriarchal and outdated role models are perpetuated, and violence is committed in the name of religion. Just as social democracy defends the right of every individual to freely practice a religious confession, it also insists on respect for other religious and non-religious worldviews. Those who claim respect for themselves must respect others and respect their freedoms. (SPÖ 2018a)

This programmatic statement clearly shows the tension caused by the SPÖ positioning itself as a defender of human rights on the one hand and as a prominent critic of the patriarchy and violence on the other hand. Although the arguments of many MPs from the SPÖ and the NEOS differ from those of the ÖVP and FPÖ, the left and liberal parties seem to be affected by contagion due to the FPÖ's dominance on this issue and the co-optation of it by the ÖVP.

Arguing for the Hijab Ban

The FPÖ had adopted a hard-line position from the very beginning. In one of several programmatic positions introduced for the first time in 2008 (FPÖ 2008a), the FPÖ argued to ban the hijab in schools, at universities, and in public service fields. Blaming the would-be victim of a hijab ban and failing to see their ban as a means of exclusion, the FPÖ argues that the hijab itself excludes Muslim women from the public sphere: "Wearing a headscarf would exclude many young girls from public life.... The headscarf is a symbol of Islamism and is perceived by many women as oppression. For this reason alone, a headscarf ban at schools, universities, and public service would be long overdue here in Austria.... The protection of women against oppression must therefore be the top priority—even above the freedom of a few who want to wear it voluntarily" (FPÖ 2015).

This obsession with freeing women contradicts the fairly patriarchal attitude of the FPÖ in general (Goetz 2021). Hence, one is inclined to regard it as projection by FPÖ members when they call the hijab a "systematic oppression" (Parlament Österreich 2019b); a symbol of patriarchic and archaic oppression that contradicts the values of a modern, open, and free society (BMEIA 2018); and a "prison made out of fabric" (FPÖ 2016). This victimization framing urges the defenders of freedom and liberty to rescue the imprisoned. While the FPÖ has never been a party that supported women's rights—indeed, it stands for a traditional concept of family and has often voted against increasing protections and supports for women—the debate on the hijab was used to position the FPÖ as a defender of "hard-won women's rights" (FPÖ 2017a). Some politicians explicitly communicated their perceptions of Muslim men as the perpetrators of this oppression (Parlament Österreich 2019b). It is especially Muslim fathers, brothers, and husbands who are framed as the enforcers of patriarchic systems (FPÖ 2019).

The ÖVP also used a discursive strategy of victimization, describing the hijab as a "symbol of oppression" (ÖVP 2019d) and asking for the support of all female leaders of Viennese political parties to rally behind the ÖVP to ban the hijab in preschool. Whereas white non-Muslim women are framed as "Western" and "enlightened," Islam stands for "oppression," which is typical of Western white feminism (Shachar 2007). In 2019, the then integration spokesperson for the ÖVP argued in this culturalized way: "It [the hijab] represents an ideological attitude that does not correspond to our Western, enlightened society. If we want to protect children and especially young girls from coercion and oppression, there is no way around a ban" (ÖVP 2019a). Another MP from the ÖVP went so far as to quote *Submission*, by the French author Michel Houllebecq, calling him a "Nietzsche of our days," in arguing that the hijab ban means "abolishing oppression" (Parlament Österreich 2019b).

The call to ban the hijab is also based on the idea that the hijab is a symbol of the sexualization of Muslim women and girls. Wearing the hijab in preschool is framed as an "early sexualization" (*Frühsexualisierung*) of young girls. Thus, proponents of the hijab ban in preschool argued that it would protect Muslim children from "religiously early indoctrination, sexualization and later stigmatization" (FPÖ 2018c). This notion of *Frühsexualisierung* is typically used by the FPÖ and conservative circles to mobilize against early sex education for children in school (FPÖ 2018b). In the context of Muslims, the term is used to blame Islam for early sexualization because the hijab is seen as a marker that makes visible the sexual maturity of young girls. This strategy is also used by the ÖVP. An ÖVP press release reads, "The children's headscarf sexualizes young girls and deprives them of the opportunity to develop. It is our duty to protect children from these influences and to provide them with a discrimination-free childhood. This is also confirmed by the experts Zana Ramadani and Professor Ebrahim Afsah" (ÖVP 2019e). By quoting Muslim agents who provided their expertise to the ÖVP in the Constitutional Committee before the bill reached Parliament, the politicians of the ÖVP used them to further legitimize the curtailing of Muslim religiosity. Hence, it is not only the dominant white Catholic society but even the brown Muslims who want to free themselves from the 'oppressive' symbols of Islam. This also reflects the aim of the ÖVP to not blatantly speak out against Islam and all Muslims, like the FPÖ, but rather to allow the "good" Muslims to partner with the ÖVP. According to the ÖVP, the hijab ban would allow a "Western-oriented Islam" to develop (ÖVP 2019b).

Another central theme is the defense and representation of Muslim women. Acknowledging the fact that Muslim girls wearing the hijab are often targeted, one MP from the FPÖ stated, "Our state must protect girls and young women. Insults and pressure must be stopped immediately. This can only be assured by banning the headscarf from school classes in general!" (FPÖ 2017c). Similarly, the FPÖ claimed in a press release that the "ban on headscarves in elementary school serves to protect our children from discrimination and early sexualization" (FPÖ 2019). Several politicians of the FPÖ lamented the nonrepresentation of liberal Islam and liberal Muslims by the Islamic Religious Association (IGGÖ) (FPÖ 2017d, 2017f). In creating a dual dichotomization of the good and the bad Muslim, the hijab becomes a central feature of the bad Muslim, while the good Muslim is framed as the liberal one who rejects traditions like the hijab. The theme of representation is also used by the ÖVP: "It must not be in a pluralistic society like ours that girls are forced to wear headscarves. The federal government acts in the interest of our children" (ÖVP 2019c). Here, the ÖVP positions itself as a political party in power representing the interests of "our children" who must be saved from systems of (male Muslim) oppression.

Another important theme of argument was integration. The hijab as well as the full-face veil, the niqab, are seen as "hindering integration" (FPÖ 2018b). Again, the phenomenon of discrimination in the job market against Muslim women wearing the hijab is taken as a reason to empower these women by banning the hijab (FPÖ 2018b). The ÖVP has also presented the hijab as a sign that indicates an inability to integrate into Austrian society and thus as a sign of willing separation. The ÖVP argues that by wearing the hijab, one is not part of Austrian society:

> The public service provides—as the term itself says—services for all and therefore has to orient itself not only along the laws but also along the cultural and value concepts of the broad Austrian public, and the headscarf is certainly not one of them, especially in schools. . . . Islamic forms of clothing have been used more and more often and more clearly in recent years as symbols of demarcation from our Western way of life and are also questionable from the point of view of women's rights. . . . Conversely, however, precisely such clothing then makes the successful integration of women into the majority society more difficult. (ÖVP 2017c)

This quote not only reveals a paternalistic perspective on Muslim women but also accuses them of demarcating themselves from the rest of society, which is homogenized as uniform. In the FPÖ, Muslim women are specially framed as passive objects who are dependent on their husbands and require saving from male dominance. One MP from the FPÖ argued, "We cannot and must not tolerate Islamist parallel societies [*Parallelgesellschaft*] and countersocieties [*Gegengesellschaften*] in Austria and must enable children to find their way to a free and self-determined development" (FPÖ 2018a). *Parallelgesellschaft* and *Gegengesellschaften* are two important concepts used in populist radical right discourses that have become quite mainstream. Speakers who use these terms claim that Muslims segregate themselves from the society in which they live, not only to remain separate but also to act against (*gegen*) the dominant society. While the notion of *Parallelgesellschaft* has become mainstream, the term *Gegengesellschaften* has been developed to identify Muslims as a threat to the rest of society. The hijab is seen as a central signifier marking Muslim women as belonging to a space outside of Austrian society. Taking off the hijab thus becomes a ticket to getting a job and becoming a "normal" part of society.

Another important theme is "political Islam." According to one MP from the FPÖ, the hijab "is far from being a purely religious symbol or even just a head covering, but in any case, [it] carries the Sharia in its luggage" (FPÖ 2017e). Then party chairman Strache argued, "The headscarf is a symbol of political Islam. . . . What Mustafa Kemal Atatürk achieved in an Islamic country almost 100 years ago must be beyond dispute today as a conditio sine qua non in a country based on Christian values" (FPÖ 2017d). Hence, Austria would only be following in the footsteps of modernized Muslim countries. Similarly, the ÖVP presented Atatürk as an example of a leader "who banned traditional Islamic clothing from the public life of his country right at the beginning of his reform path" (ÖVP

2017c). Although Muslim people are sometimes mobilized to support the argument to restrict Muslim religiosity in the public square, other Muslim voices are not taken seriously. This can be observed in the FPÖ's reasoning that the hijab "clearly contradicts the social norms of our Western community of values" (FPÖ 2017a) when it disagreed with the legal opinion of the IGGÖ that wearing the hijab is part of a religious practice. This is important because the IGGÖ is the legal representative of Austrian Muslims and its opinions are not private but have to be taken as the Islamic stance within the framework of state-church relations in Austria; ignoring them implies a break from this legal framework. The discourse on the hijab includes framing the hijab as political as well as religious. The FPÖ, for example, argued that the hijab was not necessarily "a symbol of belief" (FPÖ 2017a), but rather a symbol of political Islam, as well as a symbol of "Islamism" (FPÖ 2015) and a symbol of "radical Islamic symbolism" (FPÖ 2016). While this topos of "political Islam" is also used by the ÖVP, the hijab is not solely framed as political. It also became a symbol of a religious and ideological Other, as a press release reveals: "Children must be protected from problematic political, religious or ideological backgrounds" (ÖVP 2018b).

For the ÖVP, implementing the hijab ban at the federal level is an important tool to position itself against the SPÖ, which governs many urban centers, including the capital Vienna. The ÖVP sees the hijab ban as a way to integrate Muslim women: "I call on the City of Vienna, however, to also take action itself and to fundamentally change its attitude, to stop its subsidies for Islamic kindergartens, and to pull together with the federal government on the headscarf ban. There must be no tolerance for such conduct, which is incompatible with our leading culture [*Leitkultur*] and value system" (ÖVP 2018a). The term *Leitkultur* was introduced in Germany at the end of the 1990s by the political scientist Bassam Tibi, who discussed the place of Islam in Germany and Europe (Tibi 2001). Later, the term was primarily used to refer to Muslims not fitting into the mainstream culture, the *Leitkultur*. In the above example, the *Leitkultur* is defined by the white, non-Muslim majority that excludes symbols of Muslim visibility like the hijab.

Related to the political discourse on *Leitkultur* is the theme of enlightenment, which has been especially central in statements made by the ÖVP. For one MP, "It's about keeping the head—in the case of young girls in elementary schools—clear, keeping the head clear for development in physical, in mental, in spiritual terms. . . . It's about the enlightenment that we have to receive . . . about stepping out of the subjugation that this headscarf represents. That is, in fact, the case" (Parlament Österreich 2019b). Not covering one's head becomes a sign of physical, mental, and spiritual independence and enlightenment.

A rather inconsistent theme refers to "secularity" and "neutrality." While Austria is a secular state that follows a model of cooperation with legally recognized churches and religious communities, a Catholic dominance still pervades the political landscape. During the debate on the hijab ban, ÖVP politicians argued that the hijab in school would "undermine" (ÖVP 2019b) the neutrality of the state in general. This perspective was articulated in a press release from the former general secretary of the ÖVP: "Especially in school, there is a need for clear role models, who convey our basic understanding of a religion-friendly but secular state and transport our fundamental values such as freedom and equality" (ÖVP 2017a). Although the ÖVP calls for the protection of neutrality and secularity, the Christian cross, a religious symbol that can be found in every public building and also every school, goes unchallenged. Hence, the defense of neutrality and secularity is simply a means to defend the Christian white character and dominance of the public order. The Christian—or more specifically, the Catholic—cross in the public buildings is seen as part of the *Leitkultur* and a manifestation of fundamental rights (ÖVP 2017d).

### Arguing against the Hijab Ban

Left-wing and liberal parties have often wondered about the discourse on the hijab asking whether right-wing parties actually care about women's rights, as they claim. Traditionalist perspectives on families dominate the worldviews of both the ÖVP and the FPÖ, which have reliably voted against same-sex marriage and LGBTQI rights and have expressed little to no support for women's shelters. From the perspective of the SPÖ and the NEOS, the right-wing parties use the issue of the hijab only for the purpose of "othering" Muslims in Austria, not because they are genuinely dedicated to empowering women (SPÖ NÖ 2018; NEOS 2019a, 2019b). The SPÖ argues that banning the hijab in preschool is nonsensical, since girls at that age do not actually wear one: "And if the arguments for this course of destruction are lacking, then a headscarf ban for kindergarten children is conjured out of the hat to distract. As a mayor and state legislator who is on the road a lot in Lower Austria, I don't know a single child with a headscarf in kindergarten or in elementary school" (SPÖ NÖ 2018).

This argument that no child or only a small number of children wears a headscarf and therefore a legal solution is not necessary was presented in many of the statements by SPÖ politicians in parliamentary debates (SPÖ 2018d). Here, the hijab ban is challenged not for reasons related to moral values but because it is a non-issue. Another theme that came up frequently in the discourse is self-determination. The SPÖ argued against a ban for several reasons, several of which are conveyed in a statement released by the female spokesperson of the SPÖ: "I think it's a shame that people are calling for bans on such a sensitive topic. . . . Every woman should have the right and the opportunity to live her life in a self-determined way, independently and according to her wishes. Our goal is to encourage women in their actions and to provide the framework that is needed to be able to live freely and in dignity" (SPÖ 2016). This Social Democratic MP argued that the right to self-determination should belong to individual women and the state should not be able to dictate the lifestyle of women. The SPÖ also touched on another theme in order to satisfy its rather antireligious electorate that sees religion in general as contradictory to the ideological roots of a Social Democratic political party. The idea of "symbol politics" was used to frame the hijab ban of the populist radical right parties as a superficial means to mobilize fear. As one MP said, "We, therefore, have little to gain from the sole proposal for a headscarf ban for girls in elementary school—even if we emphasize in the same breath that it is quite clear that girls must not be forced to wear a headscarf" (NR 2019, 209). This example shows that the SPÖ tried to position itself as a political party that is not in favor of the hijab as a religious issue, but at the same time it argued that such a hijab ban would hamper the integration of these girls, since it leaves out educational empowerment. During one parliamentary debate, an MP from the SPÖ said, "I also don't want children to wear a headscarf because their parents want them to. . . . We should not break off contact with a ban. We should talk to them; we should hire social workers. We should talk to the parents" (Parlament Österreich 2019b).

Hence, to some extent, the SPÖ reproduced the image of Muslim girls being oppressed, while at the same time, it positioned itself as opposing a hijab ban. This is also the case for the NEOS, which does not question the idea of the hijab as a form of "oppression," as the ÖVP and the FPÖ argued. This is reflected in a statement made by the former party leader of the NEOS: "Young girls must never be forced to wear a headscarf" (NEOS 2018a). A press release of the NEOS reads, "Nobody wants to see children with headscarves in childcare facilities" (NEOS 2018c). Hence, the idea of a dominantly white, non-Muslim space is again reproduced.

For some politicians from the SPÖ, the hijab is intended to exclude Muslim women from the public sphere. Using themes of "differentiation," "patriarchy," and "representation of Muslim women," one MP from the SPÖ argued that Muslim women can be empowered only if they are not excluded and dictated to. Speaking to a male MP from the ÖVP, the female parliamentarian responded,

> Do you really believe that you will achieve the liberation of Muslim women with this law? . . . We are discussing an amendment to the dress code for women. These exist almost everywhere in the world. There are mullahs and religious fanatics who tell women what to wear and tell them they can't drive cars. There are dictators and despots who forbid women in public office to wear pants or let their hair down. Would we like to join them? My stomach certainly turns as a feminist when I learn or even experience that fathers, brothers, brothers-in-law— whoever—force young girls to wear a headscarf. (Parlament Österreich 2019b)

This argument reveals how successfully the ÖVP and the FPÖ were able to frame the hijab as an oppressive item. Another MP (NEOS) who argued against the hijab ban nevertheless referred to the oppressive dimension of the hijab: "To avoid any misunderstanding, I am not in favor of girls wearing headscarves in elementary school, but I am in favor of everything being done to ensure that every child has the chance to develop his or her abilities, no matter where he or she is born into" (Parlament Österreich 2019b).

Even so, some members of the NEOS defended women targeted because of their hijabs. According to the NEOS chairman, wearing a hijab should not be a reason to be mobbed (NEOS 2018a). However, in contrast to the ÖVP and the FPÖ and especially the SPÖ, the NEOS argued that a hijab ban should be extended up to the age of fourteen years (NEOS 2018b, 2019a). Hence, it voted against the hijab ban in preschool, because it would not be part of a comprehensive program to promote integration. The then chairman of the NEOS saw a hijab ban as one of many measures to ensure better integration of the otherized Muslim:

> We must always be careful with clothing regulations and bans in a liberal democracy. We will look at the government's legislative proposal. One thing is clear, however: symbolic debates can never replace a serious integration policy. . . . Young girls must never be forced to wear a headscarf. . . . However, headscarf bans alone will not solve the serious problems of integration in education. . . . For this purpose, more funds are needed, for example, to hire social workers who can provide real support in integration and mediation. (NEOS 2018a)

## CONCLUSION

With the implementation of the ban on the full-face veil in 2017, a centrist government comprised of the SPÖ and ÖVP laid the basis for regulating Muslim women's bodies. Soon, more laws were implemented, not under the leadership of the Social Democrats this time, but by the ÖVP, which sought to restrict the wearing of the hijab in educational institutions. After 2015, the IGGÖ was no longer consulted by the government and state authorities along consociationalist lines, as it had been in the past. Rather, the opposite was the case: the IGGÖ's strong objections to these laws went ignored. It was clear that the populist radical right's discourse on the hijab, which is central to all anti-Muslim discourses, had become so mainstream that it was not only fully co-opted by the ÖVP but even partially shared by opposition parties that otherwise had social-liberal agendas.

In discussions in Parliament, the hijab was negatively framed as a symbol of systematic oppression. It became a symbol of patriarchal oppression that was in conflict with a modern, open, and free society. The hijab ban was rationalized by its framing as a tool of "early sexualization" and "religiously early indoctrination, sexualization, and later stigmatization," which is seen as contradicting the social norms of "our Western values." Hence, the hijab is no longer seen as part of religious praxis, but rather as a symbol of so-called political Islam, as various members of Parliament have argued. Naturally, the solution must be to protect women and children from these devastating political influences that run counter to "social integration" or ideas of equality. The state takes on the role of a savior to allow Muslim girls self-determination. Blaming the victim of the hijab ban, MPs argued that the hijab itself excludes Muslim women from the public sphere, instead of seeing the hijab ban as a means of exclusion.

To counter this discourse, opposition MPs first put on record that there were nearly no preschool-age girls wearing a hijab. Some MPs also saw the hijab ban as being against independence and self-determination. Most interestingly, some MPs from the social-liberal NEOS reiterated that the hijab was negatively influential for young girls and even called for an extension of the ban to age fourteen, rather than ten as the coalition of the ÖVP and FPÖ had proposed. The political left—namely, the Greens, the SPÖ, and NEOS—were ill equipped to combat anti-Muslim populist rhetoric and policy initiatives due to their strong secular streaks. As defending Islam is not generally considered a winning strategy, they offered little opposition, starting with the SPÖ, which implemented the face-veil ban during its coalition with the ÖVP and supported the 15a agreement to ban the hijab in preschools.

This helped the ÖVP become the de facto leader of anti-Muslim policies.[3] After the coalition of the ÖVP and the FPÖ crumbled in May 2019 and the ÖVP formed a new coalition with the Greens, their coalition agreement included an expansion of the hijab ban to middle school, up to age fourteen (Republik Österreich 2020, 148). This was not pursued only because the Austrian Constitutional Court found that the hijab ban in elementary schools was unconstitutional because it violated the principle of equality in conjunction with the right to freedom of religion. The court's brief opinion refers to the values of openness and tolerance guaranteed in article 14 of the Federal Constitutional Law, embodied in the requirement to treat different religious and ideological convictions according to the principle of equality. The Constitutional Court stated that particularly in Austria's state-organized education sector, adherence to these constitutionally prescribed values is essential (VfGH 2020). If this decision had not been made, the coalition agreement would have been implemented. In choosing to take up the topic of the hijab, the ÖVP under Kurz could be sure to find very little opposition, even from the political left and social-liberal political parties, because many of the views of the ÖVP are shared across the political spectrum, or at least they are not fundamentally challenged.

The ÖVP's new strategy under the leadership of Sebastian Kurz was to frame its discriminatory politics toward Muslims in an acceptable way to gain maximum public support and minimize resistance by the opposition parties. Hence, the hijab ban was framed as a measure to protect Muslim girls from premature

# 6 · THE SECURITY STATE

Austria is home to three intelligence services. Two of them, the Army Intelligence Office (Heeres-Nachrichtenamt, HNaA) and the Counterintelligence Service (Abwehramt, AbwA), are both parts of the Ministry of Defense. While the HNaA, which forms part of the military, is the only intelligence service that operates as a foreign service, the AbwA is the domestic intelligence service operating under the Ministry of Defense. The third intelligence service is the Office for the Protection of the Constitution and Counterterrorism (Bundesamt für Verfassungsschutz und Terrorismusbekämpfung, BVT), which is part of the Ministry of the Interior. It emerged from the former state police and merged with a few other units to become the BVT in 2002. Following several internal conflicts and scandals that became public, the BVT was restructured in 2021 and became the Directory of State Protection and Intelligence (Direktion für Staatsschutz und Nachrichtendienst, DSN). The domestic intelligence service BVT used to publish an annual report for the public that offers an assessment of security risks on a domestic level.

## THE HISTORY OF AUSTRIA'S SECURITY POLITICS VIS-À-VIS ISLAM

The oldest annual report dates back to 1997 (BMI 1998), before 9/11 and also before Islam became a highly contested domestic issue. The report states that "the majority of Muslims are adherers of a moderate Islam and act according to the Austrian laws" (47). It also argues in favor of a differentiation between Islam as a religion, Islamic fundamentalism, and most importantly, "Islamic extremism," which the BVT defies as a "radical form of Islamic fundamentalism" (47). Hence, according to the BVT's definition, while "Islamic fundamentalism" is a form of rigorous religious lifestyle, only "Islamic extremism" is considered problematic, since it is the Islamic extremist who picks up arms (46–47). At the same time, the report refers to the IGGÖ as an institution in Austria based on the Islam Act of 1912. In another instance, it is only mentioned as a victim of a bomb threat (25). This position is maintained in the following reports. The 1999 report even states that the reason why most Muslims are not extremists is because of the legal recognition of Islam and the IGGÖ (BMI 2000, 61).

This line of reasoning can be found in the BVT's annual reports until 2001, when the discourse shifted and extensive space is given to the discussion of al-Qaeda. The next year, the 2002 report reiterated the BVT's assumption that the legal recognition of Islam and access to religious education courses in public schools are powerful tools for integration (*Integrationskraft*) and are thus more influential than the extremists in convincing potential followers. The report on 2003 (BVT 2004) and 2004 (BVT 2005) did not explicitly refer to the IGGÖ. The 2005 report included the IGGÖ again when it praised the existence of the organization. According to the BVT, the institutionalization of Islam was defined as a guarantor of better security: "The security on both sides emerges from this [the legal recognition of Islam]. Muslims in Austria have a clear and confident basis with the IGGÖ to be in dialogue with different social and state organizations. The Austrian state and its authorities, on the other hand, have the confident organs of the Islamic Religious Society as a contact person who can represent and negotiate the interests of Muslims" (BVT 2006).[1] In the 2006 report, the institutionalization of Islam in Austria was mentioned as an example to be followed by other EU member states. For a few years, the IGGÖ was not mentioned. The 2012 report mentioned that the IGGÖ distanced itself from protests against the release of the anti-Muslim video "Innocence of Muslims" (BVT 2013, 67). In the 2016 report, the IGGÖ is mentioned along with other official Muslim denominations in Europe (BVT 2016, 39), while it is again left out in 2017's report (BVT 2017). To sum up, until 2017, Austria's domestic intelligence service, the BVT, did not see the IGGÖ as a security threat. Instead, the IGGÖ was seen as a guarantor of stability. This view changed much later.

## INTRODUCING CLAIMS ABOUT "POLITICAL ISLAM" AS A THREAT

While the FPÖ had initiated its very general attack on Muslims in 2005, it was the ÖVP that explicitly used the term "political Islam" systematically and consistently. The ÖVP addresses this issue in two subchapters of its election program from 2017, titled "Showing Zero Tolerance towards Political Islam" and "Preventing Parallel Societies": "Political Islam is a combination of religious fundamentalism and political extremism and as such is a breeding ground for violence and terrorism. It aims to undermine our values and ways of life. Political Islam has no place in our society—we must fight radicalization, violence, and terrorism with all means" (ÖVP 2017b, 22). The danger of "political Islam," according to the election program, is threefold: "political Islam" is a "breeding ground for violence and terrorism . . . a totalitarian system with the ambition to produce parallel legal systems," which is promoted from abroad to "undermine our values and way of life" (23). This goes hand in hand with the project of creating an "Austrian/European-style Islam" (Hafez 2018a), especially by Sebastian Kurz since he became the state secretary in the federal Ministry of the Interior in 2011. The "Islam of Austrian character" constitutes the other side of the coin of a negatively framed "political Islam" (Hafez 2018a).

Several institutions, from academia (Hafez 2020b) to policy-driven state-affiliated institutions such as the Austrian Integration Fund, which is ideologically connected to the ÖVP, have been central in shaping the discourse on Islam. They have promoted the idea of "political Islam" as a threat to society in a quite systematic way (Hafez 2021b). With this knowledge production, several politicians of the ÖVP repeatedly framed "political Islam" as the greatest threat to Austrian society. The ÖVP's general secretary argued, "The poison of political Islam must not endanger our society.... Violent clashes, territorial conflicts, and parallel justice are on the agenda according to the executive officials and judges" (*Kronen Zeitung* 2018). By using terms like "poison," those who are framed as proponents of "political Islam" are dehumanized, which justifies any extraordinary means against them. If the bad Muslims are framed as "carriers of poison," every measure can be taken to protect oneself from this "poison." This allows political leaders to justify political measures taken against this allegedly dangerous group of people.

One can see the discursive impact of this knowledge production. The ban on the hijab in elementary school was legitimized as a means to fight "political Islam." This was widely supported in the media by "integration experts" and academics, as shown in the Austrian section of the *European Islamophobia Report* (Hafez 2019c). For Chancellor Kurz, fighting "political Islam" translated to monitoring Islamist associations and Islamist ideology on social media, and segregation in the realm of education (Renner 2019a).

In the 2017 program of the ÖVP-FPÖ coalition government, for the first time, "political Islam" was a focal point of security policies. The coalition program requires that essential sources of faith, such as the Koran, be submitted in an authorized translation, something which had been requested but not achieved in the new Islam Act of 2015. This clearly shows how much politicians are interested in managing an otherized religion that is seen as a potential threat. In addition, the program reiterates a "ban on foreign financing" and a "criminal law against political Islam" (Republik Österreich 2017). Later, numerous laws were passed to fight alleged "political Islam," especially following the inception of the new coalition formed between the ÖVP and the FPÖ.

When a coalition between the Conservative ÖVP and the populist radical right FPÖ under the leadership of Sebastian Kurz and Heinz-Christian Strache was formed in December 2017, Herbert Kickl, a longtime leader in the FPÖ (who later succeeded Strache as chairman of the FPÖ) became minister of the interior. Fearing that the intelligence service was dominated by people tied to the Conservative ÖVP (Postl 2019), Kickl attempted to replace top officials of the BVT to rebrand the intelligence service according to his wishes (Schreiber and Möchel 2019). Hence, the changes within the BVT can be seen as a shift to the right based on the governance of the populist radical right FPÖ, as well as a general move to the right within a state agency.

In the annual report published by the BVT in 2019, the intelligence service closed the chapter of cooperation and adopted the agenda of the populist radical right to criminalize Muslim actors:

> "Political Islam" in Austria
>
> Islamist actors are not exclusively concerned with matters of religious cultus in Muslim communities, such as the operation of prayer rooms (mosques), offering Muslim religious education in schools, conducting Muslim religious teacher training at universities, or organizing Muslim funerals in Austria. Rather, they are involved in much broader matters of education, social welfare, and the shaping of cultural life for Muslims. The aim of this is to create a comprehensive counter-model to the existing non-Muslim majority society in Austria and to prevent Muslims from "blending in" (assimilation) with this society.
>
> The Muslim Brotherhood is currently the most exposed actor of such political Islam in Austria. It is a network of associations and organizations and, at its core, a hierarchically structured organization. Islam is understood as a holistic model of society, it is a school of life, cultural association, social idea, and business enterprise all in one. With its universal ideology, which is aimed at all areas of society, it has significantly outperformed other Islamist movements of the 20th century. . . . The Muslim Brotherhood represents a questionable concept of integration when, on the one hand, they call for "integration through participation" and for social engagement in Austria, but on the other hand, they repeated the "victim narrative" of the (alleged) one-sided discrimination of Muslims and "Islamophobia" in Austrian society. (BVT 2019, 15–16)

For the first time in the history of modern Austria, the IGGÖ was depicted as an Islamist danger instead of a legitimate Muslim institution. The services of the IGGÖ, such as religious education in public school, the training of religious teachers, and chaplaincy in prisons and hospitals—all of which were supported by the state—were now being defined as the work of Islamists. All of these services had been implemented with the help of the state, even partly supported with state funds. By defining certain fields of the IGGÖ's primary scope as Islamist threats, the BVT report made a legally recognized religious institution, once a partner of the state, into a state enemy.

Compared to the previous work of the BVT, the terminology adopted in the 2019 document reflects the political discourse to a greater extent. While the BVT previously used terms such as "Islamism" and "jihadism" in its annual reports,

now it adopted a term known mainly from the public discourse—"political Islam."
This term has been central to the discourse of the ÖVP under the leadership of
Sebastian Kurz (Hafez 2023a, 134). Various laws, such as the hijab ban in kindergartens and primary schools and the Symbol Act, have been implemented as a
means to combat what was referred to as "political Islam" (Hafez 2019c). But
other than in one headline, the term "political Islam" was not used in the 2018
report of the BVT. It was also not defined there, and it has therefore generated a
great amount of vagueness and diffusion rather than clarity. The discourse around
political Islam, it seems, is less about providing a clear-cut definition of a phenomenon than about attempting to include different strains of Islamic groups
within one broad category to criminalize all of them (Hafez 2023b). This becomes
clear when one reads about the three future challenges that the report details.
While the first two speak of jihadist and other violent expressions of so-called
Islamic extremism, the third speaks of explicitly nonviolent Islamic movements.
According to the report, while these movements denounce the democratic constitutional state, they cooperate with parties, associations, and NGOs to have a
social and political impact. This could lead to a "strategic infiltration with the aim
of shaping and regulating the society according to social beliefs of the 'caliphate'
and 'Sharia'" (17). All of this sounds more like a blatantly Islamophobic conspiracy
pamphlet than a state agency's report. In addition, it shows the wide-reaching
changes that have occurred within the intelligence service, starting with the
FPÖ's involvement in the Ministry of the Interior.

The BVT's annual report in 2017 goes even further. While concepts and terms
such as "diversity," "inclusion," and "social cohesion" have found their way into
the jargon of societal politics, and more progressive institutions have been speaking of empowerment and positive discrimination, the BVT chose quite the
opposite position. According to the report, Islamists use education, social welfare services, and the organization of cultural life to create a "countersociety." The
goal of Islamists was to prevent "assimilation," asserts the BVT—which reveals
the goal of the intelligence service. While "integration" often is nothing more
than a euphemism for assimilation, never has any state authority made this so
explicit in an official document. With this statement, the BVT goes beyond its
scope, not only discussing security threats in society but also laying down a societal agenda. As it alleges that Islamists are following an agenda to create an alternative society, it appears that the BVT itself is following a clear agenda that aims
to render Muslims invisible through assimilation. The annual report of the BVT
seems to reflect the contemporary political discourse rather than to relate to the
previous work of the BVT. This is further evidenced by the report that followed
in 2020, which did not mention the IGGÖ at all.

The BVT's annual report of 2017 suggests a major shift in the relationship
between a legally recognized religious society and a state authority. Whereas
churches and religious societies are normally associated only with the Cultural

Affairs Office (*Kultusamt*), only the Jewish community has a systematic relationship with the Ministry of the Interior, but this relationship is defined by the protection of synagogues. In the case of the IGGÖ, the 2017 annual report of the BVT represents the first time a religious society became a target of a state authority. Most of the IGGÖ's major services, such as religious education, the training of religion teachers, and the organization of chaplaincy in prisons and hospitals, are funded by the state. When these services are placed under state scrutiny, all religious institutions attached to the IGGÖ, which were legally connected after the Islam Act of 2015, are targeted. In the past, Muslim associations had been free to act independently of the IGGÖ, but the Islam Act of 2015 put them all under one roof. As a consequence, they are all at risk of surveillance by the state.

## COMBATING "POLITICAL ISLAM"

### Banning Symbols of "Extremism"

After the Second World War, Austria outlawed symbols of National Socialism by issuing the Prohibition Act of 1947. Seventy years later, following the rise of al-Qaeda and later, ISIS, this ban was extended to other groups. The coalition formed by the New ÖVP and the Social Democrats outlawed the use of the symbols of al-Qaeda and ISIS in 2014 (BGBl 2014) after the rise of ISIS that went hand in hand with the civil war in Syria and Iraq and the subsequent influx of refugees from these areas. There were no objections to this ban from any civil society organization or state body or from any Muslim institution (Parlament Österreich 2014b).

Later on, in 2018, the Symbol Act of 2014 was amended to include not just designated terrorist organizations. During the coalition government of the ÖVP and the FPÖ, the government proposed widening the scope of the act to include other organizations that were not on any terrorist list. The ban was extended to include the Marxist Kurdistan Workers' Party (PKK); Hamas; the military part of Hizbullah; the Muslim Brotherhood; the Turkish nationalist "Grey Wolves"; the Croatian fascist Ustashe; and "organizations which are declared as terrorist ones by EU legal acts" (BGBl 2019). According to the interior minister, "The symbols and gestures of the organizations mentioned in the amended law are against the constitution and contradict our basic democratic values" (BMI 2018).

There are at least three noteworthy characteristics of the groups that were later included under the Symbol Act. First, organizations that are defined as terrorist on a national or European level, like the PKK, are included alongside organizations that are not declared terrorist, like the Muslim Brotherhood, which had not been deemed extremist in Austria on any level. That is, organizations that are, legally speaking, terrorist organizations, like ISIS and al-Qaeda, are lumped together with groups that are not. Hence, symbols of "terrorism" and symbols of political and/or religious extremism are banned under the same pretenses. The affected organizations all share only one central trait: they have their roots outside of Austria. So more precisely, the Symbol Act was a foreign symbols ban. Second, the BVT produces an annual report that surveils numerous populist radical right organizations, such as the Identitarian Movement. It is striking that no Austrian white nationalist organization was included in the act, but it is perhaps understandable given that the FPÖ was in government at the time and many of these radical right organizations have personal links to members of the FPÖ, a party that was originally established by ex-Nazis for ex-Nazis (Pelinka 2002), and which has tried hard to reposition itself as pro-Jewish, anti–anti-Semitic, and purely Islamophobic (Hafez 2014c). People caught using the banned symbols can be fined up to 4,000 euros and (10,000 euros for repeat offenses), whereas using banned Nazi symbols carries a maximum fine of 4,000 euros. Third, a very important detail of this legislation states that the minister of the interior can at any time expand this list to include other groups by mere decree. According to article 1.10, any group that is part of a successor organization of the aforementioned can also be banned. This enables the minister to potentially crack down on any "foreign" civil society organization that the government labels a threat.

Other than in 2014, when the first version of the act was deliberated, several institutions voiced their discontent with the newly amended law. The Council of the Kurdish Society in Austria (FEYKOM) pointed out that many white nationalist symbols had not been included in the ban, but its objection focused primarily on the fact that the PKK's symbols were outlawed, and it asked for the removal of the PKK from the banned list (FEYKOM 2018).[2] The Ombudsoffice for Children and Youths (KIJA) was one of the few institutions to criticize the general expansion of the Symbol Act of 2014, arguing that children and youth might use these symbols as a form of provocation and that the penalities outlined in the act would be disproportionate for them (KIJA 2018). One NGO that provides legal advice for antiracist organizations even welcomed the law (Klagsverband 2018).

The IGGÖ argued that adding the symbols of organizations on the EU terrorist list would be reasonable, but it criticized the inclusion of the Muslim Brotherhood based on a report by U.S. academic who has been accused of spreading anti-Muslim conspiracy theories. This report, which was commissioned by the Austrian Integration Fund and also included the logo of the BVT, had already received plenty of criticism from other Muslim associations (Hafez 2018d). The IGGÖ argued in its opinion on the law that this report was suffering "scientific inadequacy and ideological bias . . . massive empirical deficiencies, a large number of incorrect source references and violations of good scientific practice" (IGGÖ 2018, 1). More alarming for the IGGÖ was that:

a large number of people who belong to the IGGÖ are directly or indirectly associated with the "Muslim Brotherhood" in the report without any factual basis. Thus, completely false, empirically, and factually unprovable claims are made. Such an unqualified report as a legal basis for interpreting far-reaching and completely undefined and completely indeterminate prohibitions and ordinances cannot be reconciled with any constitutional guarantees and contradicts the principle of legality.... Each of the groups mentioned in the above problematic report... can thus potentially fall under a ban under the Symbols Act and thus be stigmatized and criminalized. (2)

The IGGÖ saw itself as under threat by the expansion of the Symbol Act. In addition, the interpretation of the law did not draw on the BVT's annual report, which had not yet been published (the report is usually published a year later, in late summer), but instead drew on information from Bavaria's intelligence service. The IGGÖ pointed out that "no Austrian material for the evaluation of Austrian circumstances is referred to. Austrian facts and circumstances require Austrian empirical surveys" (2).

The Symbol Act of 2014 was again renewed by the government coalition of the New ÖVP and the Greens in 2021. This amendment further expanded the outlawing of symbols of various groups, including the white supremacist Identitatarian Movement.[3] Since the law allows the minister of the interior to extend the symbols ban to other "affiliated" organizations by mere decree, potentially every organization that a government may want to target can be affected.

The official interpretation of the law by the lawmakers held that in the case of the symbols of the Muslim Brotherhood, the state is not targeting the Muslim Brotherhood itself but rather those Muslim civil society organizations that criticize the government for its anti-Muslim politics. The interpretation drew extensively on a report written by a biased scholar connected to a think tank whose many fellows systematically target the most vocal Muslim civil society organizations across Europe to criminalize them and subsequently exclude them from the public sphere (Hafez 2018d). This reminds us of similar initiatives in the United States, where critical experts have repeatedly warned that the call to outlaw the Muslim Brotherhood is nothing but an attempt to crack down on critical political opposition. For instance, the Network Against Islamophobia (NAI), a project of the Jewish Voice for Peace, argued that the Trump administration could easily "use this legislation [proposed Muslim Brotherhood ban] and an executive order to target national and local Muslim civil liberties and other organizations that work on behalf of Muslim communities" (NAI 2018). This seems also to be the case in Austria.

It is also worth mentioning that one of the leading Islamophobic figures in the United States, Daniel Pipes, argued in a piece for the *Washington Times* that something unprecedented had taken place in Austria. "For the first time in

Western Europe, a government took power that advocates anti-immigration and anti-Islamization policies," he stated (Pipes 2018). In the eyes of neocon hawkish Islamophobes, Austria has become a laboratory for the implementation of institutionalized Islamophobia.

## Closing Mosques

One of the first measures of the ÖVP-FPÖ coalition was an attempt to close two mosques—those of a Turkish nationalist association and the Arab Islamic Society, which is a legal body of the IGGÖ. Since the Islam Act of 2015 forced all Islamic religious associations to become part of the IGGÖ, these institutions have also become public bodies. The leadership of the government—Chancellor Sebastian Kurz, Vice Chancellor Heinz-Christian Strache, the interior minister. and the minister for cultural affairs—announced in a press conference on the last Friday of the Muslims' holy month of Ramadan that eight mosques would be closed to fight "political Islam" (AFP 2018). The decision was to close the Arab Islamic Society and an additional mosque of the Turkish Federation (allegedly belonging to the Grey Wolves), which was also part of the IGGÖ. In addition, the expulsions of forty imams of the Turkish-Islamic Union for Cultural and Social Cooperation in Austria (ATIB) mosques that are connected to the Turkish Ministry of Religious Affairs were announced (ORF 2019c).

At the time, Chancellor Kurz framed the government's initiative as a means to protect ordinary Muslims from "political Islam." The cultural affairs minister (ÖVP) argued that it was "no contradiction to be a believing Muslim and a proud Austrian" (Gigler and Jungwirth 2018). According to the minister, the mosques were home to the Salafi people, who would not have a "positive attitude towards the state and society" (Temel, Kapeller, and Ichner 2018). Hence, he believed that the Arab Islamic Society, along with seven of its mosques and the Turkish Federation's mosque, had to be shut down. Yet, the Islam Act of 2015 had declared that a mosque or a cultural society (*Kultusgemeinde*) could be recognized only if it has a "positive basic attitude towards society and the state" (paragraph 4(3)). Regarding the supposed Grey Wolves' mosque, the expansion of the Symbol Act of 2014 can be seen as a precursor to legitimating its closure. Muslim spokespersons who supported this measure argued that the mosques had broken the law and that Austria had in the past failed to recognize the threat of political Islam and should systematically close down mosques of the Muslim Brotherhood. Nonetheless, it can be argued that although the closed mosques tended to represent the Egyptian community that was more aligned with the Egyptian state, which had outlawed the Muslim Brotherhood as a terrorist organization.

While the mosque of the alleged Grey Wolves was reopened shortly after the press conference, following a visit by the IGGÖ and state officials (ORF 2018b), the representatives of the Arab Islamic Society (which is a part of the IGGÖ) litigated against the government's attempt to dissolve the institution (Mittelstaedt

2018). Later, the Vienna Administrative Court declared that the government's decision of non-suspensive character (which would have suggested immediately implementing it without any possibility of appeal) was unlawful and announced a final verdict for the case in the spring of 2019 (Bischof 2018). Although the government had announced that the initiative was to target Erdoğan-affiliated mosques, the ban had affected those who were least equipped to defend themselves in terms of human and financial resources. No opposition party in Parliament stood up against these measures. The general secretary of the SPÖ even declared this to be the first "reasonable measure" taken by the government (ORF 2018a). The closed mosques were framed as a symbol of "political Islam." Hence, although there is no clear-cut definition and especially no legal definition of what "political Islam" constitutes, the concept had grown powerful.

Following a complaint by the mosques, the Viennese Court of Administration ruled half a year later that the government's initiative was unlawful (ORF 2019a). The government vowed to appeal the verdict at the Federal Administrative Court. The minister for cultural affairs argued that if this meant changing the Islam Act of 2015, then that would be done by the federal government (Ichner 2019b). Simultaneously, several mosques in Vienna and Lower Austria were visited by personnel of the Cultural Affairs Office (Kultusamt) without prior notification. The IGGÖ protested, saying this was an "exceedance of one's level of competency." The officials told the community members and imams that they would "check if everything is fine" (Renner 2019b), clearly transgressing their competencies as described in the Islam Act of 2015, which allowed the Cultural Affairs Office to check the prerequisites for the legal recognition of entities of the IGGÖ but did not give it any power to police institutions of the IGGÖ. These court-imposed restrictions on the government authorities were then used as a basis for adding new powers in an amended Islam Act, as laid out in the program of the ÖVP-Greens coalition:

Strengthening the Cultural Affairs Office with the Law:
- Ensure efficient monitoring of the ban on foreign financing of religious societies introduced in 2015 and consistent enforcement of the Islam Act by the Office of Cultural Affairs
- Expand existing provisions to prevent circumvention of the ban on foreign financing in the Islam Act (e.g., foundations)
- Strengthen the Cultural Affairs Office as the competent association authority for those associations that back religious societies. (Republik Österreich 2020, 159)

As the legal scholar specializing on law and religion Richard Potz had argued, the Cultural Affairs Office was more and more turning into a "Religion Police" (Potz

2017). Following the publication of the governmental program, other scholars of religion criticized the authoritarian moves of the Austrian government:

> The fact that the government has placed religious affairs in the Ministry of Integration, expanded the Cultural Affairs Office and gave it supervisory authority with the right to intervene, and decreed that integration is the task of religious instruction ("religious instruction that promotes integration") illustrates the religious police impetus with which the government wants to shape religion such that corresponds to its political concerns. The government seems to prefer a religion that does not get too much in the way and ideally produces well-behaved citizens. (Lauxmann 2020)

Part of this new policy was the surveillance of what the ÖVP had identified as one of the main problems: political Islam.

### An Institution of Surveillance: The Documentation Center for Political Islam

In July 2020, the Documentation Center for Political Islam was established. It had been announced on the second day of the ÖVP-Greens coalition that took power in January 2020; the integration minister, Susanne Raab (ÖVP), had stated that this was a high priority and it would be finalized within the first 100 days of government (ORF 2020b). The center was designed to be a monitoring facility that tracks religious extremism, conducts research, and documents and archives it (ORF 2019b). It was established on 15 July 2020 and launched by the minister of cultural affairs (ÖVP) alongside two scholars, Mouhanad Khorchide and Lorenzo Vidino (Bridge Initiative Team 2020c). The Documentation Center for Political Islam has been presented as "part of the national strategy of extremism prevention and deradicalization" (*Wiener Zeitung* 2020). It has a yearly budget of 1,700,000 euros. According to Minister Raab, the center makes it possible "for the first time in Austria, . . . to independently and scientifically deal with the dangerous ideology of political Islam and offer insights into the previously hidden networks" (*Kronen Zeitung* 2020). The board includes several well-known authors whose views on the matter have been considered rather one-sided, including Susanne Schröter (Bridge Initiative Team 2021), Lorenzo Vidino (Bridge Initiative Team 2020c), and Heiko Heinisch (Bridge Initiative Team 2020b). During the opening, the minister declared, "Political Islam is poison for our social coexistence and must be fought with all means. With the establishment of the Documentation Center for Political Islam, Austria thus becomes a pioneer in Europe" (BKA 2021). Minister Raab called for an annual report on extremism as well as the "creation of an overview map of problematic networks and associations in Austria that can be attributed to political Islam. The aim is to make visible the structures, actors, and goals of the representatives of this dangerous ideology.

Financial, organizational and ideological connections (abroad) are also to be inves-tigated and disclosed"; in addition, the center ought to present a "detailed analysis of the individual networks operating in secret" (BKA 2020b). This is what hap-pened nearly one year later, when the infamous "Islam Map" was relaunched, draw-ing harsh criticism from Muslims for showing all Muslim institutions and their addresses, including some of the home addresses of people representing those organizations (Farzan 2021). The introduction of the map led to protests from sev-eral NGOs as well as international organizations, including the Council of Europe, which argued that the map was "hostile to Muslims and potentially counterpro-ductive" (Council of Europe 2021). During the presentation, Khorchide said that "political Islam" is "wrapped with a cloak of democracy." He further suggested that the proponents of political Islam would engage in *taqiyya*—dissimulation or denial of religious belief in the face of persecution—by masking their "inwardly" values (BKA 2020b). According to this logic, whatever Muslims do, they cannot be trusted. While Susanne Raab reaffirmed that this monitoring center was not target-ing Islam as a religion, Muslim activists argued that it might become an "institution of surveillance" (ORF 2020a). One could add that it might become an institution for criminalizing Muslimness, with regularly issued reports insinuating that Mus-lims and their institutions are waging a war because they participate in society.

## "POLITICAL ISLAM" AS A CRIMINAL OFFENSE

By 2017, the head of the populist radical right FPÖ had called for a ban on "fas-cistic Islam," taking up a term that was coined by one of the leading hawkish neoconservative authors in the United States, Norman Podhoretz, who saw "Islamofascism" as the new enemy for a coming crusade in his *New York Times* bestseller *World War IV* (2007). Vice Chancellor Heinz-Christian Strache used this notion intentionally to follow a strategy to reframe Islam as a political ideol-ogy rather than a religion. He argued that by banning the symbols of "fascistic Islam," he was putting an end to the "creeping Islamization," a favorite reference point of the populist radical right in Europe.

During the coalition of the ÖVP with the FPÖ, the latter's parliamentary party leader Johann Gudenus announced a new act for mid-2019 forbidding the promotion of "political Islam" (*Der Standard* 2019). However, this was not accomplished during their term because the coalition broke up in mid-2019. The idea was later revived by Chancellor Sebastian Kurz following the murder of four people in a terrorist attack in Vienna by a former ISIS sympathizer on 2 Novem-ber 2020. The Greens pushed back against the legislation and watered down the bill so that it banned "religiously motivated extremism" in general, but the new integration affairs minister (ÖVP) declared during the presentation of the law that it is directed against "political Islam" (Gaigg and Schmidt 2020). So far, the government has not offered a legal definition of "political Islam," but one could deduce from the implemented policies what the government means when they accuse Muslims of following "political Islam": wearing a hijab or running a mosque (Hafez 2023a, 2023b).

As part of the antiterror package that was presented a few months after the terrorist attack in downtown Vienna on 2 November 2020, the Symbol Act was changed in July 2021. More importantly, this package included a ban on "political Islam."

Many expert institutions, such as the Association of Austrian Lawyers (Vereinigung der österreichischen Richterinnen und Richter), argued that there was no need to include religious motivation in the reasons of motivation of a criminal offense (RIV 2021). Several opinions authored by scholars of criminal law also argued that there was "no need to aggravate terrorism criminal law" (Institut für Rechts- und Kriminalsoziologie 2021; Schwaighofer and Venier 2021). Even the Ombud for Equal Treatment (Gleichbehandlungsanwaltschaft), which is part of the Austrian Chancellery, argued that such a law would further anti-Muslim racism:

> Even if the offense "religiously motivated extremist association" is now formulated in a religion-neutral way, contrary to what was initially reported in the media, only Islam is mentioned in the explanations, and the term "political Islam" is also used here. As the Ombud for Equal Treatment is aware from many years of consulting experience, laws create awareness for problematic situations and conflicts and are essential for reducing discrimination in people's minds. Anti-Muslim racism is a prevalent problem in Austria. Since the explanations focus purely on Islam, a discriminatory effect cannot be ruled out, which could exacerbate this problem. (Ombud for Equal Treatment 2021, 4–5)

The Austrian Bishops' Conference (Österreichische Bischofskonferenz) went even further, criticizing as problematic the way political Islam is discussed in the interpretation of the law. Quoting the German intelligence service, which stated that Islamism was not only a "personal, private issue, but a societal and political [one]," the Austrian Bishops' Conference argued:

> Contrary to the statements made in this passage, it is precisely an expression of the right to freedom of expression that every citizen and every institution in the state has the right, through their political and social activities, to work toward a society and thus also a legal system that corresponds to their values. Taking a clear position on sociopolitical issues is seen as the core task of a wide variety of civil society initiatives and non-governmental organizations (NGOs). Such legitimate influence on the process of political decision-making is the right of every citizen and every institution, and thus naturally also of the recognized churches and religious societies. Moreover, religion cannot be reduced to a purely private

matter. Article 15 of the Austrian Constitution of 1867 already protects the right of legally recognized churches and religious societies to practice their religion together in public. (Austrian Bishops' Conference 2021)

The Protestant Church made it even more explicit by saying that this "ad hoc legislation is directed against one religion only, Islam. This is clear from the explanatory notes, which place 'political Islam' in the foreground. Either this is an unequal treatment between Islam and other religions, which must be strictly rejected, or the legislator generally assumes that religions are not allowed to be and act politically" (Protestant Church 2021, 1). Similarly, the Austrian Bar Association (Österreichische Rechtsanwaltskammertag) saw the inclusion of "religiously motivated extremist associations" as being against the principle of equality and discriminating against Muslims (2021, 10). Many written opinions, including by the directors of the OSCE (2021) and Amnesty International Austria (2021), protested the inclusion of "religiously motivated extremist associations," but the language was finally adopted by all political parties with a great majority (Parlament Österreich 2021).

Part of the anti-terror package was a renewal of the Islam Act of 2015. It included two important amendments. First, it gave the chancellor additional power by enabling them to close legal institutions of the IGGÖ. Previously, this was solely in the hands of the IGGÖ. It also gave the Cultural Affairs Office the power to demand the IGGÖ's accounts, which is not the case with other churches or religious societies. Second, it authorized the chancellor to ask for a list of all religious officeholders, which was publicly known to be a list of imams. Again, no comparable legislation exists with respect to other churches or religious societies (BGBl. 2021). Amnesty International Austria criticized these regulations on the grounds they would create a specific regulation of Islam not found with any other church or religious society. It argued that these regulations amounted to interference in the internal affairs of a religious society and thus are against the principles of religious freedom.

## CONCLUSION

After the ÖVP introduced the term "political Islam" into its platforms, the phrase found its way into the party's coalition agreements, first in the ÖVP-FPÖ coalition and then in the ÖVP-Greens coalition. The coalition of the centrist-right ÖVP with the populist radical right FPÖ facilitated the implementation of several policies and measures that fundamentally changed the relationship between the state authorities and Muslims. Under the governance of an interior minister from the FPÖ, for the first time since its inception, the BVT regarded the IGGÖ as an institution with problematic tendencies. Gone were the days when the IGGÖ was seen as a partner against extremism.

Lawmakers introduced bills such as the Symbol Act of 2014 that gradually widened the range of movements and organizations to be targeted, finally including even parts of the IGGÖ. With the initiative to close mosques and ban the hijab in the name of the fight against "political Islam" (which was later rescinded by a court), the government showed that fighting "political Islam" was not about cracking down on violence or extremist ideology but about questioning Muslims' fundamental freedoms, such as freedom of association and freedom of religion. Although many of these initiatives had to be rescinded by the Constitutional Court and Administration Courts, the government continued along this path by making "political Islam" a criminal offense in July 2021. Gone were the days of consociational policymaking, where the IGGÖ was regarded as a reliable partner of state authorities and even a factor of stability and an ally in terms of societal security. The new policies, whose origins can be traced to the ÖVP's leadership in various coalition governments, saw the IGGÖ and adherents of the religion of Islam as a security threat based on the framing of "political Islam" as a matter of security concern.

# 7 · ATTITUDES AND PERCEPTIONS OF AUSTRIAN VOTERS TOWARD MUSLIMS

In this chapter, we address the situation of Muslims in Austria from an empirical perspective based on a series of survey data. We also look for evidence of whether these attitudes have increased or declined over time. These findings can give us an idea of what it is like to be a Muslim in a country that has historically seen itself as Roman Catholic but has since become largely secular. As a result, attitudes toward Muslims are shaped less by religious beliefs per se than by cultural perceptions. As described elsewhere in this book, Austrian political culture was long divided between a Catholic population rooted in the rural or middle-class milieus on the one hand and a Social Democratic, secular, and even atheist working class or an urban progressive milieu on the other. As this division has faded, religious symbols and holy days from Christmas to Easter have become predominantly cultural events and traditions. In some cases, they have even revived in response to globalization and resurgent identity politics. When the leaders of the populist radical right Freedom Party speak of Europe as the bulwark of Christianity against Islam, they are acting not as representatives of devout Christians, but rather as guardians of certain cultural constructs that, in the minds of many, represent the essence of Austrian and European culture (Hafez, Heinisch, and Miklin 2019). Religion has thus become a marker of identity and an instrument of exclusion. The rise of identity politics is likely a general reaction to modernization and globalization, which have increased the desire for national autonomy and the preservation of accustomed practices. As religious foundations dwindle, their rituals and outward appearance become more important.

## AUSTRIA'S AMBIVALENT NATIONAL IDENTITY

Austria is not exceptional in that people desire a strong national identity as these trends can be observed elsewhere as well. However, Austria differs from other countries in that no clearly defined national (political) identity has emerged. This is due to the complicated past of its predominantly Catholic, German-speaking population in a multiethnic empire, which ended up as an independent country more or less by an accident of history. When the Austro-Hungarian monarchy collapsed in 1918, the political elites of the newly created Austrian Republic intended for the country to join Germany, but this was prevented by the powers victorious in World War I. Nonetheless, many people in the new country saw themselves as the ethnic German remnant of the old empire and thus regarded the German nation state as their natural homeland. Catholic conservatives were, however, least enthusiastic about the prospect of a unification with Germany as the latter was decidely less Catholic in orientation. In short, Catholicism was an important marker of Austrian identity for those favoring national independence.

Moreover, instead of having a national political and civic identity, Austrians identified strongly with the respective political milieus in which they had been socialized—Catholic conservatism and Austro-Marxist social democracy. The two political camps offered substitute identities and became states within the state. The divisions eventually proved insurmountable; after increasingly violent clashes between the armed militias of both sides, the conservative forces succeeded in establishing an authoritarian Austrofascist state in 1934. Armed social democratic resistance was put down by force.

Social divisions persisted after World War II, but the political elites in both camps were now committed to national independence and democracy. To ensure that ideological differences and mutual distrust did not again threaten the country's stability, a consocialist model of government was created in which the interests of both sides were represented on the basis of proportionality. Liberalization, increasing prosperity, and generational change in the wake of the postwar baby boom softened the old divisions. By the 1970s, a new, more liberal middle class had emerged, giving the centrist Social Democrats three successive absolute majorities (1971, 1975, and 1979) in Parliament (Heinisch 2002, 39–47).

This period of liberalization and modernization was followed by what has been called the silent counterrevolution (Bale and Rovira Kaltwasser 2021), which led to a strengthening of conservative political and cultural trends and, in particular, to the rise of the populist radical right (Heinisch and Werner 2021). With German nationalism politically tainted and traditional Catholicism no longer enjoying widespread appeal, the Austrian right had no clear political tradition to draw on. In response, the emerging Austrian identity became an amalgam that blended the revival of local folk customs and regional traditions with select and popular aspects of Austrian imperial heritage, Christian rituals, and in many cases, also esoteric ideas about spiritual naturalism. Austrians are quite conservative in orientation and thus skeptical about modernization and change. In fact, Austrians are among the three EU member states least likely to agree with the statement that the "overall influence of science and technology on society is positive" (European Commission 2021).

Another feature of Austria's postwar identity is its insularity. Despite being at the center of Europe and fully economically dependent on the Single European Market, Austria has been one of the most Euroskeptical countries in the EU. Although surrounded by NATO member states, Austria has also maintained its stated commitment to neutrality in matters of military defense. This can be observed in the Austrian right's pronounced skepticism of U.S.-led Western liberalism (e.g., *Die Presse* 2016). The perceived encroachment of foreign culture on the perceived Austrian way of life—whether it is the displacement of a local restaurant by a McDonalds or the disappearance of traditional pork from the menu at school or in business meetings to accommodate non-Christians—has become the source of far-right mobilization (OTS 2010). Not surprisingly, the FPÖ has occasionally demanded that eating pork in kindergartens and schools be made obligatory (e.g., *Profil* 2019).

We must also not forget that in Austria many cultural traditions have religious connotations, as they are rooted in the country's religious past. Even in the secular modern state, religious ceremonies are part of public and state functions. For example, a church service on the first day of school or a religious invocation at the beginning of a university semester are still common practices, and crucifixes are regularly present in schools and courtrooms. Most traditional festivals have a religious origin, usually celebrating the feast of the local patron saint, and most national holidays have a church connection.

At the same time, church attendance in Austria has massively declined. From 2010 to 2020 the number of people attending Sunday's service dropped from approximately 659,000 to 359,000 (Mohr 2022a). At the same time, the share of Catholics in society decreased from 64.2 percent to 53.8 percent. Christian holidays play a role mainly because people receive time off for them as public holidays. Christian festivals are thoroughly commercialized, as they are everywhere, and politicians publicly criticize even the influential Catholic Church when it supports politically unpopular causes, such as standing up for asylum seekers. In order to avoid paying church tax, many Catholics and Protestants leave their respective denominations every year. Therefore, Austrians, much like people in other European countries, are often "feel-good" Catholics who maintain religious traditions on high holidays or see them more as a moral canon that is helpful for raising children.

## CONFLATING MUSLIMS WITH IMMIGRANTS

The construction and perception of Muslims as cultural Others often results in the conflation of Muslims with immigrants. As such, the political debates about immigration and integration are difficult to separate from those about Muslims.

Here, it is important to remember that Austria is a reluctant and unacknowledged country of immigration (Heiss and Rathkolb 1995; Bauböck et al. 2006). Although government officials generally avoid admitting it, the share of the foreign-born population in Austria increased from less than 2 percent in the early 1960s to about 17 percent in 2020. This means that about one in five people living in Austria was born abroad (Mohr 2022b, 2023). If we add those born in Austria to foreign-born parents (about 5.6%), the share of Austrians with a migration background amounts to over 20 percent. This means that the resident population has become very diverse and multicultural in a relatively short time. In schools, the proportion of people with an immigrant background is even higher. In elementary schools, it increased by four percentage points to 21 percent in the ten years leading up to 2017 (Salchegger et al. 2017). In fact, about one in four people under the age of twenty-nine and almost one in three people between the ages of thirty and forty-four have a migration background; this applies to only one in eight people over the age of sixty (Gruber 2018, 8–9). Nevertheless, Austria has some of the most restrictive citizenship laws in Western Europe, even for those born and raised in Austria. Thus, the share of the resident population with an international background is about 22 percent, while the share of citizens with such a background is only 5 percent (Statistik Austria, reported in Gruber 2018, 8–9). This means that the vast majority of people who immigrated to Austria or were born into such a family do not have the same rights as citizens and cannot participate in the political process. Of course, not all people with a migration background are Muslim or come from Muslim-majority countries. Nevertheless, they make up a large proportion, and the lack of political access, even if they were born in Austria, prevents these groups from influencing their situation. Austria also neglected to ensure that non-EU citizens obtain the right to vote and run for office in local elections after 5 years of residency, which was critically noted in the country report on Austria by the European Commission against Racism and Intolerance (ECRI 2010, 33).

Moreover, the issue of immigration and asylum ranks high on the list of political concerns, along with unemployment, the economy, and other pressing issues (European Commission 2011). In comparative surveys on standard indicator questions, Austrians tend to express negative views of foreigners (Friesl, Polak, and Hamachers-Zuba 2009; Gruber, Mattes, and Stadlmair 2015; Ulram 2009, 5). National tabloid media routinely paint a picture of immigrants and refugees that casts them in a negative light (Allen and Nielsen 2002, 311) and associates them with crime and illegality. In public debate, we often find a generally undifferentiated depiction of non-European immigrants as wanting to exploit Austria's well-meaning population and welfare system (Weiss 2000, 6). This well-established aversion to immigration is not only directed toward Muslims or even to non-Europeans, yet the widespread dislike of foreigners, and the implicit perception of Muslims as such, taints their public image in a doubly negative way.

Finally, the question of immigration also intersects with the issue of nationality and ethnicity. A large part of the Muslim population in Austria is of Turkish or Bosnian origin. This has at times further complicated bilateral relations between Austria and Turkey, whereby nationalist sentiments on both the Turkish and Austrian sides influence the Turkish community in Austria and how it is perceived by others. Similarly, the conflict between Bosnians and Kosovars as well as other ethnic groups in the Balkans, especially Serbs, has resulted in latent animosities between these groups in Austria, which can be exploited by anti-Muslim political actors such as the FPÖ.

In short, while immigration and the situation of Muslims in Austria are fundamentally separate issues, we must recognize that they are often congruent in public and political perceptions and therefore conflated in public opinion. We need to keep this in mind when we examine Austrians' attitudes toward Islam in the next section.

## WHAT THE DATA TELL US

It is important to note that the empirical data presented here provide a general overview of the situation of Muslims in Austria. Nevertheless, specific conditions can vary widely, as shown by the fact that in Vienna, with a population of about two million, the number of people calling themselves Catholics is only about 584,000, while the number of Muslims has risen to 200,000 (Mohr 2022b. In comparison, the ratio of Catholics to other religious groups is significantly higher in Austria's western provinces.

Despite the rise in the Muslim population in Austria, which includes a substantial and growing indigenous Muslim community, the attitudes of many Austrians toward Islam are shaped less by personal interactions than by public and political discourse about Muslims and Islam. These discourses are subject to a variation not only in framing, but also in intensity.

Figure 7.1 based on the work of Josh Klier (2022) shows the results of a quantitative text analysis using topical modeling examining 30,010 speeches (on average 834 per year) given by FPÖ members in Parliament from 1986 through 2021 on the topic of Islam in conjunction with the words referencing "terrorism" or "terrorist." The topical model suggests that there is an initial increase in frequency in these topical associations in the second half of the 1990s, coinciding with the Freedom Party's turn toward identity politics after a poor showing in the 1994 elections. Then we observe a further rise in frequency related to September 11, 2000, and another increase after 2003, when the party was in a downward spiral and wanted to appeal to its core voters. Lasting at least until the 2008 national parliamentary elections, FPÖ and BZÖ were engaged in an intense rivalry. As the BZÖ faded away after 2008, the frequency of FPÖ speeches on the

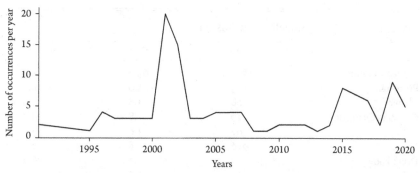

FIGURE 7.1 Frequency of FPÖ MPs connecting Islam-related topics with terrorism in parliamentary speeches 1986–2021. (Klier 2022: 16)
NOTE: Topical analysis of 30,010 speeches overall (834 speeches per year) identifying topical connections between Islam and terrorism as mentioned by FPÖ party members.

subject declined somewhat in the wake of global financial crisis as other issues took precedent (Hauser and Heinisch 2016). This changed again after the FPÖ was excluded as a potential government partner by the other parties in the 2013 elections. The subsequent refugee crisis and competition with the ÖVP, which had also begun to mobilize voters through immigration and identity as a central focus in its own campaign, coincided with further marked increases in the FPÖ discourse associating Islam and terrorism.

The issue subsides again somewhat after the change in government in 2019 when the FPÖ is embroiled in a major public scandal causing two subsequent leadership changes. Then, in the wake of the COVID-19 pandemic, the Issue of Islam losed further traction in the FPÖ discourse in 2021. The topical analysis shows clearly that Islam has been regularly associated in this discourse with terrorism, crime, military operations, security, and threats to freedom. Although Muslims are now the second-largest religious group in Austria, they form only a small percentage of the citizenry and thus the voters in the country. This means that they remained significantly underrepresented in Austrian politics and their needs go often unheard because electorally, political parties have little incentive to take up their issues. Moreover, since the majority of Muslims have practically no voice in Austrian politics, only vocal and radical minorities occasionally take to the street in political protest, which in turn contributes to a public perception of all Muslims as radicals. With data collected from a representative sample of Austrians of legal voting age, table 7.1 shows that the percentage of citizens who identify themselves as Muslims amounts to about 1.8 percent, compared with 65.2 percent Roman Catholics, 5 percent Protestants, and 23.8 percent with no religious affiliation.

TABLE 7.1    Religious Affiliations in Austria

|  | Frequency | Valid % | Cumulative % |
|---|---|---|---|
| Roman Catholic | 2506 | 65.2 | 65.2 |
| Protestant | 193 | 5.0 | 70.2 |
| Islamic | 68 | 1.8 | 71.9 |
| Christian Orthodox | 29 | .8 | 72.7 |
| Other | 62 | 1.6 | 74.3 |
| None | 916 | 23.8 | 98.1 |
| Don't know | 10 | .3 | 98.4 |
| Refused | 62 | 1.6 | 100.0 |
| Total | 3846 | 100.0 |  |

SOURCE: Authors' calculations based on AUTNES Comparative Study of Electoral Systems Post-Election Survey 2017, see Aichholzer et al. 2018.

## ATTITUDES TOWARD ISLAM IN AUSTRIA

If we turn to the general attitudes toward Muslims in Austria, using data from the Austrian National Election Study (Aichholzer et al. 2018), we see in table 7.2 that when asked whether Muslim and European lifestyles are easily compatible, only a small percentage (6.3%) fully agree with this statement. Another 34.3 percent agree somewhat or partly agree and party disagree. More than half of all Austrians find that a Muslim lifestyle, however defined, is not easily compatible with the local way of life, not only in Austria but in Europe in general. The largest group (33.4%) are those who reject compatibility the most. Even assuming that this strongly negative response refers to the "ease" of compatibility and not to compatibility as such, this result is indicative of how widespread the perception of Muslims as the "Other" is.

As can be seen in table 7.3, when breaking down voters' attitudes about the compatibility of Muslim and European lifestyles according to respondents' likely party choice, some differences emerge depending on political ideology. Potential voters of more socioculturally liberal parties such as the NEOS and the Greens or the left-wing Social Democrats tend to be more willing to agree on lifestyle compatibility, while supporters of parties of the center right (the ÖVP) and the populist radical right (FPÖ) predominantly view Muslims as incompatible.

Not surprisingly, the strongest opposition on this issue comes from voters of the populist radical right FPÖ, where more than 80 percent reject the idea of an easy compatibility of Muslim and European lifestyles. It should be noted from table 7.3, however, that only in the case of the Greens does the majority of an electorate actually believe in the compatibility of Islam with a European lifestyle. Thus, even the majority of people who voted for the NEOS and the Social Democrats, as shown in table 7.3, are skeptical about the cultural suitability of

TABLE 7.2     Compatibility of European and Muslim Lifestyles, according to Austrians

|  | Frequency | Valid % | Cumulative % |
|---|---|---|---|
| Completely agree | 113 | 6.3 | 6.3 |
| Somewhat agree | 206 | 11.5 | 17.8 |
| Partly agree/disagree | 410 | 22.8 | 40.6 |
| Somewhat disagree | 429 | 23.9 | 64.5 |
| Completely disagree | 600 | 33.4 | 97.9 |
| Don't know | 21 | 1.2 | 99.1 |
| Refused | 16 | .9 | 100.0 |
| Total | 1795 | 100.0 |  |

SOURCE: Authors' calculations based on AUTNES Comparative Study of Electoral Systems Post-Election Survey 2017, see Aichholzer et al. 2018.

TABLE 7.3     Compatibility of European and Muslim Lifestyles according to Austrians, by Party Choice

|  | Agree % | Partly agree/ disagree % | Disagree % | Total % | N |
|---|---|---|---|---|---|
| SPÖ | 23.7 | 25.6 | 50.7 | 100.0 | 270 |
| List Sebastian Kurz—the New ÖVP | 12.1 | 21.3 | 66.6 | 100.0 | 422 |
| FPÖ | 6.4 | 11.4 | 82.2 | 100.0 | 219 |
| Greens | 38.1 | 36.4 | 25.4 | 100.0 | 118 |
| NEOS | 20.7 | 31.0 | 48.3 | 100.0 | 58 |
| Team Stronach | 50.0 | — | 50.0 | 100.0 | 4 |
| Other party | 27.0 | 43.2 | 29.7 | 100.0 | 37 |
| Will vote invalid | 30.0 | 15.0 | 55.0 | 100.0 | 20 |
| Total | 17.8 | 23.0 | 59.2 | 100.0 | 1148 |

SOURCE: Authors' calculations based on AUTNES Comparative Study of Electoral Systems Post-Election Survey 2017, see Aichholzer et al. 2018.

Muslims. This is important insofar as the immigration debate is often framed by the right in terms of people's ability to integrate, which presupposes a certain cultural suitability. The idea of *Integrierbarkeit* (integrability) is de facto code for arguing for the exclusion of non-European immigrants based on their purported inability to "blend in." Thus, the refusal of admission to Austria is ostensibly made not for racist reasons, as this would be constitutionally problematic, but for reasons of cultural compatibility. Since many asylum seekers, or in other cases immigrants, come from Muslim-majority countries in the Middle East and Africa, the alleged cultural incompatibility of Islam with European society is a means of justifying an exclusionary position. The implications of the political

TABLE 7.4    Austrians Saying They Feel like a Stranger due to the Prevalence of Muslims

|  |  | Frequency | Percent % | Valid % | Cumulative % |
|---|---|---|---|---|---|
| Valid | Agree | 666 | 17.0 | 38.1 | 38.1 |
|  | Partly agree/disagree | 296 | 7.6 | 16.9 | 55.0 |
|  | Disagree | 787 | 20.1 | 45.0 | 100.0 |
|  | Total | 1749 | 44.8 | 100.0 |  |
| Total |  | 3908 | 100.0 |  |  |

SOURCE: Authors' calculations based on AUTNES Comparative Study of Electoral Systems Post-Election Survey 2017, see Aichholzer et al. 2018.

discourse on Islam show that both the traditionalist right and the secular left are reasonably consistent in their skepticism of Islam as something that does not belong in Western societies. While Conservatives and the far right tend to view Muslims in terms of cultural exclusivism, the left tends to question their presence for fear of jeopardizing social advances such as secularization and women's rights.

The widespread aversion to Islam is also evident in another set of survey results that captures a person's alienation from his or her own society because of the presence of "Others." Table 7.4 shows that only 45 percent of Austrians could definitively rule out feeling like a stranger due to the prevalence of Muslims, which means that more than half of respondents agree in some form with the statement or are at least unsure about how they feel. When we analyze this result by age and gender, we find that this attitude is very common among younger respondents, with the youngest cohort agreeing almost as much (82.3%) as the middle cohort (86.6%) (see table 7.5). This corresponds to findings of qualitative small-N studies that were conducted with adults and youth (Schönberger 2010) as well as with young people only (Herzog 2012). This perception is also more common among men than women, whose social progress is supposedly more threatened by Muslims in society. In fact, as table 7.5 shows, young men up to age thirty are the group least likely to disagree (39.1%) with the idea of feeling like a stranger due to the prevalence of Muslims. Older voters of both sexes are less likely to report such alienation.

If we once again correlate the estrangement from one's own society due to the presence of Muslims in that society, we notice again the clear differences based on the prospective party vote (see table 7.6a). The supporters of the Greens, the SPÖ, and NEOS are most likely to disagree with the statement that they are strangers in their own society due to the prevalence of Muslims. This also shows a difference regarding the question of cultural compatibility, which indicates skeptical attitudes among voters of both left-wing and right-wing parties. On the question of alienation, it is only the right that asserts intense feelings of alienation.

TABLE 7.5    Austrians Saying They Feel like a Stranger due to the Prevalence of Muslims, by Age and Gender

|  |  |  | Agree % | Partly agree/ disagree % | Disagree % | Total % |
|---|---|---|---|---|---|---|
| Male | Age interval 3 | 30 and under | 43.1 | 17.8 | 39.1 | 100.0 |
|  |  | 31–50 | 43.8 | 13.8 | 42.4 | 100.0 |
|  |  | 51 and over | 33.8 | 17.4 | 48.8 | 100.0 |
|  | Total |  | 39.2 | 16.3 | 44.5 | 100.0 |
| Female | Age interval 3 | 30 and under | 39.2 | 18.6 | 42.3 | 100.0 |
|  |  | 31–50 | 42.8 | 15.6 | 41.6 | 100.0 |
|  |  | 51 and over | 30.6 | 18.5 | 50.8 | 100.0 |
|  | Total |  | 36.5 | 17.6 | 45.9 | 100.0 |
| Total | Age interval 3 | 30 and under | 41.2 | 18.2 | 40.7 | 100.0 |
|  |  | 31–50 | 43.3 | 14.7 | 42.1 | 100.0 |
|  |  | 51 and over | 32.3 | 18.0 | 49.7 | 100.0 |
|  | Total |  | 37.9 | 16.9 | 45.2 | 100.0 |

SOURCE: Authors' calculations based on AUTNES Comparative Study of Electoral Systems Post-Election Survey 2017, see Aichholzer et al. 2018.

TABLE 7.6A    Austrians Saying They Feel like a Stranger due to the Prevalence of Muslims, by Party Choice—2017

|  | Agree % | Partly agree/ disagree % | Disagree % | Total % |
|---|---|---|---|---|
| SPÖ | 24.2 | 16.4 | 59.5 | 100.0 |
| List Sebastian Kurz—the New ÖVP | 38.9 | 21.6 | 63.4 | 100.0 |
| FPÖ | 78.3 | 11.3 | 10.4 | 100.0 |
| Greens | 7.5 | 10.0 | 82.5 | 100.0 |
| NEOS | 27.1 | 23.7 | 49.2 | 100.0 |
| Team Stronach | 50.0 | 25.0 | 25.0 | 100.0 |
| Other party | 18.9 | 13.5 | 67.6 | 100.0 |
| Will vote invalid | 31.6 | 26.3 | 42.1 | 100.0 |
| Total | 38.4 | 17.1 | 44.5 | 100.0 |

SOURCE: Authors' calculations based on AUTNES Comparative Study of Electoral Systems Post-Election Survey 2017, see Aichholzer et al. 2018.

Still, the differences between Conservatives and radical right populists is startling. The latter are almost twice as likely to feel alienated as Conservatives, who are closer overall to the supporters of other parties than to those of the populist radical right. In the latter case, almost 80 percent of respondents say they feel alienated because of the prevalence of Muslims in their society.

An interesting finding is presented in table 7.6b, which shows the responses to the same question by party choice, but in the context of the 2013 national

TABLE 7.6B    Austrians Saying They Feel like a Stranger due to the Prevalence of Muslims, by Party Choice—2013

|  | Agree % | Partly agree/ disagree % | Disagree % | Total % | N |
|---|---|---|---|---|---|
| SPÖ | 23.0 | 61.3 | 15.7 | 100.0 | 421 |
| ÖVP | 21.6 | 62.6 | 15.8 | 100.0 | 278 |
| FPÖ | 58.1 | 40.0 | 1.9 | 100.0 | 473 |
| BZÖ | 29.5 | 62.8 | 7.7 | 100.0 | 78 |
| Greens | 4.4 | 51.6 | 44.0 | 100.0 | 341 |
| NEOS | 11.2 | 58.0 | 30.8 | 100.0 | 169 |
| Team Stronach | 33.9 | 56.7 | 9.4 | 100.0 | 127 |
| KPÖ | 7.7 | 50.0 | 42.3 | 100.0 | 52 |
| Pirates | 13.5 | 48.6 | 37.8 | 100.0 | 37 |
| CPÖ (Christian Party of Austria) | 50.0 | 50.0 | 0.0 | 100.0 | 4 |
| Other party | 25.8 | 71.0 | 3.2 | 100.0 | 31 |
| Will vote invalid | 15.2 | 67.4 | 17.4 | 100.0 | 46 |
| Total | 27.1 | 54.2 | 18.7 | 100.0 | 2057 |

SOURCE: Authors' calculations based on AUTNES Online Panel Survey 2013, see Kritzinger et al. 2020.

elections with data taken from the Austrian National Election of 2013 (Kritzinger et al. 2020). We see a clear difference between the Conservative party voter in 2013 and in 2017. In 2013, the average Conservative party voter expressed much less estrangement due to Muslims compared to in the 2017 study. In fact, in 2013, fewer ÖVP voters agreed and more also disagreed with the assertion that they felt like strangers, compared to supporters of the SPÖ. These two studies give us insight into the differences among voters of the "old" ÖVP and the repositioned "new" ÖVP under Chancellor Kurz, which focused on anti-Islamic and anti-immigration themes. This suggests that focusing the ÖVP's agenda on anti-Muslim mobilization was able to affect the attitudes of its constituency in this regard.

If one compares the answers to the question of whether one feels like a stranger due to the prevalence of Muslims by province, considerable regional differences become apparent (table 7.7.). Agreement is highest in the small eastern province of Burgenland (51.5%) and lowest in the western province of Tyrol (20.8%). Both outliers are somewhat surprising, as Burgenland has a relatively small Muslim population and has reliably elected Social Democrats to public office, while Tyrol is considered a bastion of traditionalism and Catholicism, where Conservatives dominate. While it is true that Tyrol is an affluent province and that western Austrian conservatism tends to be more liberal, the difference between this province and its neighbors, especially Salzburg, is surprising given the cultural similarities. The responses from the provinces with the relatively largest Muslim populations, Vienna and Vorarlberg, are roughly in the middle. Tangentially, we find that the presence of Muslims is not responsible for this perception. Rather,

TABLE 7.7    Austrians Saying They Feel like a Stranger due to the Prevalence of Muslims, by State

| Austrian state and resident Muslim population | Agree % | Partly agree/ disagree % | Disagree % | Total % |
|---|---|---|---|---|
| Vorarlberg (12.4%) | 36.4 | 18.2 | 45.5 | 100.0 |
| Tyrol (8.7%) | 20.8 | 17.6 | 61.6 | 100.0 |
| Salzburg (6.5%) | 43.8 | 13.5 | 42.7 | 100.0 |
| Upper Austria (8.4%) | 38.0 | 16.2 | 45.8 | 100.0 |
| Carinthia (5.5%) | 37.0 | 10.0 | 53.0 | 100.0 |
| Styria (5.1%) | 39.9 | 16.7 | 43.5 | 100.0 |
| Burgenland (2.2%) | 51.5 | 18.2 | 30.3 | 100.0 |
| Lower Austria (4.9%) | 39.4 | 18.5 | 42.1 | 100.0 |
| Vienna (14.8%) | 38.1 | 18.1 | 43.8 | 100.0 |
| Total (8.3%) | 38.1 | 16.9 | 45.0 | 100.0 |

SOURCE: Authors' calculations based on AUTNES Comparative Study of Electoral Systems Post-Election Survey 2017, see Aichholzer et al. 2018.

TABLE 7.8    Austrians Saying They Do Not Want Muslims as Neighbors

| | | Frequency | Valid % | Cumulative % |
|---|---|---|---|---|
| Valid | Mentioned | 355 | 22.4 | 22.4 |
| | Not mentioned | 1233 | 77.6 | 100.0 |
| | Total | 1588 | 100.0 | |
| Total | | 1644 | | |

SOURCE: Authors' calculations based on the European Values Study 2017, see EVS 2022.

the opposite is true—namely, that respondents in regions with a lower proportion of Muslims tend to perceive greater alienation. This finding is consistent with other studies that show that radical rightwing populists are most successful in areas with the fewest immigrants or Muslims (Skenderovic 2008, 26). Table 7.7 compares the shares of the resident Muslim population per state with the percentage of responses given in each category.

We will now examine how Austrian respondents react to Muslims on a personal level. The European Values Study 2017 (EVS 2022) and the Values in Crisis Survey (Aachauer et al. 2021) provide us with two indicators to measure this sentiment for Austria. The first question, the results of which are shown in table 7.8., asks whether people would not want Muslims as neighbors, and the second asks whether it would be okay with them if their daughter or son were to marry "someone from a Muslim country" (table 7.9).

On the first question, 22.4 percent of Austrians mentioned in the survey that they would not want Muslims as neighbors. Thus, about three-quarters did not mention this as a problem for them.

TABLE 7.9    Austrians Saying It Would Be Okay with Them If Their Son/
Daughter Were to Marry Someone from a Muslim Country

|  |  | Frequency | Valid % | Cumulative % |
|---|---|---|---|---|
| Valid | Yes, definitely | 310 | 15.4 | 15.4 |
|  | Perhaps yes | 408 | 20.2 | 35.6 |
|  | Rather not | 507 | 25.1 | 60.7 |
|  | Under no circumstances | 520 | 25.8 | 86.5 |
|  | Don't know | 273 | 13.5 | 100.0 |
|  | Total | 2018 | 100.0 |  |

SOURCE: Authors' calculations based on the Values in Crisis Austria 2021, see Aschauer et al. 2021.

When asked whether people would be okay if their daughter or son married someone from a Muslim country, only 15.4 percent were clearly supportive of that idea and a further 20.2 percent were leaning in that direction. By contrast, 25.8 percent were strictly opposed, and 25.1 percent rather unfavorably disposed to such a marriage.

If we break down the responses by gender and age, as shown in table 7.10, we find that younger Austrians are more open to such marriages than older ones. Men and women aged thirty and younger are most supportive of such liaisons as 47.4 percent men and 53.5 percent of women indicate their agreement. Nonetheless, an overall majority of all age groups and both genders (51%) together has mixed feelings and a significant minority is opposed (13.5%). In general, younger female respondents are slightly more positive about this idea than young male respondents, but overall women are more skeptical than their male counterparts as the findings reported in table 7.10 suggest. We also find that female respondents are more polarized on this issue, as they are the group most in favor and most opposed to the idea overall. The main difference between these subgroups of women is their age. There is a 27 percent difference in favorability between women under thirty and those aged thirty-one to fifty. These numbers may reflect not only differences in intergenerational attitudes toward cultural diversity, but also personal experiences as Austrian neighborhoods and especially schools have become more culturally diverse. Nowadays, younger non-Muslim Austrians have more personal contact with Muslims and can therefore draw on their own experiences when assessing these issues. The views of older Austrians are more likely to be influenced more by public and political discourse.

If we then analyze how attitudes differ according to the degree of urban or rural background, we find that opinions are relatively uniform across all segments of the population (see table 7.11). Only those who live in the big city of Vienna are more open-minded. The other categories—suburbs and exurbs, medium-sized cities and towns, villages, and living on farms and in the countryside—show

TABLE 7.10    Austrians Saying It Would Be Okay with Them If Their Son/ Daughter Were to Marry Someone from a Muslim Country, by Gender and Age Group

|  |  |  | Agree % | Partly agree/ disagree % | Disagree % | Total % |
|---|---|---|---|---|---|---|
| Male | Age interval 3 | 30 and under | 47.4 | 42.9 | 9.7 | 100.0 |
|  |  | 31–50 | 30.3 | 54.5 | 15.2 | 100.0 |
|  |  | 51 and over | 34.2 | 56.4 | 9.4 | 100.0 |
|  | Total |  | 36.2 | 52.4 | 11.4 | 100.0 |
| Female | Age interval 3 | 30 and under | 53.5 | 36.2 | 10.3 | 100.0 |
|  |  | 31–50 | 26.3 | 57.4 | 16.3 | 100.0 |
|  |  | 51 and over | 31.2 | 50.9 | 17.9 | 100.0 |
|  | Total |  | 34.9 | 49.6 | 15.5 | 100.0 |
| Total | Age interval 3 | 30 and under | 50.4 | 39.6 | 10.0 | 100.0 |
|  |  | 31–50 | 28.3 | 56.0 | 15.7 | 100.0 |
|  |  | 51 and over | 32.7 | 53.6 | 13.8 | 100.0 |
|  | Total |  | 35.5 | 51.0 | 13.5 | 100.0 |

SOURCE: Authors' calculations based on the Values in Crisis Austria 2021, see Aschauer et al. 2021.

TABLE 7.11    Austrians Saying It Would Be Okay with Them If Their Son/ Daughter Were to Marry Someone from a Muslim Country, by Area of Residence, Urban to Rural

|  |  | Agree % | Disagree % | Don't know % | Total % |
|---|---|---|---|---|---|
| Residence | Metropolis | 39.8 | 45.7 | 14.5 | 100.0 |
|  | Suburbs | 32.9 | 56.3 | 10.7 | 100.0 |
|  | Exurbs/medium-sized cities | 34.2 | 53.3 | 12.5 | 100.0 |
|  | Towns/villages/farms | 34.9 | 50.7 | 14.4 | 100.0 |
|  | Countryside | 32.5 | 52.5 | 15.0 | 100.0 |
| Total |  | 35.6 | 50.9 | 13.5 | 100.0 |

SOURCE: Authors' calculations based on the Values in Crisis Austria 2021, see Aschauer et al. 2021.

more or less the same attitudes. While almost 40 percent of respondents in the big city see no problem with their son or daughter marrying a person from a Muslim country, the percentage of respondents in the suburbs who feel the same is only 33 percent, which is hardly different from the percentage of respondents from very rural areas. The difference between metropolitan residents and those from other residential areas undoubtedly reflects not only more tolerant attitudes toward diversity, but also the relatively high proportion of people with a cultural background from Muslim-majority countries.

## ATTITUDES TOWARD THE TREATMENT
## OF MUSLIMS IN AUSTRIAN SOCIETY

When Austrians are asked whether they think Muslims have fewer opportunities in society, a relative majority of 40 percent disagree with this statement (see table 7.12). In comparison, 34.7 percent agree and another 25.3 percent partly agree. This means that about 60 percent feel that life could be more difficult for Muslims in Austrian society than for non-Muslims. Not surprisingly, this result varies by both age and gender. For both genders, it is the oldest cohorts who are most aware of these difficulties (see table 7.13). As many as 40.6 percent of men over fifty and 37.4 percent of women in the same age group believe that Muslims "have fewer opportunities." Women are overall more likely to disagree with this statement than are men and of both genders together, the thirty-one to fifty age group is least likely to think that Muslims have fewer opportunities when compared to other age cohorts.

When we break down these responses by party preference, we see in table 7.14 that supporters of the Greens (66.4%) are more likely than voters of other parties to believe that Muslims have fewer opportunities. A relative majority of Austrians who vote for the NEOS and the Social Democrats acknowledge the difficulties Muslims face in Austrian society. In contrast, majorities of Conservative and populist radical right voters disagree with the statement that Muslims have fewer opportunities. The largest party group in this regard is FPÖ voters, 60.8 percent of whom reject the idea that Muslims are disadvantaged in Austrian society. In addition, a high percentage (50%) of potential nonvoters—that is, people who are alienated from the established political system—also reject the idea that Muslims have fewer opportunities.

In the following section, we focus on how Austrians would react to discrimination against Muslims in society. Specifically, we examine survey data that capture whether Austrians say they become "angry" when Muslims are discriminated against because of their faith. Table 7.15 shows that 43.1 percent completely or somewhat agree with this statement, while 30.6 percent completely or somewhat disagree. About 22 percent remained unsure as to how they feel.

When asked whether Muslims are treated worse than non-Muslims in Austria, significant majorities reject this notion, as shown in table 7.16. Not surprisingly, the proportion is highest among FPÖ voters (79.4%), but it is also high among Conservative voters (63.2%), Social Democratic voters (40.4%), and potential nonvoters (65%). NEOS voters also tend to disagree rather than agree with this statement by a significant margin (37.9% vs. 25.9%). The notable exception are Green voters, a majority of whom (55.6%) agree with the statement that Muslims treated worse than non-Muslims. Across all voter categories, Austrians are more than twice as likely to disagree as to agree with the statement. This

**TABLE 7.12** Austrians Saying that Muslims Have Fewer Chances in Society

|  |  | Frequency | Valid % | Cumulative % |
|---|---|---|---|---|
| Valid | Agree | 589 | 34.7 | 34.7 |
|  | Partly agree/disagree | 430 | 25.3 | 60.0 |
|  | Disagree | 680 | 40.0 | 100.0 |
|  | Total | 1699 | 100.0 |  |

SOURCE: Authors' calculations based on AUTNES Comparative Study of Electoral Systems Post-Election Survey 2017, see Aichholzer et al. 2018.

**TABLE 7.13** Austrians Saying that Muslims Have Fewer Chances in Society, by Gender and Age Group

|  |  |  | Agree % | Partly agree/ disagree % | Disagree % | Total % |
|---|---|---|---|---|---|---|
| Male | Age interval 3 | 30 and under | 30.6 | 30.1 | 39.3 | 100.0 |
|  |  | 31–50 | 31.5 | 21.4 | 47.1 | 100.0 |
|  |  | 51 and over | 40.6 | 24.9 | 34.5 | 100.0 |
|  | Total |  | 35.4 | 24.9 | 39.8 | 100.0 |
| Female | Age interval 3 | 30 and under | 29.9 | 29.9 | 40.2 | 100.0 |
|  |  | 31–50 | 30.8 | 26.6 | 42.6 | 100.0 |
|  |  | 51 and over | 37.4 | 23.3 | 39.3 | 100.0 |
|  | Total |  | 33.5 | 25.9 | 40.6 | 100.0 |
| Total | Age interval 3 | 30 and under | 30.3 | 30.0 | 39.7 | 100.0 |
|  |  | 31–50 | 31.2 | 23.8 | 45.0 | 100.0 |
|  |  | 51 and over | 39.1 | 24.1 | 36.8 | 100.0 |
|  | Total |  | 34.5 | 25.3 | 40.2 | 100.0 |

SOURCE: Authors' calculations based on AUTNES Comparative Study of Electoral Systems Post-Election Survey 2017, see Aichholzer et al. 2018.

**TABLE 7.14** Austrians Saying that Muslims Have Fewer Chances in Society, by Prospective Party Choice

|  | Agree % | Partly agree/ disagree % | Disagree % | Total % |
|---|---|---|---|---|
| SPÖ | 41.5 | 25.7 | 32.8 | 100.0 |
| List Sebastian Kurz—the New ÖVP | 29.6 | 27.4 | 43.0 | 100.0 |
| FPÖ | 20.6 | 18.7 | 60.8 | 100.0 |
| Greens | 66.4 | 19.8 | 13.8 | 100.0 |
| NEOS | 46.4 | 26.8 | 26.8 | 100.0 |
| Team Stronach | 25.0 | 50.0 | 25.0 | 100.0 |
| Other party | 36.1 | 30.6 | 33.3 | 100.0 |
| Will vote invalid | 15.0 | 35.0 | 50.0 | 100.0 |
| Total | 35.3 | 24.8 | 39.8 | 100.0 |

SOURCE: Authors' calculations based on AUTNES Comparative Study of Electoral Systems Post-Election Survey 2017, see Aichholzer et al. 2018.

TABLE 7.15    Austrians Saying They Get Angry When Muslims Are Discriminated against due to Their Faith

|  | Frequency | Valid % | Cumulative % |
|---|---|---|---|
| Completely agree | 373 | 20.8 | 20.8 |
| Somewhat agree | 401 | 22.3 | 43.1 |
| Partly agree/disagree | 401 | 22.3 | 65.5 |
| Somewhat disagree | 231 | 12.9 | 78.3 |
| Completely disagree | 317 | 17.7 | 96.0 |
| Don't know | 43 | 2.4 | 98.4 |
| Refused | 29 | 1.6 | 100.0 |
| Total | 1795 | 100.0 |  |

SOURCE: Authors' calculations based on AUTNES Comparative Study of Electoral Systems Post-Election Survey 2017, see Aichholzer et al. 2018.

TABLE 7.16    Austrians Saying that Muslims Are Treated Worse due to Their Faith, by Prospective Party Choice

|  | Agree % | Partly agree/ disagree % | Disagree % | Total % |
|---|---|---|---|---|
| SPÖ | 28.5 | 31.1 | 40.4 | 100 |
| List Sebastian Kurz—the New ÖVP | 12.3 | 24.5 | 63.2 | 100 |
| FPÖ | 7.3 | 13.3 | 79.4 | 100 |
| Greens | 55.6 | 17.9 | 26.5 | 100 |
| NEOS | 25.9 | 36.2 | 37.9 | 100 |
| Team Stronach | 50.0 | - | 50.0 | 100 |
| Other party | 37.8 | 13.5 | 48.6 | 100 |
| Will vote invalid | 15.0 | 20.0 | 65.0 | 100 |
| Total | 21.3 | 23.3 | 55.4 | 100 |

SOURCE: Authors' calculations based on AUTNES Comparative Study of Electoral Systems Post-Election Survey 2017, see Aichholzer et al. 2018.

suggests that sensitivity to how difficult life can be for a religious minority in Austria tends to be limited to urban and more progressive voter groups.

We are also interested in the breakdown by province of how Austrians view the treatment of Muslims compared to non-Muslims. As shown in table 7.17, we find the most agreement with the statement that Muslims are treated worse because of their faith in the federal states of Tyrol and Vienna and the most disagreement in Carinthia, followed at some distance by Lower Austria, Salzburg, and Vorarlberg and Styria (tied). Since these provinces differ greatly in terms of size, urbanization, prosperity, and political orientation, it is difficult to discern a clear pattern. Nevertheless, even here, we find more agreement with the idea that Muslims are discriminated against in those federal states with relatively larger

TABLE 7.17     Austrians Saying that Muslims Are Treated Worse due to
Their Faith, by State

| Austrian state and resident Muslim population | Agree % | Partly agree/ disagree % | Disagree % | Total % |
|---|---|---|---|---|
| Vorarlberg (12.4%) | 20.9 | 20.9 | 58.2 | 100.0 |
| Tyrol (8.7%) | 26.7 | 20.8 | 52.5 | 100.0 |
| Salzburg (6.5%) | 19.1 | 22.5 | 58.4 | 100.0 |
| Upper Austria (8.4%) | 20.3 | 24.6 | 55.2 | 100.0 |
| Carinthia (5.5%) | 12.9 | 21.8 | 65.3 | 100.0 |
| Styria (5.1%) | 18.3 | 23.5 | 58.2 | 100.0 |
| Burgenland (2.2%) | 21.9 | 23.4 | 54.7 | 100.0 |
| Lower Austria (4.9%) | 19.1 | 22.1 | 58.9 | 100.0 |
| Vienna (14.8%) | 25.8 | 27.1 | 47.1 | 100.0 |
| Total (8.3%) | 20.9 | 23.7 | 55.4 | 100.0 |

SOURCE: Authors' calculations based on AUTNES Comparative Study of Electoral Systems Post-Election Survey 2017, see Aichholzer et al. 2018.

Muslim populations. This is undoubtedly due to both the slightly larger share of Muslims reflected in the sample and probably the more numerous personal interactions between Muslims and non-Muslims in these provinces. As shown in table 7.17, Austrians are more than twice as likely to disagree than agree with this statement. The table also shows the share of the resident Muslim population by province, which differs significantly from the share of Muslims eligible to vote, given Austria's restrictive citizenship policy with regard to immigrants.

## A LOOK BACK IN TIME AND ACROSS TIME

In the study on the 2013 Austrian parliamentary elections, people were asked whether they believed that Muslims get more than they deserve. In many ways, this is the opposite sentiment to the one presented in table 7.17. The 2013 results are quite revealing, as shown in table 7.18. A quarter of respondents fully agree with this statement, and nearly half (44.3%) fully or somewhat concur with the assertion. In comparison, the percentages of those who tend to disagree or strongly disagree with this view are 12.3 percent and 11.3 percent, respectively. It should be emphasized again, however, that these data come from the Austrian National Election Study (AUTNES) Online Panel Survey 2013, as more recent data were not available.

The same 2013 survey also asked Austrians whether they thought Muslims were responsible for racial tension in the country. Again, as shown in table 7.19, large percentages (40.7%) completely or somewhat agreed with this statement. In fact, less than 10 percent fully disagreed with the idea that Muslims themselves were provoking racial problems.

TABLE 7.18    Austrians Saying that Muslims Get More than They Deserve

|  | Frequency | Valid % | Cumulative % |
|---|---|---|---|
| Completely agree | 790 | 25.6 | 25.6 |
| Somewhat agree | 577 | 18.7 | 44.3 |
| Partly agree/disagree | 587 | 19.0 | 63.4 |
| Somewhat disagree | 379 | 12.3 | 75.6 |
| Completely disagree | 349 | 11.3 | 87.0 |
| Don't know | 387 | 12.5 | 99.5 |
| Refused | 15 | .5 | 100.0 |
| Total | 3084 | 100.0 |  |

SOURCE: Authors' calculations based on the AUTNES Comparative Study of Electoral Systems Post-Election Survey 2013, see Kitzinger et al. 2020.

TABLE 7.19    Austrians Saying Muslims Are Responsible for Racial Tension

|  | Frequency | Valid % | Cumulative % |
|---|---|---|---|
| Completely agree | 671 | 21.8 | 21.8 |
| Somewhat agree | 585 | 19.0 | 40.7 |
| Partly agree/disagree | 921 | 29.9 | 70.6 |
| Somewhat disagree | 446 | 14.5 | 85.1 |
| Completely disagree | 281 | 9.1 | 94.2 |
| Don't know | 163 | 5.3 | 99.4 |
| Refused | 17 | .6 | 100.0 |
| Total | 3084 | 100.0 |  |

SOURCE: Authors' calculations based on the AUTNES Comparative Study of Electoral Systems Post-Election Survey 2013, see Kritzinger et al. 2020.

The 2013 study also shows how much unease many Austrians feel toward Muslims. Nothing says this more clearly than the overwhelming two-thirds agreeing with the demand that Muslims should assimilate, as table 7.20 indicates. While the idea of Muslim assimilation in the form of "integration" became a very salient concept in the political campaigns at the time and thereafter, the question leaves open what the respondents precisely mean by "assimilation." Instead of using the term assimilation which carries negative overtones, the public political discourse centers on integration. Like assimilation, the term integration encompasses a variety of notions ranging from language, values, outward appearance, change of cultural habits, and the like. Here we have to recall that the overwhelming majority of Muslims in Austria are Turks and Bosnians and therefore Europeans. Their attitudes, education levels, and lifestyles are generally shaped by class affiliation rather than religion, as Austria in the past specifically recruited

TABLE 7.20  Austrians Saying Muslims Should Assimilate

|  | Frequency | Valid % | Cumulative % |
|---|---|---|---|
| Completely agree | 1258 | 40.8 | 40.8 |
| Somewhat agree | 785 | 25.5 | 66.2 |
| Partly agree/disagree | 723 | 23.4 | 89.7 |
| Somewhat disagree | 122 | 4.0 | 93.6 |
| Completely disagree | 91 | 3.0 | 96.6 |
| Don't know | 88 | 2.9 | 99.4 |
| Refused | 17 | .6 | 100.0 |
| Total | 3084 | 100.0 | |

SOURCE: Authors' calculations based on the AUTNES Comparative Study of Electoral Systems Post-Election Survey 2013, see Kritzinger et al. 2020.

workers for factories and low-level service jobs. Moreover, the term "guest worker" implied that these laborers would one day return to their homelands and encouraged the maintaining of close ties with their home countries and cultures. Opportunities for social and economic advancement remained largely closed to the first generation of migrants. This is not only because their presence was intended to be temporary, but also because socioeconomic advancement was difficult even for working-class Austrians, given the importance of class affiliation and early tracking in the Austrian school system. Moreover, the term "assimilation" implies a defined understanding of Austrian culture into which one can integrate, which, as our earlier discussion showed, is difficult to conceptualize given Austrian history. Therefore, assimilation seems to imply "blending in" and disappearing in appearance and lifestyle rather than adopting a particular set of values and ideas.

Finally, we look at changes in attitudes over time. Unfortunately, there are few questions used at two different points in time that would allow us to make this comparison. In table 7.21, we show three such attitudes over time. First, we compare the results of the 2008 European Values Study with the 2018 results, when Austrians were asked whether they would like Muslims as neighbors. Over ten years, between 2008 and 2018, the share of people who expressed not wanting Muslims as neighbors dropped significantly, from 30.9 percent to 22.4 percent. When it comes to feeling like a stranger due to the presence of Muslims, the sample mean has risen slightly, also reflecting a slight increase in negative sentiment. We have seen in table 7.6b that this was especially due to the change in attitude among ÖVP voters. The question about the compatibility of Muslims with European lifestyle has remained roughly the same. Viewed from a different perspective, we may say that despite the politicization of Islam among Austrian political elites, especially on the right, the popular attitudes have remained largely stable or even point toward greater acceptance.

TABLE 7.21   Comparison of Selected Attitudes toward Muslims over Time

| Comparison of means | 2008 | 2018 |
|---|---|---|
| Don't like Muslims as neighbors | 30.9% | 22.4% |

SOURCE: European Values Study 2008 and 2017–2018.

| Comparison of means | 2013 | 2018 |
|---|---|---|
| Feel like a stranger due to the presence of Muslims | 2.80 | 3.13 |
| Muslim compatibility with European lifestyle | 3.71 | 3.68 |

SOURCES: Authors' calculations based on the AUTNES Comparative Study of Electoral Systems Post-Election Survey 2013 (Kritzinger et al. 2020) and on AUTNES Comparative Study of Electoral Systems Post-Election Survey 2017 (Aichholzer et al. 2018).

Overall, the survey results suggest that Islam is not perceived as a threat to religion, but rather as a challenge to national culture. Muslims clearly represent the cultural Other to most Austrian, especially when they are noticed as a distinct group. Public discourse about the need to "integrate" immigrants is often a poorly disguised call for Muslims to assimilate and disappear into the majority population. The data also betray a deep insecurity about their own identity on the part of the majority population, a sentiment that is indicated by the sense of alienation when they perceive that too many Muslims are present. These feelings are strongest among radical right and Conservative Austrians but are certainly not exclusive to them. They are particularly pronounced among men aged thirty-one to fifty and in federal states with the relatively lower shares of Muslim residents.

## CONCLUSION

The empirical findings examined strongly suggest that Muslims remain the cultural Other despite their growing presence in Austria. The decline of Catholicism and increasing secularization have not necessarily increased the acceptance of Muslims in parts of society. Rather, the general decline in traditional religiosity has heightened the mistrust of Islam if it is publicly visible as a premodern, illiberal, and possibly radical and irrational belief system that potentially poses a threat to society and from which "vulnerable" groups, such as women and children, must be protected. The long and progressive tradition of treating Islam as an equal religion before the law and granting the Muslim community relative autonomy is not reflected in the attitudes of the majority of Austrians surveyed.

Many Austrians are aware of the difficulties Muslims face, and clearly see Muslim culture as not fully compatible with European values and lifestyles. The results also strongly suggest that these attitudes are not limited to older and right-wing Austrians but are shared also by progressives who fear that Islam and liberalism are mutually exclusive. However, there are also hopeful signs. The data also indicate that where Muslims and non-Muslims interact regularly, attitudes are less polarized and more accepting, which is a good sign and bodes well for the future. In general, people from different cultural backgrounds live together peacefully in Austria, and ethnic clashes or intercultural violence are virtually nonexistent compared with other parts of Europe. Multicultural change is noticeable in all parts of the country, but especially in Vienna, the various provincial capitals, and the major industrial areas. The data also do not show a significant deterioration in views toward Muslims despite the so-called refugee crisis in 2015 and 2016 and the common conflation of immigration and Muslims in Austria. Moreover, the conflation of immigrants and Muslims cuts both ways in that it is likely that to some extent the negative attitudes toward Muslims are actually not directed at the religion per se but at people perceived to be foreign and not Austrian or European. Thus, when our measures indicate a response to a question about Muslims, we may actually be measuring Austrians grappling with their own concerns about identity and their country's role in a globalizing world.

On a morning bus ride in any Austrian city, you see crowds of young people effortlessly switching between German and Turkish, Bosnian, or Arabic. Young women wearing headscarves mingle with those who do not. Imams are invited to public ceremonies, as are representatives of Christian denominations. Muslim cultural practices are becoming better known and understood among the non-Muslim population. These developments are taking place against a backdrop of deliberate mobilization of anti-Muslim and anti-immigrant sentiment for political purposes. We also found that the surveyed population is aware of the difficulties faced by Muslims, and many are deaf to calls for exclusion. The main problem remains political in that a large proportion of the resident Muslim population and other longtime foreign residents remain excluded from voting because of the hurdles to citizenship that exist in Austria. The fact that this group includes an increasingly large percentage of people born and raised in Austria is a political injustice and a potential source of political conflict in the future. It is only when Muslims and other politically underrepresented groups gain the political weight that reflects their numerical presence in society that significant political changes toward greater inclusiveness are likely to occur in Austria.

# 8 · CONCLUSION

We have attempted to explain the politicization of Islam and the evolution of Islam politics in Austria, which we define as as the activities by the government, interest groups, and other political actors that have influenced political conditions and perceptions of Islam and the Muslim community in our case study. The country's somewhat paradoxical relationship with Islam is one of the reasons why we believe that the Austrian case deserves more attention. Although imperial Austria had no overseas colonies, it extended its power to territories with a significant Muslim population through the annexation of Bosnia-Herzegovina in the late nineteenth century. Like colonies elsewhere, these Balkan lands were exploited by the empire and served as eroticized southern outposts to the national elites. However, the takeover of Bosnia and Herzegovina also led to the inclusion of the local Muslim population in a comparatively progressive legal framework that granted them full religious recognition and autonomy in their affairs—something that has survived to this day. This is a remarkable feat, not only in light of the political changes that have occurred during this extended period of time, but also considering the fact that today's Austria and imperial Austria have little in common and, more importantly, that Bosnia and Herzegovina has not been linked to Austria since 1918. Yet, the Islam Act of 1912 survived despite or perhaps because of the de facto absence of a Muslim population in Austria until the 1960s, when migrant laborers arrived from the former Yugoslavia and Turkey. When the Muslim community began to grow again, they were seen not as a new community but rather, like other migrant laborers, as temporary "guest workers," so neither Islam nor immigration was part of the public consciousness until political actors on the far right discovered identity politics as a means of mobilizing and winning support. Our central argument for explaining the change in Islam politics and, in particular, the politicization of Islam in Austria emphasizes the role of party competition. First, this provides the key causal mechanism in the form of competition between two far-right parties competing for voters after the collapse of the populist radical right Freedom Party of Austria in government in 2005. We then show how the radicalized discourse subsequently spread to other parties and found particular appeal among the Austrian Conservatives. As their political fortunes faltered, they began to pursue anti-Islamic identity politics to regain voters back from the far right, which, in turn, further politicized Islam. Our book therefore uses the neoinstitutionalist framework to show how a path-dependent development can explain Austrian Islam politics up to the early 2000s, including the founding of the IGGÖ in 1979. Based on the 1912 Islam Act, the Austrian state followed the established institutional pattern of church-state relations and applied the principles of parity and autonomy to the Muslim community, its main representative body. The political authorities generally viewed the IGGÖ as a partner, whether in terms of the education system or security policy. This approach contrasts markedly with the more recent Islam-focused policies that were pursued by the same governing coalition of SPÖ and ÖVP that had previously favored consociational policies toward Islam. The former approach also stands in stark contrast to those of the ÖVP and the populist radical right FPÖ (2017–2019) and more recently, the Greens (2020–). The change in direction initially culminated in the 2015 Islam Act and new burdensome legal requirements that de facto apply exclusively and selectively to Muslim students in educational institutions.

Our analysis echoes research by Bale, who has shown that center-right parties often focus on immigration and cultural issues, as does the radical right (Bale 2003). Thus, our book builds on a growing literature centered on explaining the impact of the rise of radical right parties and identity-based movements (Biard, Bernhard, and Betz 2019; Heinisch 2021). It also allows us to develop empirical expectations about whether and under what conditions such parties enter public office. Moreover, it shows us the lasting effects of such political change—even when the radical right is no longer in power, as illustrated by the ÖVP's continued policy toward Islam and Muslims. First, we were able to demonstrate that this shift in Islam-related policies came about after a highly effective public mobilization campaign by the FPÖ in an attempt to rebuild the party's strength after its near-collapse in 2005. The issues of Islam and Austrian identity were thrust into the party contest to allow the FPÖ to gain issue dominance in the ensuing discourse. To this, the other parties responded by adopting the FPÖ's anti-Muslim populist demands and making them their own. While Islam had long been part of Austria's narrative of pluralism and coexistence, dating back to the Habsburg monarchy, the political discourse changed significantly after 2005 with the FPÖ's focus on this issue.

As we show in chapter 3, Islam and Muslims in Austria were presented as an object of mystification that was tolerated by most members of the political elite and seen as an asset to a cosmopolitan city like Vienna. The idea of the good Bosnian Muslim, one who is loyal to political authority, resonated with the idea of the good Austrian Muslim. When the FPÖ discovered Islam as a wedge issue in 2005 and began to mobilize against Muslims, this naturally affected the debate about Islam and Muslims in Austria. Slowly but steadily, mainstream politicians took more law-and-order positions on this issue and even adopted some of the FPÖ's demands. Chapter 4 shows what impact this discourse had on the legal framework. The analysis of the 2015 Islam Act clearly reveals that the legal prerogatives of the IGGÖ have been severely compromised. In the past, the IGGÖ had been considered one among several co-equal institutions with their own interests and concerns, which the state and politicians usually respected as an equal partner and approached with the intent of achieving consensus. Now the tradition of pluralistic inclusion of different religions had given way to viewing Islam through the prism of securitization and its cultural compatibility with Austrian values. The IGGÖ was treated differently from other religious communities and denominations, and the principle of equality of all confessions as well as the principle of cooperation as equals were called into question. The new Islam Act stands for two new tendencies. On the one hand, the IGGÖ is strengthened vis-à-vis the lower authorities, private initiatives, and associations of its respective religious societies, the Kultusgemeinden that it oversees. On the other hand, the Muslim religious societies, including the IGGÖ, are subjected to more state control. The Islam Act of 2015 also changed a fundamental privilege—namely, the singularity of the IGGÖ as the only religious community subject to the Islam Act. As soon as the new Islam Act of 2015 was applied to two already existing Muslim religious communities, the IGGÖ and the Alevi Islamic Religious Association (ALEVI), as well as to potential future Islamic religious communities, the dominant and unique position of the IGGÖ changed. This also implied that the IGGÖ's unique authority on issues related to the Islamic faith, which had been taken for granted by legislators in the past, had been changed.

Chapter 5 examines how the regulation of the hijab changed from a regime of tolerance and protection to policies that prohibited women from wearing religious garments. First, a ban on full-face veils was introduced in 2017 by the SPÖ-ÖVP government. When the conservative ÖVP and the populist radical right FPÖ formed a coalition government, the ban on wearing the hijab in educational institutions—first in preschool and then in elementary school—soon followed. The Islamophobic discourse had grown to such an extent that this policy was eventually fully adopted by the ÖVP as well as by opposition parties that otherwise favored a socioculturally liberal outlook. The discourse strategy of the New ÖVP under the leadership of Sebastian Kurz was to frame its discriminatory policies toward Muslims in such a way as to gain maximum public support and minimize resistance by the opposition parties. Thus, the hijab ban was framed as a measure to protect Muslim girls from premature sexualization and gender segregation, which sounds very positive at first glance. As the reactions of opposition parties show, this strategy worked to some extent. Another relatively successful strategy has been to claim that one is fighting against "political Islam," asserting that it is not Islam and Muslims that are being targeted and that Muslims' fundamental freedoms—such as the freedom of religion, enshrined in the constitution—have not been violated It should be emphasized once again that the terminology used by the ÖVP-led federal government did not even refer to "Islamists," or "radical Islam," or "radical politics," as was the case in other countries, but simply to "political Islam." The shortened German-language term *politischer Islam* is so all-encompassing and ambiguous that any organized group of Muslims with any political interests and goals would by definition fall into this category. This represents a break with the ÖVP's own tradition, which has its roots in political Catholicism. If any party should understand that religious communities have legitimate political interests and seek involvement in the national political discourse, it would be the ÖVP, as the representative of the Christian Democratic tradition in Austria. The idea of strictly separating the religious from the political runs counter to the ÖVP's own party programs, which find their basis in Christian values and a Christian image of society.

Security policy, which we discuss in chapter 6, is the other policy area that supports our argument. The ÖVP referred to "political Islam" not only as a cultural threat but also as a security challenge in its election programs as well as in its coalition agreements, first in the ÖVP-FPÖ coalition (2017) and later in the ÖVP-Green coalition (2020). Several laws and measures in the area of security changed the Austrian state's relationship with religiously organized Muslims. The 2014 Symbol Act gradually expanded the circle of movements and organizations targeted, eventually including even parts of the IGGÖ as terrorist threats. The Documentation Center for Political Islam published several reports on various IGGÖ institutions. The closure of IGGÖ mosques and the banning of the hijab in the name of the fight against "political Islam"—both overturned by the judiciary—indicated that the days the state viewed the entire IGGÖ as a partner against extremism, were gone. Gone were also the days when the IGGÖ was seen as a factor of stability and an ally in matters of social security. The new policy, which was implemented by the various ÖVP-led coalition governments, viewed large parts of the IGGÖ and Muslims as a security threat, relying on the framing of "political Islam" as a security-related issue. "Political Islam" was eventually declared a criminal offense in July 2022.

The empirical findings discussed in chapter 7 clearly suggest that negative attitudes toward Muslims in Austria persist, notwithstanding the increase in the number of Muslims in the Austrian population as a whole. Given that the historically more tolerant tradition of treating Islam as an equal religion before the law and granting the Muslim community relative autonomy is not reflected in the attitudes of the majority of Austrians surveyed, it is not surprising that it was an easy decision for right-wing political parties to make the exclusion of Islam and Muslims an election issue and to enact laws that discriminate against Muslims. Moreover, while there is a clear difference in the attitudes of potential voters of more socioculturally liberal parties, such as the NEOS and the Greens or the left-wing Social Democrats, on the one hand, and supporters of right-wing parties (Kurz/ÖVP) and the populist radical right (FPÖ) on the other, distrust remains high among sympathizers of several left-wing parties. As the empirical findings show, only among the liberal NEOS electorate does a majority actually believe Islam is compatible with a European lifestyle. There are clear majorities, even among voters on the left (Greens and Social Democrats), that indicate skepticism about the cultural suitability of Muslims. This means that the issue of Islam enables parties on the radical right fringe to appeal even to supporters of liberal and leftist parties. Thus, the SPÖ supported the closure of mosques by the ÖVP-FPÖ coalition, the NEOS advocated for an even more comprehensive hijab ban (up to age fourteen), and the Green justice minister coordinated with the minister of the interior in carrying out a highly publicized, massive police raid involving nearly 1,000 police forces, Operation Luxor, mainly to project an image of toughness and police competence in order to gain public approval. The raid was later ruled to have been unlawful, with zero convictions as one case after another was dropped (Hafez 2023).

ÖVP leader Kurz was thus able to make the issue his own, at least among the established parties, and take a position between the center and the far right, leaning more toward the latter. This approach was clearly designed to appeal to voters who, like many in the Conservative ÖVP, support the preservation of Catholic culture and view the growth of Islam with alarm. Kurz's approach seemed intent on appealing to an electorate concerned about immigration but for whom the FPÖ was too radical and controversial. Finally, the ÖVP's tougher stance on integration and policing of the Muslim community also helped solidify its reputation as the party of law and order during uncertain times.

We conclude from our observations that path dependency and consociationalism no longer characterize Austria's Islam-related politics. Instead, recent election campaigns and new identity politics have introduced a new discourse on Islam, in which the populist radical right and the center-right try to compete on sociocultural issues, including immigration, traditional culture, and Islam. The political left, the Social Democrats, and even the Greens have strong secular leanings and view certain religious practices (such as the wearing of headscarves or traditional methods of slaughtering animals) as problematic in general. Consequently, they are ill equipped to counter anti-Muslim populist rhetoric and policy initiatives. In a fragmented and contested political marketplace and given the dominant voter attitudes toward Muslims and Islam, defending Islam is generally not seen as a successful political strategy. As long as Islam remained merely an issue of religion, consociationalism was well equipped to deal with state-community relations. Once Islam became politicized—that is, once it was introduced as an issue in the arena of partisan political competition—state-community relations began to change. The Islam Act of 2015 was the first outcome of this change. What had initially manifested itself in a new discourse on Islam and Muslims came together in the Islam Act and subsequently spilled over into other policy areas, from the regulation of the hijab to security policy, providing further evidence of the change in Austrian Islam politics.

While the ÖVP was able to monopolize the issue of Islam within the coalition, thus demonstrating its competence in this area, the SPÖ blurred its position due to divergences in its approach, leaving room for a rivalry between the established Conservative party and the extreme right. Indeed, in the 2017 parliamentary campaign, the Conservatives under Kurz and the FPÖ under Strache competed over who would be tougher on immigrants and refugees. The Conservatives' positions coincided with those of the FPÖ to the extent that the latter felt compelled to launch a campaign titled "Vordenker-Spätzünder" (thought leader–thought follower) to remind voters who had actually been the first to shape the Islamophobic populist discourse in Austria. Nevertheless, even after the ÖVP-FPÖ coalition imploded in 2019, the ÖVP continued its anti-Islam policies with little resistance from its junior coalition partner, the Greens. Following the work of Rovny (2012), we conclude that the ÖVP has moved from blurring the issue of integration of religious minorities to a strategy of emphasizing it as a core competence. In doing so, the Conservatives at the federal level were following a pattern already observed at the regional level, whereby the ÖVP for some time had held a clear position on banning mosques and minarets (Hafez 2010a, 2010b). Finally, given the emerging majorities of voters with anti-Muslim attitudes in various European countries, Austria is both an important starting point for analysis and a useful comparative case to identify similar patterns in party competition.

We began working on this book at a time when both Sebastian Kurz, former leader of the New ÖVP, and Heinz-Christian Strache, former leader of the FPÖ, were leading the coalition government and announcing one discriminatory measure or law after another. When the final lines of this book were written, Strache had long since resigned, after a video surfaced in 2019 showing him in a highly compromising situation (Noack and Mekhennet 2019). A year later, Kurz resigned first as chancellor in the wake of a major corruption investigation involving his government and party. He then left as party leader and announced his intention to quit politics (Karnitschg 2021). Moreover, most of this government's legislative and political measures were overturned by the Constitutional Court and administrative courts, from the ban on the hijab to the closure of mosques to Operation Luxor, the largest illegal police raid in postwar Austria, which had claimed to be targeting "political Islam." This relatively new development in the court's defense of Muslims' rights might also serve as a basis for politicians in the future to determine how to redefine the issue of Islam and Muslims. Indeed, following the Constitutional Court's decision to lift the ban on the hijab in schools, the ÖVP-Green government did not include the ban on the hijab in preschool in the 2022 framework agreement between the federal government and the nine provinces governing such regulations. It remains to be seen whether this relatively recent development will create a new pattern based on court decisions, as ÖVP politicians (BKA 2023) as well as security experts (Sablatnig 2023) working for the intelligence service remain eager to fight what they call political Islam. At the same time, we might wonder whether an already heightened voter awareness of the difficulties faced by Muslims, as was evident in the survey data primarily among Green voters and to a lesser extent among NEOS and SPÖ voters, might be reinforced by these developments on the judicial front.

There is another development to consider, as our empirical data show: where Muslims and non-Muslims interact regularly, attitudes are notably less polarized and more accepting, which is a good sign and bodes well for the future, particularly in urban areas (especially in provincial capitals), where most Muslims live. The number of Muslims doubled from 4 percent to 8 percent of the total population between 2001 and 2017. According to various scenarios, the Muslim population in Austria will be at least 12 percent and at most 21 percent in 2046 (assuming zero immigration) (Goujon, Jurasszovich, and Potančoková 2017, 33–34). In a city like Vienna, the share of Muslims in the total population would amount to 30 percent in the highest forecasts (35). Given these significant shifts, it may become a disadvantage for political parties to continue supporting anti-Muslim demands in the long run.

# ACKNOWLEDGMENTS

This book is a collaborative endeavor that started as a research project at the University of Salzburg in 2014, the same year the government presented a new Islam Act, marking the beginning of a new era in Austria's Islam politics. Since then, we have shared many panels with discussants at various places to examine these changes. We, the authors, want to thank the many scholars who have been part of this intellectual journey: Raoul Kneucker, Helga Druxes, Franz Gmainer-Pranzl, Jessica Fortin-Rittberger, Dudu Kücükgöl, Rijad Dautović, Astrid Mattes, Ivan Kalmar, Alexander Yendell, and Shadi Hamid, as well as the journal editors of *Juridikum, Patterns of Prejudice, Discourse and Society, Politics and Religion,* and *ReOrient,* where some pieces leading to this work have been published. In addition, we are especially grateful to the anonymous reviewers for their critical reading that helped develop the manuscript into its final form. We also want to gratefully acknowledge the assistance of Krista Bolton, Diana Hofmann, and Katrin Winkler in editing and revising the manuscript. We also wish to thank our many colleagues whose counsel and helpful comments on various chapters have helped improve them and have enriched this book.

# NOTES

## CHAPTER 2 THE CONTEXT

1. The quotation is taken from an article on debates about mosques in politics. See Otto Friedrich, "Muslime wollen in Sicht sein," *Die Furche*, 11 March 2008, http://www.furche.at /system/showthread.php?t=325.
2. On the international law dimension, see Dautović 2019a.
3. Literally translated, the word *Abendland* means "Occident," marking a geographical and cultural contrast with the Muslim "Orient." The term is often translated to mean "Western," but I believe this would be a mistake here because of the clear ideological—especially Catholic—connotations of the term.

## CHAPTER 3 THE DISCOURSE ABOUT ISLAM

1. This analysis builds on the CDA research on racism (Van Dijk and Wodak 2000; Van Dijk, 2000, 2002, 2004) and Islamophobic populism (Hafez 2010a, 2017a) in parliamentary debates and attempts to contribute to long-neglected analyses of parliamentary debates (Ilie 2010, 5; 2015; Ilie et al. 2016).
2. Monika Mühlwerth.
3. Reinhold Lopatka.
4. Peter Wittmann.
5. Nikolaus Alm.
6. Nikolaus Scherak.
7. Wolfgang Zinggl.
8. Efgani Dönmez.
9. Elisabeth Grimling.

## CHAPTER 4 LEGAL STATUS OF ISLAM

1. While "formal parity" (*formelle Parität*) is given in case of provisions that apply to all churches and religious societies, for provisions that apply to only one or some churches and religious societies "substantive parity" is the benchmark, meaning that formally different provisions for different churches and religious societies are admissible (with regard to specificities such as self-conception, social relevance, minority position, etc.) if they are objectively justified (Kalb, Potz, and Schinkele 2003, 62–63). Schima (2015) argued that substantive parity may also allow different treatment due to, e.g., a different number of members. For example, in the case of *Jehovah's Witnesses v. Austria*, the ECHR held that a ten-year waiting period before legal recognition (established by the Confessional Communities Law of 1998, BGBl. I Nr. 19/1998) was a violation of article 9 and 14 ECHR, since it could not be justified in the case of religious communities with a long-standing existence (Potz and Schinkele 2016, 85). In the case of a new and small religious community, the decision may have been different.
2. Only when its president—its main leader, who legally represents the IGGÖ—positioned himself reconciled with the law and even praised the new Islam Act as exemplary (ORF 2015). For a detailed discussion, see Hafez 2017c.

3. Article 15 of the Basic State Law (Staatsgrundgesetz, StGG 1867); article 9 of the ECHR.

4. Note that apart from in this first sentence of section 1 in both laws, which constitutes the most important legal statement, legal recognition is—unlike in the Protestant Act of 1961, the Orthodox Law of 1967, and the Oriental Churches Law of 2003—a case of "dynamic reference" (*dynamische Verweisung*), which could be accidental. But considering the common legal tendencies of the two laws, it might indicate the intention to create different statuses for the religious societies.

5. Compare to article 2, Concordat 1934; section 2, Orthodox Law of 1967; and section 1, Oriental Churches Law of 2003.

6. Richard Potz and Brigitte Schinkele state in their assessment on section 1 of the draft of the Islam Act that the provision "facilitates prima vista the impression of a certain programmatic meaning directed to an approach to state organization structures with a stronger governmental cultus supervision" (Potz and Schinkele 2010). Compare with the opposing view of Wolfgang Wieshaider, Zur Rechtspersönlichkeit gesetzlich anerkannter Religionsgesellschaften (öarr 2/2013, 336).

7. The example of the IGGÖ elections shows that this scenario of installing a custodian is not hypothetical. A letter from the office of the former IGGÖ president, Fuat Sanac, dated 25 March 2016 and addressed to all affiliated associations and stakeholders, presents a tightly scheduled plan for the restructuring of the IGGÖ and the election of its executive organs according to the new constitution. The letter ends with the noteworthy sentence "Everything has to be completed by 26 June 2016, otherwise, a custodian will be applied for"; this ignores the fact that according to article 30 of the IGGÖ constitution, "all elected organs execute their office until the organs are constituted according to this constitution" (IGGÖ 2016).

8. Another example would be paragraph 30 of the Islam Act 2015, which gives the federal chancellor (minister) the power to reverse decisions of religious societies that (in his opinion) are not complying with the religious society's constitution or statutes, by inflicting fines or using other legally provided means, which is incompatible with freedom of religion (and the autonomy of internal affairs according to article 15 StGG 1867 and article 9 ECHR). For more details, see Dautović and Hafez (2019).

9. According to this provision, "the authorities may prohibit gatherings and events of religious purpose if they pose an immediate danger to the interests of public safety, law, and order, health, or the rights and freedoms of others. Dangers, on the occasion of the event, originating from third parties, do not compose a reason for the prohibition." This is how the provision appears in the Israelite Act, whereas the Islam Act gives one more reason for prohibition: "national security." We can only speculate about the reason for this difference.

10. At this point, we would like to give the reader an idea of the practical background of this potentially invasive provision. According to section 31, subparagraph 2 of the Islam Act 2015, the IGGÖ was obliged to pass a new constitution (including a description of its teachings) adjusted to the requirements of the new law. It was not until December that the competent Council of Scholars (Consulting Council) of the IGGÖ was presented with a forty-one-page document on "faith teachings," which seemingly was supported by the Federal Chancellery (or the Cultural Affairs Office). The Council of Scholars refuted the contents of the document, drafted their own (nine pages in total), and sent it on to the legislative organ of the IGGÖ, the Shura Council, to pass the new constitution (including the short document on teachings), and then forwarded it to the Cultural Affairs Office. The Cultural Affairs Office responded on 5 February 2016 (BKA-KA9.070/0001-KULTUSAMT/2016), suggesting that the constitution (including teachings) in that form would have to be rejected, because of the IGGÖ's definition of who is a Muslim and therefore a member (which is clearly a question of internal affairs and religious teachings), and other objections to the part of the constitution

on teachings. Thus, bypassing the authority of the competent organs of the IGGÖ, the application was changed and a constitution with a section on teachings different from what was passed by the Shura Council was permitted (and came into effect).

11. Article 15 StGG 1867; article 9 ECHR.

12. Specifically, inconsistent with article 15 StGG.

13. Freedom of association is protected by article 13 StGG 1867 and article 11 ECHR. Since there was a lot of legal confusion around these regulations, worries and fears of possible dissolution (many of the associations in question own a large amount of property, such as mosque buildings and schools, which would have been liquidated in the case of dissolution) made most Islamic associations change their statutes in ways that meant their purpose was no longer the propagation of Islamic teachings. This now makes them dependent on the IGGÖ, since partner bodies (cultus communities and "facilities according to the internal act of the religious society with legal personality") within the IGGÖ have to be founded by members of the associations, which are now the official providers of all religious services and activities, while the associations themselves were reduced to handling tasks in the administration of the associations' properties and cultural activities.

14. In a broader perspective, the two main dimensions of discrimination seem to be embedded in a larger trend of preserving Catholic hegemony. One dimension is that a special status for Muslims emerges with the new Islam Act, in contrast to the Israelite Act of 2012. The other dimension is general discrimination, which is also present in the Israelite Act and seems to exist in a new tradition of return to state-church sovereignty. This can be dated back to the enactment of the Confessional Communities Law of 1998, which was introduced to postpone the legal recognition of the Jehovah's Witnesses (Mayer 1997, 2), which happened only in 2009, after they had fulfilled all legal requirements. The fact that all three acts (the Confessional Communities Law of 1998, the Israelite Act of 2012, and the Islam Act 2015) were introduced and passed under the direction of the ÖVP suggests that the government was interested in stabilizing the hegemony of the Catholic Church against minority churches and religious societies. In the case of Islamic religious societies, it seems that governmental politics have promoted further fragmentation and that the Islam Act of 2015 is the latest piece in this plan. Regarding the registration of the Islamic-Shiite Community in Austria (as a confessional community), Potz and Schinkele wrote, "In light of the still persisting embeddedness of the Shiite majority in the Islamic Religious Society in Austria (IGGÖ), according to this interpretation the registration of a Jafarite (Twelver-Shiite) Minority, the Islamic-Shiite Religious Society would have been impermissible" (Potz and Schinkele 2010, 14).

## CHAPTER 5 MUSLIM HEADSCARF—AUSTRIAN CULTURE WAR

1. After the introduction of the full-face veil ban, passersby on the street felt justified in making Muslims with face veils aware of the ban. In total, there were thirty official acts in the first two weeks, only four of which involved a Muslim woman wearing a face veil. The rest were Muslim women wearing a hijab. The most notable symbolic act was directed against the parliamentary mascot, who was asked by police to take off his face covering. See Hafez 2018c, 70.

2. One of the first critiques targeting the government was in response its plan to disestablish the AUVA, a social security institution that takes care of people who have been left with physical or psychological disabilities following accidents.

3. This move by the Austrian government changes the very notion of citizenship itself by introducing the difference of Muslims as a basis for different treatment. In this way, the government is questioning the idea of religious freedom and thus of the equality of citizens of different religious backgrounds, as defined in article 9 of the European Convention on

Human Rights (ECHR). The government argued that this was also the case in Turkey before the AK Party came to power (*Die Presse* 2018c), seemingly ignoring the fact that a system of de facto military tutelage is nothing a democratic country in Western Europe should long for. Consequently, these policy initiatives speak an unambiguous truth: equality no longer includes every citizen. Witnessing the abandonment of the principle of equality as a basis for democracy, which ought to secure the equal treatment of all its citizens—not only de facto but also de jure—means we are witnesses to a re-emerging political order. Nevertheless, the trend of regulating the female Muslim body was stopped by the Constitutional Court in December 2020.

## CHAPTER 6    THE SECURITY STATE

1. "Aus dieser Situation ergibt sich Sicherheit für beide Seiten, die Muslime und den Staat. Die Muslime in Österreich, unbeschadet ob österreichische Staatsangehörige oder nicht, haben über die Islamische Glaubensgemeinschaft eine klare und sichere Basis, über die sie mit den verschiedensten gesellschaftlichen und staatlichen Organisationen in einen Dialog treten können. Der österreichische Staat und seine Behörden hingegen haben die Sicherheit, in den Organen der Islamischen Glaubensgemeinschaft einen Ansprechpartner zu haben, der die Interessen der Muslime vertreten und verhandeln kann."

2. According to the Austrian government, the PKK has around 4,000 sympathizers in Austria. Their symbols are frequently used during demonstrations on their core issues and also when PKK-sympathetic organizations rally alongside other organizations on an array of issues. This is also true for the military wing of Hizbullah, although the symbols of this organization are far less prevalent on the streets. Another symbol that is even more common in youth culture among Turkish-origin youth is the sign of the Grey Wolves, the so-called wolf greeting. Rather than being a symbol specific to the Grey Wolves organization or its Turkish mother party, the Milliyetçi Hareket Partisi (MHP), it is frequently used to demonstrate Turkish nationalist pride. These organizations' symbols are the most widespread and hence the ones immediately affected by the legislation.

3. The renewed legislation in 2021 banned the symbol not only of the militant wing of Hizbullah, but Hizbullah in general, Hizb ut-Tahrir, the Caucasus Emirates, and another leftist group named the DHKP-C. Since the populist radical right FPÖ was no longer part of the coalition government, for the first time, the symbols of two white nationalist organizations were banned—those of the Identitarian Movement and its successor organization, The Austrians (*Die Österreicher*; DO5) (BGBl 2021, 2).

# REFERENCES

Abu-Lughod, Lila. 2013. *Do Muslim Women Need Saving?* Cambridge, MA: Harvard University Press.

Abuzahra, Amani. 2022. "Das österreichische Islamgesetz—Von der Duldung zum Respekt und retour?" In *Islamophobia Studies Yearbook 2022*, vol. 12, edited by Farid Hafez, 73–96. Vienna: New Academic Press.

Adam, Heribert. 2015. "Xenophobia, Asylum Seekers, and Immigration Policies in Germany." *Nationalism and Ethnic Politics* 21 (4): 446–464.

Adamovich, Ludwig. 1979. Brief betreffend Anerkennung einer islamischen Religionsgemeinde in Wien. GZ 602212/1-VI/5/79. 6 April 1979.

Aichholzer, Julian, Sylvia Kritzinger, Markus Wagner, Nicolai Berk, Hajo Boomgaarden, and Wolfgang C. Müller. 2018. "AUTNES Comparative Study of Electoral Systems Post-Election Survey 2017 (SUF edition)." Austrian Social Science Data Archive. https://doi.org/10.11587/IMKDZI.

Akkerman, Tjitske. 2012. "Comparing Radical Right Parties in Government: Immigration and Integration Policies in Nine Countries (1996–2010)." *West European Politics* 35 (3): 511–529.

Al-Azhar. 1976. Brief des Großimams der Al-Azhar, Abdal-Halim Mahmud an Islamil Balic, Präsident der Vereinigung der österreichischen Muslime [personal letter of the Grand Imam of Al Azhar Abdal-Halim Mahmud to Islamil Balic, president of the Association of Austrian Muslims] 13 February 1976.

Albertazzi, Daniele, and Duncan McDonnell. 2010. "The Lega Nord Back in Government." *West European Politics* 33 (6): 1318–1340.

Allen, Christopher, and Jørgen S. Nielsen. 2002. *Summary Report on Islamophobia in the EU after 11 September 2001*. European Monitoring Center on Racism and Islamophobia (EUMC). Vienna, May 2002. https://fra.europa.eu/sites/default/files/fra_uploads/199-Synthesis-report_en.pdf.

Alm, Niko. 2014. "Der Entwurf zum Islamgesetz." 18 September 2014. https://alm.net/der-entwurf-zum-islamgesetz/.

Amir-Moazami, Shirin. 2011. "Pitfalls of Consensus-Orientated Dialogue: The German Islam Conference." *Approaching Religion* 1 (1): 2–15.

Asad, Talal. 2003. *Formations of the Secular: Christianity, Islam, Modernity*. Stanford, CA: Stanford University Press, 2003.

Altwanger, Konrad, and Werner Zögernitz. 2006. *Nationalrat-Geschäftsordnung samt Verfahrensordnung für parlamentarische Untersuchungsausschüsse und umfangreiche Anmerkungen*. Vienna: Manz.

Aschauer, Wolfgang, Alexander Seymer, Martin Ulrich, Markus Kreuzberger, Franz Höllinger, Anja Eder, Markus Hadler, Johann Bacher, Dimitri Prandner. 2021. "Values in Crisis Austria—Wave 1 and Wave 2 Combined (SUF edition)." Austrian Social Science Data Archive. https://doi.org/10.11587/6YQASY.

Bader, Veit. 2007. "The Governance of Islam in Europe: The Perils of Modelling." *Journal of Ethnic and Migration Studies* 33 (6): 871–886.

Bader, Veit. 2014. "Dilemmas of Institutionalisation and Political Participation of Organised Religions in Europe. Associational Governance as a Promising Alternative." RECODE Online Working Paper no. 25, 1–25. https://www.recode.info/wp-content/uploads/2014/01/Final_Final-TITLE-PAGE-25-Bader_fin.pdf.

Bail, Christopher. 2014. *Terrified: How Anti-Muslim Fringe Organizations Became Mainstream.* Princeton, NJ: Princeton University Press.

Bale, Tim. 2003. "Cinderella and Her Ugly Sisters: The Mainstream and Extreme Right in Europe's Bipolarising Party Systems." *West European Politics* 26 (3): 67–90.

Bale, Tim, and Cristóbal Rovira Kaltwasser, eds. 2021. *Riding the Populist Wave: Europe's Mainstream Right in Crisis.* Cambridge: Cambridge University Press.

Bauböck, Rainer, Albert Kraler, Marco Martiniello, and Bernhard Perchinig. 2006. "Migrants' Citizenship: Legal Status, Rights and Political Participation. The Dynamics of International Migration and Settlement in Europe." In *The Dynamics of International Migration and Settlement in Europe,* edited by Karen Kraal, Rinus Penninx, and Maria Berger, 65–98. Amsterdam: Amsterdam University Press.

Bauböck, Rainer, and Bernhard Perchinig. 2006. "Migrations- und Integrationspolitik." In *Politik in Österreich,* edited by Herbert Dachs, Peter Gelich, Herbert Gottweis, Helmut Kramer, Volkmar Lauber, Wolfgang C. Müller, and Emmerich Tálos, 726–743. Vienna: Mainz Verlag.

Bennett, Andrew, and Alexander L. George. 2005. *Case Studies and Theory Development in the Social Sciences.* Cambridge, MA: MIT Press.

Berghahn, Sabine and Petra Rostock, eds. 2009. *Der Stoff, aus dem Konflikte sind: Debatten um das Kopftuch in Deutschland, Österreich und der Schweiz.* Bielefeld: transcript Verlag.

Beyer, Jürgen. 2006. *Pfadabhängigkeit: Über institutionelle Kontinuität, anfällige Stabilität und fundamentalen Wandel.* Schriften aus dem Max-Planck-Institut für Gesellschaftsforschung, Bd. 56. Frankfurt am Main: Campus Verlag.

Biard, Benjamin, Laurent Bernhard, and Hans-Georg Betz, eds. 2019. *Do They Make a Difference? The Policy Influence of Radical Right Populist Parties in Western Europe.* London: ECPR.

Biegelbauer, Peter, and Erich Grießler. 2009. "Politische Praktiken von MinisterialbeamtInnen im österreichischen Gesetzgebungsprozess." *Österreichische Zeitschrift für Politikwissenschaft* 38 (1): 61–78.

Biegelbauer, Peter, Christoph Konrath, and Benedikt Speer. 2014. "Die wissenschaftliche (Nicht-)Beschäftigung mit der Verwaltung und ihrem Verhältnis zur Politik in Österreich." *Austrian Journal of Political Science* 43 (4): 349–365.

Birt, Jonathan. 2006. "Good Imam, Bad Imam: Civic Religion and National Integration in Britain Post-9/11." *Muslim World* 96 (4): 687–705.

Bischof, Günter, Anton Pelinka, and Hermann Denz, eds. 2005. *Religion in Austria.* Contemporary Austrian Studies 13. New Brunswick, NJ: Transaction.

Bleich, Erik. 2009. "State Responses to 'Muslim' Violence: A Comparison of Six West European Countries." *Journal of Ethnic and Migration Studies* 35 (3): 361–379.

BMBWK. 2004. "Abschrift des Erlasses vom 23.06.04, das Tragen von Kopftüchern durch muslimische Schülerinnen betreffend." Bundesministerium für Bildung Wissenschaft und Kultur (BMBWK). http://www.forum-muslimische-frauen.at/index.php?page=erlass-vom-juni-2004-zum-kopftuchtragen-an-schulen.

Bracke, Sarah, and Luis Manuel Hernández Aguilar. 2021. "Thinking Europe's 'Muslim Question': On Trojan Horses and the Problematization of Muslims." *Critical Research on Religion* 10 (2): 1–21.

Bridge Initiative Team. 2020a. "Factsheet: Counter-Jihad Movement." Bridge, a Georgetown University Initiative. 17 September 2020. https://bridge.georgetown.edu/research/factsheet-counter-jihad-movement/.

Bridge Initiative Team. 2020b. "Factsheet: Heiko Heinisch." Bridge, a Georgetown University Initiative. 3 March 2020. https://bridge.georgetown.edu/research/factsheet-heiko-heinisch/.

Bridge Initiative Team. 2020c. "Factsheet: Lorenzo Vidino." Bridge, a Georgetown University Initiative. 22 April 2020. https://bridge.georgetown.edu/research/factsheet-lorenzo-vidino/.

Bridge Initiative Team. 2020d. "Factsheet: Wiener Akademikerbund (WAB, Viennese Association of Academics)." Bridge, a Georgetown University Initiative. 2 June 2020. https://bridge.georgetown.edu/research/factsheet-wiener-akademikerbund-wab-viennese-association-of-academics/.

Bridge Initiative Team. 2021. "Factsheet: Susanne Schröter." Bridge, a Georgetown University Initiative. 13 January 2021. https://bridge.georgetown.edu/research/factsheet-susanne-schroter/.

Bromley-Trujillo, Rebecca, and John Poe. 2020. "The Importance of Salience: Public Opinion and State Policy Action on Climate Change." *Journal of Public Policy* 40 (2): 280–304.

Bruckmüller, Ernst. 1994. *Österreichbewußtsein im Wandel*. Schriftenreihe des Zentrums für Angewandte Politikforschung 4. Vienna: Signum-Verlag.

Brünner, Christian. 2002. "Zum Geleit (Plädoyer für eine verfassungskonforme, den Rollen von Staat und Religionsgemeinschaften im Kooperationsmodell adäquate Ausgestaltung des Staatskirchenrechts)." In *Die "Anerkennung" von Religionsgemeinschaften*, edited by Richard Potz and Reinhard Kohlhofer, 13–23. Vienna: Verlag Österreich.

Bunzl, Matti. 2005. "Between Anti-Semitism and Islamophobia: Some Thoughts on the New Europe." *American Ethnologist* 32 (4): 499–508.

Bunzl, John, and Farid Hafez, eds. 2009. *Islamophobie in Österreich*. Vienna: Studienverlag.

Çakır, Alev. 2011. "Governance religiöser Diversität in Österreich." PhD diss., University of Vienna.

Casanova, José. 2011. "Cosmopolitanism, the Clash of Civilizations and Multiple Modernities." *Current Sociology* 59 (2): 252–267.

Cesari, Jocelyne. 2010. "Securitization of Islam in Europe." In *Muslims in the West after 9/11: Religion, Politics and Law*, edited by Jocelyne Cesari, 9–27. New York: Routledge.

Ciornei, Irina, Eva-Maria Euchner, and Ilay Yesil. 2021. "Political Parties and Muslims in Europe: The Regulation of Islam in Public Education." *West European Politics* 45 (5): 1003–1032.

Collier, Paul. 2011. *Wars, Guns, and Votes: Democracy in Dangerous Places*. London: Random House.

Crepaz, Markus M. L. 1994. "From Semisovereignty to Sovereignty: The Decline of Corporatism and Rise of Parliament in Austria." *Comparative Politics* 27 (1): 45–65.

Crouch, Colin, and Franz Traxler. 1995. *Farewell to Labour Market Associations? Organized versus Disorganized Decentralization as a Map for Industrial Relations*. Avebury: Aldershot, 3–19.

Csigó, Monika. 2006. *Institutioneller Wandel durch Lernprozesse. Eine neo-institutionalistische Perspektive*. Wiesbaden: Verlag für Sozialwissenschaften.

Dachs, Herbert, Peter Gerlich, Herbert Gottweis, Helmut Kramer, Volkmar Lauber, Wolfgang C. Müller, and Emmerich Tálos. 2006. *Politik in Österreich: Das Handbuch*. Vienna: Manz.

Dannhauser, Claudia. 2007. "Prammer: Kopftuch als, Symbol untergeordneter Frauenrolle." *Die Presse*. 27 September 2007. https://www.diepresse.com/332797/prammer-kopftuch-als-symbol-untergeordneter-frauenrolle.

Dautović, Rijad. 2019a. "Der völkerrechtliche Hintergrund der Anerkennung der islamischen Glaubensgemeinschaft in Österreich. Zur Genese des Art. 4 des Protokolls vom 26. Februar 1909 und seiner Bedeutung für die Rechtsstellung der Muslime in Österreich." In *Die Islamische Glaubensgemeinschaft in Österreich. 1909–1979–2019: Beiträge zu einem neuen Blick auf ihre Geschichte und Entwicklung*, edited by Farid Hafez and Rijad Dautović, 45–72. Vienna: New Academic Press.

Dautović, Rijad. 2019b. "40 Jahre Islamische Glaubensgemeinschaft in Österreich? Vom historischen Missverständnis zu Alter und Wesen der IGGÖ." In *Die Islamische Glaubensgemeinschaft in Österreich. 1909–1979–2019: Beiträge zu einem neuen Blick auf ihre Geschichte und Entwicklung*, edited by Farid Hafez and Rijad Dautović, 175–186. Vienna: New Academic Press.

Dautović, Rijad. 2019c. "40 Jahre seit Wiederherstellung der IRG-Wien. Warum die Islamische Religionsgemeinde Wien nicht erst 1979 gegründet wurde." In *Die Islamische Glaubensgemeinschaft in Österreich. 1909–1979–2019: Beiträge zu einem neuen Blick auf ihre Geschichte und Entwicklung*, edited by Farid Hafez and Rijad Dautović, 99–124. Vienna: New Academic Press.

Dautović, Rijad, and Farid Hafez. 2015. "MuslimInnen als BürgerInnen zweiter Klasse? Eine vergleichende Analyse des Entwurfes eines neuen Islamgesetzes 2014 zum restlichen Religionsrecht." In *Jahrbuch für Islamophobieforschung 2015*, edited by Fariz Hafez, 26–54. Vienna: Studienverlag.

Dautović, Rijad, and Farid Hafez. 2019. "Institutionalising Islam in Contemporary Austria: A Comparative Analysis of the Austrian Islam Act of 2015 and Austrian Religion Acts with Special Emphasis on the Israelite Act of 2012." *Oxford Journal of Law and Religion* 8 (1) (February): 28–50.

De Cillia, Rudolf, Teresa Distelberger, and Ruth Wodak. 2009. "Österreichische Identitäten in politischen Gedenkreden des Jubiläumsjahres 2005." In *Gedenken im Gedankenjahr. Zur diskursiven Konstruktion österreichischer Identitäten im Jubiläumsjahr 2005*, edited by Rudolf de Cillia and Ruth Wodak, 29–77. Vienna: Studienverlag.

De Cillia, Rudolf, and Ruth Wodak. 2009. *Gedenken im 'Gedankenjahr'. Zur diskursiven Konstruktion österreichischer Identitäten im Jubiläumsjahr 2005*. Vienna: Studienverlag.

De Cillia, Rudolf, Ruth Wodak, and Martin Reisigl. 1999. "The Discursive Construction of National Identities." *Discourse & Society* 10:149–173.

Deschouwer, Kris. 1989. "Patterns of Participation and Competition in Belgium." *West European Politics* 12 (4): 28–41.

Dolezal, Martin, Marc Helbling, and Swen Hutter. 2010. "Debating Islam in Austria, Germany and Switzerland: Ethnic Citizenship, Church-State Relations and Right-Wing Populism." *West European Politics* 33 (2): 171–190.

Du Bois, W. E. B. 2006. *The Souls of Black Folk*. University Park: Pennsylvania State University Press.

ECRI. 2010. *ECRI Report on Austria*. European Commission against Racism and Intolerance. 10 March 2010. https://www.refworld.org/publisher,COECRI,,AUT,513dc1f52,0.html.

Ehs, Tamara. 2011. "Politics & Law. So nah und doch so fern." *Österreichische Zeitschrift für Politikwissenschaft* 40 (2): 197–205.

El-Sehity, Magda Mariam. 2009. "Islamophobie in den österreichischen Tageszeitungen- eine kritische Diskursanalyse." Diplomarbeit am Institut für Publizistik- und Kommunikationswissenschaft an der Universität Wien.

Elster, Jon. 1992. *Local Justice: How Institutions Allocate Scarce Goods and Necessary Burdens*. New York: Russell Sage Foundation.

Euchner, Eva-Maria. 2018. "Regulating Islamic Religious Education in German States." *Zeitschrift für Vergleichende Politikwissenschaft* 12:93–109.

EUMC. 2006. *Muslims in the European Union. Discrimination and Islamophobia*. European Monitoring Center on Racism and Islamophobia (EUMC). https://fra.europa.eu/sites/default/files/fra_uploads/156-Manifestations_EN.pdf.

European Commission. 2011. "European Citizens' Knowledge and Attitudes towards Science and Technology." Eurobarometer. September 2021. Standard Eurobarometer 75–Spring 2011. https://europa.eu/eurobarometer/surveys/detail/1019.

European Commission. 2021. "European Citizens' Knowledge and Attitudes towards Science and Technology." Eurobarometer. September 2021. https://europa.eu/eurobarometer /surveys/detail/2237.

European Values Study 2008: Integrated Dataset (EVS 2008). 2022. GESIS Data Archive, Cologne. ZA4800 Data file Version 5.0.0, https://doi.org/10.4232/1.13841.

European Values Study 2017: Integrated Dataset (EVS 2017). 2022. GESIS Data Archive, Cologne. ZA7500 Data file Version 5.0.0. https://doi:10.4232/1.13897.

European Values Study 2017–2018: Integrated Dataset (EVS 2017)—Sensitive Data. 2022. GESIS Data Archive, Cologne. ZA7501 Data file Version 2.0.0, https://doi.org/10.4232/1 .13898.

Fallend, Franz. 2012. "Populism in Government: The Case of Austria (2000–2007)." In *Populism in Europe and the Americas: Threat or Corrective for Democracy?*, edited by Cas Mudde and Christóbal Rovira Kaltwasser, 113–135. Cambridge: Cambridge University Press.

Fetzer, Joel S., and J. Christopher Soper. 2004. *Muslims and the State in Britain, France and Germany*. Cambridge: Cambridge University Press.

Friedrich, Otto. 2008. "Muslime Wollen in Sicht Sein," *Die Furche*, 11 March 2008. http://www .furche.at/system/show thread.php?t=325.

Friesl, Christian, Thomas Hofer, and Renate Wieser. 2009. "Die Österreicher/-innen und die Politik." In *Die Österreicher/-innen: Wertewandel 1990–2008*, edited by Christian Friesl, Regina Polak, and Ursula Hamachers-Zuba, 207–293. Vienna: Czernin Verlag.

Friesl, Christian, Regina Polak, and Ursula Hamachers-Zuba, eds. 2009. *Die Österreicher Innen: Wertewandel 1990–2008*. Vienna: Czernin Verlag.

Furat, Ayşe Zişan. 2012. "A Cultural Transformation Project: Religious and Educational Policy of the Austro-Hungarian Empire in Bosnia (1878–1918)." In *Balkans and Islam: Encounter, Transformation, Discontinuity, Continuity*, edited by Ayşe Zişan and Hamit Er, 63–84. Newcastle upon Tyne: Cambridge Scholars.

Furat, Ayşe Zişan. 2019. "Bosnian Muslims' Relations with Istanbul: Religious and Sovereign Rights in the Context of 1909 Autonomy Statute." In *Die Islamische Glaubensgemeinschaft in Österreich. 1909–1979–2019: Beiträge zu einem neuen Blick auf ihre Geschichte und Entwicklung*, edited by Farid Hafez and Rijad Dautović, 73–95. Vienna: New Academic Press.

Fürlinger, Ernst. 2013. *Moscheebaukonflikte in Österreich: Nationale Politik des religiösen Raums im globalen Zeitalter*. Vienna: V&R Unipress.

Geden, Oliver. 2005. "Identitätsdiskurs und politische Macht: Die rechtspopulistische Mobilisierung von Ethnozentrismus im Spannungsfeld von Opposition und Regierung am Beispiel von FPÖ und SVP." In *Populisten an der Macht. Populistische Regierungsparteien in West- und Osteuropa*, edited by Susanne Frülich-Steffen and Lars Rensmann, 69–83. Vienna: Braumüller Verlag.

Gerlich, Peter. 1985. *Sozialpartnerschaft in der Krise—Leistungen und Grenzen des Neokorporatismus in Österreich*. Vienna: Böhlau.

Getzner, Michael, and Reinhard Neck. 2001. *Die Entwicklung der Staatsausgaben in Österreich*. Vienna: Ludwig Boltzmann-Institut zur Analyse Wirtschaftspolitischer Aktivitäten.

Gingrich, Andre. 1998. "Frontier Myths of Orientalism: The Muslim World in Public and Popular Culture of Central Europe." In *MESS—Mediterranean Ethnological Summer School*, edited by Bojan Baskar and Borut Bromen, vol. 2, 99–127. Ljubljana: Inštitut za Multikulturne raziskave zavod.

Gingrich, Andre. 2015. "The Nearby Frontier: Structural Analyses of Myths of Orientalism." *Diogenes* 60 (2): 60–66.

Goetz, Judith. 2021. "Traditionelle Geschlechterordnungen und importierte Unterdrückung. Die antifeministischen Geschlechterpolitiken der FPÖ." *L'Homme* 32 (1): 127–134.

Goodwin, Jeff, and James M. Jasper. 1999. "Caught in a Winding, Snarling Vine: The Structural Bias of Political Process Theory." *Sociological Forum* 14 (1): 27–92.

Goujon, Anne, Sandra Jurasszovich, and Michaela Potančoková. 2017. "Religious Denominations in Austria: Baseline Study for 2016—Scenarios until 2046." Vienna Institute of Demography Working Papers, no. 09/2017, Austrian Academy of Sciences (ÖAW), Vienna Institute of Demography (VID). Vienna, August 2017. https://www.econstor.eu/bitstream/10419/184837/1/WP2017_09.pdf.

Gresch, Nora, and Leila Hadj-Abdou. 2009. "Selige Musliminnen oder marginalisierte Migrantinnen? Das österreichische Paradox der geringen Teilhabe von Kopftuchträgerinnen bei 'toleranter' Kopftuchpolitik." In *Der Stoff, aus dem Konflikte sind: Debatten um das Kopftuch in Deutschland, Österreich und der Schweiz*, edited by Sabine Berghahn and Petra Rostock, 73–99. Bielefeld: Transcript Verlag.

Gresch, Nora, Leila Hadj-Abdou, Sieglinde Rosenberger, and Birgit Sauer. 2008. "Tu Felix Austria? The Headscarf and the Politics of 'Non-issues.'" *Social Politics: International Studies in Gender, State & Society* 15 (4): 411–432.

Gresch, Nora, Leila Hadj-Abdou, Sieglinde Rosenberger, and Birgit Sauer. 2012. "Hijabophobia revisited: Kopftuchdebatten und -politiken in Europa. Ein Überblick über das Forschungsprojekt VEIL." In *Migration und Geschlechterverhältnisse. Kann die Migrantin sprechen?*, edited by Eva Hausbacher, Elisabeth Klaus, Ralph Poole, Ulrike Brandl, and Ingrid Schmutzhart, 198–212. Wiesbaden: Verlag für Sozialwissenschaften.

Gruber, Helmut. 1991. *Antisemitismus im Mediendiskurs: Die Affäre "Waldheim" in der Tagespresse*. Wiesbaden: Verlag für Sozialwissenschaften.

Gruber, Oliver. 2018. "Diversität und Integration im Schulsystem. Empirische Befunde zur Ungleichheit und ihre bildungspolitischen Konsequenzen." *GW Unterricht* 151 (3): 5–19.

Gruber, Oliver, Astrid Mattes, and Jeremias Stadlmair. 2015. "Die meritokratische Neugestaltung der österreichischen Integrationspolitik zwischen Rhetorik und Policy." *Home* 45 (1): 65–79.

Haddad, Yvonne Yazbeck, and Tyler Golson. 2007. "Overhauling Islam: Representation, Construction, and Cooption of 'Moderate Islam' in Western Europe." *Journal of Church and State* 49 (3): 487–515.

Hafez, Farid. 2009a. "Islamophobe Diskursstrategien in Grün und Blau. Eine diskursanalytische Analyse eines Interviews des Grünen Bundesrat Efgani Dönmez." In *Islamophobie in Österreich*, edited by John Bunzl and Farid Hafez, 168–182. Vienna: Studienverlag.

Hafez, Farid. 2009b. "Zwischen Islamophobie und Islamophilie: Die FPÖ und der Islam." In *Islamophobie in Österreich*, edited by John Bunzl and Farid Hafez, 105–125. Vienna: Studienverlag.

Hafez, Farid. 2010a. *Islamophober Populismus: Moschee- und Minarettbauverbote sterreichischer Parlamentsparteien*. Wiesbaden: Verlag für Sozialwissenschaften.

Hafez, Farid. 2010b. "Österreich und der Islam—eine Wende durch FPÖVP? Anmerkungen zur Rolle von Islamophobie im politischen Diskurs seit der Wende." In *Die beschämte Republik: Zehn Jahre nach Schwarz-Blau in Österreich*, edited by Frederick Baker and Petra Herczeg, 130–141. Vienna: Czernin Verlag.

Hafez, Farid. 2012a. *Anas Schakfeh. Das österreichische Gesicht des Islams*. Vienna: Braumüller GmbH.

Hafez, Farid. 2012b. "Jörg Haider and Islamophobia." In *From the Far Right to the Mainstream Islamophobia, Party Politics and the Media*, edited by Humayun Ansari and Farid Hafez, 45–68. Frankfurt: Campus Verlag.

Hafez, Farid. 2013. "One Representing the Many: Institutionalized Austrian Islam." In *Debating Islam: Negotiating Religion, Europe, and the Self*, edited by Samuel Behloul, Susanne Leuenberger, and Andreas Tunger-Zanetti. Bielefeld: Transcript Verlag.

Hafez, Farid. 2014a. "Disciplining the 'Muslim Subject': The Role of Security Agencies in Establishing Islamic Theology within the State's Academia." *Islamophobia Studies Journal* 2 (2): 43–57.

Hafez, Farid. 2014b. "Gedenken im 'islamischen Gedankenjahr.' Zur diskursiven Konstruktion des österreichischen Islams im Rahmen der Jubiläumsfeier zu 100 Jahren Islamgesetz." In *Wiener Zeitschrift für die Kunde des Morgenlandes* 104:63–85.

Hafez, Farid. 2014c. "Shifting Borders: Islamophobia as the Cornerstone for Building Pan-European Right-Wing Unity." *Patterns of Prejudice* 48 (5): 1–21.

Hafez, Farid. 2015a. "Das IslamG im Kontext islamophober Diskurse. Eine Policy Frame-Analyse zum Politikgestaltungsprozess des IslamG 2015." *Juridikum* 2:160–165.

Hafez, Farid. 2015b. "Die österreichische 'Islam-Lehrer'-Studie. Mediale Berichterstattung und politische Implikationen." In *Jahrbuch für Islamophobieforschung 2015*, edited by Fariz Hafez, 100–122. Vienna: Studienverlag.

Hafez, Farid. 2016. "Ostarrichislam: Gründe der korporatistischen Hereinnahme des Islams in der Zweiten Republik." *Österreichische Zeitschrift für Politikwissenschaft* 45 (3): 1–11.

Hafez, Farid. 2017a. "Debating the 2015 Islam Law in Austrian Parliament: Between Legal Recognition and Islamophobic Populism." *Discourse and Society* 28 (4): 392–412.

Hafez, Farid. 2017b. "Muslim Protest against Austria's Islam Law: An Analysis of Austrian Muslim's Protest against the 2015 Islam Law." *Journal of Muslim Minority Affairs* 37 (3): 267–283.

Hafez, Farid. 2017c. "Thematisierung von 'Religion' in der österreichischen Politikwissenschaft. Status Quo, Tendenzen und kritische Anmerkungen." *Interdisciplinary Journal for Religion and Transformation in Contemporary Society* 3 (1): 41–61.

Hafez, Farid. 2018a. "Alte neue Islampolitik in Österreich? Eine postkoloniale Analyse der österreichischen Islampolitik." *ZfP—Zeitschrift für Politik* 65 (1): 22–44.

Hafez, Farid. 2018b. "Banning Symbols of Extremism in Austria: Targeting Extremism or Civil Society?" SETA Perspectives, no. 49. Istanbul, December 2018. https://setav.org/en/assets/uploads/2018/12/49_Perspective.pdf.

Hafez, Farid. 2018c. "Islamophobia in Austria: National Report 2017." In *European Islamophobia Report 2017*, edited by Enes Bayraklı and Farid Hafez, 49–84. Istanbul: SETA.

Hafez, Farid. 2018d. "Muslim Civil Society under Attack: The European Foundation for Democracy's Role in Defaming and Delegitimizing Muslim Civil Society." In *Islamophobia and Radicalization: Breeding Intolerance and Violence*, edited by Iner Derya and John Esposito, 117–137. Cham: Springer International.

Hafez, Farid. 2019a. *Feindbild Islam. Zur Salonfähigkeit von Rassismus*. Vienna: Böhlau Verlag & V&R Unipress.

Hafez, Farid. 2019b. "Islamophobe Denkfabriken: Strategien der systematischen Diffamierung und Delegitimierung muslimischer zivilgesellschaftlicher AkteurInnen am Beispiel der Denkfabrik 'European Foundation for Democracy.'" In *Jahrbuch für Islamophobieforschung 2019*, edited by Fariz Hafez, 7–30. Vienna: Studienverlag.

Hafez, Farid. 2019c. "Islamophobia in Austria: National Report 2018." In *European Islamophobia Report 2018*, edited by Enes Bayraklı and Farid Hafez, 87–126. Istanbul: SETA.

Hafez, Farid. 2019d. "From Jewification to Islamization: Political anti-Semitism and Islamophobia in Austrian politics then and now." *ReOrient* 4 (2): 197–220.

Hafez, Farid. 2020a. "Islamophobia in Austria: National Report 2019." In *European Islamophobia Report 2019*, edited by Enes Bayraklı and Farid Hafez, 79–113. Istanbul: SETA.

Hafez, Farid. 2020b. "Rassismus im Bildungswesen: Zur Disziplinierung des muslimischen 'Anderen' im Bildungswesen am Beispiel des Diskurses zu islamischen Kindergärten in Österreich." In *Nationalpopulismus bildet? Lehren für Unterricht und Bildung*, edited by

Manfred Oberlechner, Reinhard Heinisch, and Patrick Duval, 100–122. Frankfurt am Main: Wochenschau Verlag.

Hafez, Farid, ed. 2021a. *Das "Andere" Österreich: Leben in Österreich abseits männlich-weiß-heteronormativ-deutsch-katholischer Dominanz.* Vienna: New Academic Press.

Hafez, Farid. 2021b. "Surveilling and Criminalizing Austrian Muslims: The Case of 'Political Islam.'" *Insight Turkey* 23 (2): 11–22.

Hafez, Farid, ed. 2023. *Operation Luxor: Eine kritische Aufarbeitung der größten rassistischen Polizeioperation Österreichs.* Bielefeld: Transcript Verlag.

Hafez, Farid. 2023a. "Das Dispositiv 'politischer Islam' in der österreichischen Bundespolitik," *Frankfurter Zeitschrift für Islamische Theologie* 6:121–142.

Hafez, Farid. 2023b. "Criminalizing Muslim Agency in Europe: The Case of 'Political Islam' in Austria, Germany, and France." *French Cultural Studies* 34 (3): 313–328.

Hafez, Farid, and Reinhard Heinisch. 2018. "Breaking with Austrian Consociationalism: How the Rise of Rightwing Populism and Party Competition Have Changed Austria's Islam Politics." *Politics and Religion* 11 (3) (September): 649–678.

Hafez, Farid, and Reinhard Heinisch. 2019. "The Political Influence of the Austrian Freedom Party in Austria." In *Do They Make a Difference? The Policy Influence of Radical Right Populist Parties in Western Europe,* edited by Benjamin Biard, Laurent Bernhard, and Hans-Georg Betz, 145–164. New York: Rowman & Littlefield.

Hafez, Farid, Reinhard Heinisch, and Eric Miklin. 2019. "The New Right: Austria's Freedom Party and Changing Perceptions of Islam." Center for Middle East Policy, Brookings Institution. Washington, DC, 24 July 2019. https://www.brookings.edu/articles/the-new-right-austrias-freedom-party-and-changing-perceptions-of-islam/.

Hafez, Kai. 2002a. *Das Nahost- und Islambild in der deutschen überregionalen Presse.* Baden-Baden: Nomos Verlag.

Hafez, Kai. 2002b. *Die politische Dimension der Auslandsberichterstattung: Das Nahost- und Islambild der deutschen überregionalen Presse.* Baden-Baden: Nomos Verlag.

Hafez, Kai. 2014. *Islam in Liberal Europe: Freedom, Equality, and Intolerance.* Plymouth: Rowman & Littlefield.

Haider, Jörg. 1993. *Die Freiheit, die ich meine.* Vienna: Ullstein.

Hall, Peter A., and Rosemary C. R. Taylor. 1996. "Political Science and the Three New Institutionalisms." *Political Studies* 44:936–957.

Halm, Dirk. 2008. *Der Islam als Diskursfeld.* Wiesbaden: VS Verlag für Sozialwissenschaften.

Hanisch, Ernst. 1977. *Die Ideologie des politischen Katholizismus in Österreich 1918–1938.* Vienna: Geyer.

Hanisch, Ernst. 1994. *"Der lange Schatten des Staates": Österreichische Gesellschaftsgeschichte im 20. Jahrhundert, 1890–1990.* Vienna: Ueberreuter.

Hauptmann, Ferdinand. 1985. "Die Mohammedaner in Bosnien-Hercegowina." In *Die Habsburgermonarchie 1848–1918,* vol. 4, *Die Konfessionen,* edited by Adam Wandruszka, XI–XVI. Vienna: VÖAW.

Hauser, Kristina, and Reinhard Heinisch. 2016. "The Mainstreaming of the Austrian Freedom Party: The More Things Change..." In *Radical Right-Wing Populist Parties in Western Europe: Into the Mainstream?,* edited by Tjitske Akkerman, Sarah L. de Lange, and Matthijs Rooduijn, 46–62. London: Routledge.

Heine, Susanne, Rüdiger Lohlker, and Richard Potz. 2012. *Muslime in Österreich. Geschichte, Lebenswelt, Religion, Grundlagen für den Dialog.* Vienna: Styria.

Heinisch, Reinhard. 1999. "Modernization Brokers—Austrian Corporatism in Search of a New Legitimacy." *Current Politics and Economics of Europe* 9 (1): 65–94.

Heinisch, Reinhard. 2000. "Coping with Economic Integration: Corporatist Strategies in Germany and Austria in the 1990s." *West European Politics* 23 (3): 67–96.

Heinisch, Reinhard. 2001. "Defying Neo-liberal Convergence: Austria's Successful Supply-Side Corporatism in the 1990s." *Journal of Government and Policy* 19 (1): 29–44.

Heinisch, Reinhard. 2002. *Populism, Proporz, and Pariah—Austria Turns Right: Austrian Political Change, Its Causes and Repercussions.* Huntington, NY: Nova Science.

Heinisch, Reinhard. 2003. "Success in Opposition—Failure in Government: Explaining the Performance of Right-Wing Populist Parties in Public Office." *West European Politics* 26 (3): 91–130.

Heinisch, Reinhard. 2008. "Right-Wing Populism in Austria: A Case for Comparison." *Problems of Post-Communism* 55 (3) (May/June): 40–56.

Heinisch, Reinhard, Steven Saxonberg, Annika Werner, and Fabian Habersack. 2021). "The Effect of Radical Right Fringe Parties on Main Parties in Central and Eastern Europe: Empirical Evidence from Manifesto Data." *Party Politics* 27 (1): 9–21.

Heinisch, Reinhard K., and Annika Werner. 2021. "Austria: Tracing the Austrian Christian Democrats' Adaptation to the Silent Counter-Revolution." In *Riding the Populist Wave: Europe's Mainstream Right in Crisis,* edited by Tim Bale and Cristóbal Rovira Kaltwasser, 91–112. Cambridge: Cambridge University Press.

Heiss, Gernot, and Oliver Rathkolb, eds. 1995. *Asylland wider Willen: Flüchtlinge in Österreich im europäischen Kontext seit 1914.* Vol. 25. Vienna: J & V Edition.

Helms, Ludger. 2004. "Einleitung: Politikwissenschaftliche Institutionenforschung am Schnittpunkt von Politischer Theorie und Regierungslehre." In *Politische Theorie und Regierungslehre. Eine Einführung in die politikwissenschaftliche Institutionenforschung,* edited by Ludger Helms and Uwe Jun, 13–44. Frankfurt am Main: Campus Verlag.

Hernández Aguilar, Luis Manuel. 2015. "Welcome to Integrationland: On Racism and the German Islam Conference." PhD diss., Goethe-University, Frankfurt am Main.

Hernández Aguilar, Luis Manuel. 2017. "Suffering Rights and Incorporation: The German Islam Conference and the Integration of Muslims as a Discursive Means of Their Racialization." *European Societies* 19 (5): 623–644.

Hernández Aguilar, Luis Manuel. 2018. *Governing Muslims and Islam in Contemporary Germany: Race, Time, and the German Islam Conference.* Leiden: Brill.

Herzog, Eva-Maria. 2012. "'Bilder in unseren Köpfen': Eine soziologische Studie zum Selbst- und Fremdbild von MuslimInnen." In *Jahrbuch für Islamophobieforschung 2012,* edited by Farid Hafez, 142–153. Vienna: Studienverlag.

Hödl, Klaus. 2010. "Islamophobia in Austria: The Recent Emergence of Anti-Muslim Sentiments in the Country." *Journal of Muslim Minority Affairs* 30 (4): 443–456.

Hofhansel, Claus. 2010. "Accommodating Islam and the Utility of National Models: The German Case." *West European Politics* 33 (2): 191–207.

Horvath, Elisabeth. 2009. *Heinz Fischer. Die Biografie.* Vienna: Kremayr & Scheriau.

Hummel, Daniel. 2021. *Prejudice and Policymaking: Islamophobia in the United States and the Diffusion of Anti-Sharia Laws.* London: Rowman & Littlefield.

Huntington, Samuel P. 1993. "The Clash of Civilizations." *Foreign Affairs* 72 (3) (Summer): 22–49.

Ilie, Cornelia. 2010. "Introduction." In *European Parliaments under Scrutiny: Discourse Strategies and Interaction Practices,* edited by Cornelia Ilie. Amsterdam: John Benjamins.

Ilie, Cornelia. 2015. "Parliamentary Discourse." In *The International Encyclopedia of Language and Social Interaction,* edited by Karen Tracy, Cornelia Ilie, Todd Sandel, 1113. New York: Oxford University Press.

Ilie, Cornelia, Ihalainen Pasi, and Kari Palonen, eds. 2016. *Parliament and Parliamentarism: A Comparative History of a European Concept.* New York: Berghahn Books.

Inglehart, Ronald. 1997. *Modernization and Postmodernization: Cultural, Economic, and Political Change in 43 Societies.* Princeton, NJ: Princeton University Press.

Jenny, Marcelo. 2011. "Austria." *European Journal of Political Research Political Data Yearbook* 50:907–908.

Joppke, Christian. 2013. *Legal Integration of Islam.* Cambridge, MA: Harvard University Press.

Kaag, Mayke, and Farid Tabarki. 2010. "Muslims in Amsterdam." At Home in Europe Project, Open Society Foundations. New York. www.opensocietyfoundations.org/uploads /91973b57-9f21-4cf4-bfc1-6d6e81bb2818/a-muslims-amsterdam-report-en-20101123_0.pdf.

Kalb, Herbert, Richard Potz, and Brigitte Schinkele. 2003. *Religionsrecht.* Vienna: WUV Universitätsverlag.

Karčić, Fikret. 1999. *The Bosniaks and the Challange of Modernity: Late Ottoman and Habsburg Times.* Sarajevo: El-Kalem.

Karlhofer, Ferdinand, and Emmerich Talos.1999. *Zukunft der Sozialpartnerschaft: Veränderungsdynamik und Reformbedarf,* vol. 19. Vienna: Signum-Verlag.

Kastoryano, Riva. 2004. "Religion and Incorporation: Islam in France and Germany." *International Migration Review* 38 (3): 1234–1255.

Katzenstein, Peter J. 1976. *Disjoined Partners: Austria and Germany since 1815.* Berkeley: University of California Press.

Katzenstein, Peter J. 1985. *Small States in World Markets: Industrial Policy in Europe.* Ithaca, NY: Cornell University Press.

Kern, Thomas. 2008. *Soziale Bewegungen: Ursachen, Wirkungen, Mechanismen.* Wiesbaden: Springer-Verlag.

Kettell, Steven. 2012. "Has Political Science Ignored Religion?" *PS: Political Science & Politics* 45 (1): 93–100.

Kingdon, John W. 1984. *Agendas, Alternatives, and Public Policies.* Boston: Little, Brown.

Klestil, Thomas. 2005. *Der Verantwortung verpflichtet: Ansprachen und Vorträge 1992–2004.* Vienna: Verlag Österreich.

Klier, Josh. 2022. "36 Years of Textual Data on Populism: Using a Dynamic Topic Model and a Novel National Parliament Dataset to Analyze Austrian Right-Wing Populism." Working paper presented in the Department of Political Science, University of Salzburg. Salzburg, June 5. https://www.plus.ac.at/wp-content/uploads/2023/10/Klier_36-Years-of-Textual -Data-on-Populism_2022.pdf.

Knappskog, Tom. 2001. "Consociationalism: Theoretical Development Illustrated by the Case of Belgium." *Res Publica* 43 (4): 529–550.

Knight, Robert. 2017. *Slavs in Post-Nazi Austria: Carinthian Slovenes and the Politics of Assimilation, 1945–1960.* London: Bloomsbury.

Koenig, Mathias. 2007. "Europeanising the Governance of Religious Diversity: An Institutionalist Account of Muslim Struggles for Public Recognition." *Journal of Ethnic and Migration Studies* 33 (6): 911–932.

Korb, Sebastian, Tugba Ceren Deniz, Bengi Ünal, Alasdair Clarke, and Giorgia Silani. 2022. "Emotion Perception Bias Associated with the Hijab in Austrian and Turkish Participants." *Quarterly Journal of Experimental Psychology* 75 (5): 796–807.

Krasner, Stephen D. 1984. "Approaches to the State: Alternative Conceptions and Historical Dynamics." *Comparative Politics* 16 (2): 223–246.

Kriechbaumer, Robert. 2004. *Die Ära Kreiksy: Österreich 1970–1983.* Vienna: Böhlau.

Kritzinger, Sylvia, Kathrin Thomas, Christian Glantschnigg, Julian Aichholzer, Konstantin Glinitzer, David Johann, Markus Wagner, and Eva Zeglovits. 2020. "AUTNES Comparative Study of Electoral Systems Post-Election Survey 2013 (SUF edition)." https://doi.org /10.11587/5ZO48V.

Kundnani, Arun. 2014. *The Muslims Are Coming! Islamophobia, Extremism, and the Domestic War on Terror.* New York: Verso.

Kuru, Ahmet T. 2009. *Secularism and State Policies toward Religion: The United States, France, and Turkey.* Cambridge: Cambridge University Press.

Langer, Armin. 2020. "'Judaism Is Not a Religion, but a Political Organization': German Jews under Suspicion in the Age of Enlightenment and Parallels to Contemporary Islamophobic Discourses." In "Muslims under General Suspicion: Perspectives on the Prevention of So-Called Islamist Extremism," edited by Farid Hafez and Sinyan Qasem. Special issue, *Islamophobia Studies Yearbook* 11:91–110.

Laurence, Jonathan. 2006. "Managing Transnational Islam: Muslims and the State in Western Europe." In *Immigration and the Transformation of Europe*, edited by Craig Parsons and Timothy M. Smeeding, 253–275. Cambridge: Cambridge University Press.

Laurence, Jonathan. 2012. *The Emancipation of Europe's Muslims: The State's Role in Minority Integration.* Princeton, NJ: Princeton University Press.

Lehmbruch, Gerhard. 1984. "Interorganisatorische Verflechtungen im Neokorporatismus". In *Politische Willensbildung und Interessenvermittlung: Verhandlungen der Fachtagung der DVPW, vom 11.–13. Oktober 1983 in Mannheim*, edited by Fachtagung der DVPW, Jürgen W. Falter, Christian Fenner, Michael Th Greven, Deutsche Vereinigung für Politische Wissenschaft, 467–482. Opladen: Westdeutscher Verlag.

Lehmbruch, Gerhard. 1985. "Constitution-Making in Young and Aging Federal Systems." In *The Politics of Constitutional Change in Industrial Nations: Redesigning the State*, edited by Keith G. Banting and Ricard Simeon, 30–41. London: Palgrave Macmillan.

Lijphart, Arend. 1977. *Democracy in Plural Societies: A Comparative Exploration.* New Haven, CT: Yale University Press.

Lipset, Seymour Martin, and Stein Rokkan. 1967. "Cleavage Structures, Party Systems, and Voter Alignments: An Introduction." In *Party Systems and Voter Alignments: Cross-National Perspectives*, edited by Seymour Martin Lipset and Stein Rokkan, 3–64. New York: Free Press.

Loobuyck, Patrick, Jonathan Debeer, and Petra Meier. 2013. "Church-State Regimes and Their Impact on the Institutionalization of Islamic Organizations in Western Europe: A Comparative Analysis." *Journal of Muslim Minority Affairs* 33 (1): 61–76.

Luther, Kurth R. 2003. "The Self-Destruction of a Right-Wing Populist Party? The Austrian Parliamentary Election of 2002." *West European Politics* 26 (2): 136–152.

Luther, Kurth R. 2008. "Electoral Strategies and Performance of Austrian Right-Wing Populism, 1986–2006." In *The Changing Austrian Voter*, edited by Günter Bischof and Fritz Plasser, 101–122. New Brunswick, NJ: Transaction.

Lynch, Cecelia, and Tanya B. Schwarz. 2016. "Religion in International Relations." In *Oxford Research Encyclopedia of Politics*, edited by William R. Thompson. New York: Oxford University Press. https://oxfordre.com/politics/display/10.1093/acrefore/9780190228637.001 .0001/acrefore-9780190228637-e-122.

Mandaville, Peter. 2010. *Global Political Islam.* London: Routledge.

Mattes, Astrid. 2011. "Vorbild oder Fehlentwicklung—Wie Österreichs Medien über das Schweizer Minarettbauverbot berichten." In *Jahrbuch für Islamphobieforschung 2011*, edited by Farid Hafez, 25–37. Vienna: Studienverlag.

Maussen, Marcel. 2007. "The Governance of Islam in Western Europe: A State of the Art Report." IMISCOE Working Paper no. 16. University of Amsterdam, June 2007. https:// opendata.uni-halle.de/bitstream/1981185920/106612/181/568428552.pdf.

Mayer, Heinz. 1997. Rechtsgutachten zur Regierungsvorlage für ein Bundesgesetz über die Rechtspersönlichkeit von religiösen Bekenntnisgemeinschaften, 1997. Vienna, 21 November 1997. https://jehovas-zeugen.at/wp-content/uploads/sites/7/2022/11/19971121_Gutachten_Mayer.pdf.

McAdam, Doug. 1996. "Conceptual Origins, Problems, Future Directions." In *Comparative Perspectives on Social Movements: Political Opportunties, Mobilizing Structures, and Cultural Framings*, edited by Doug McAdam, John D. McCarthy, and Mayer N. Zald, 23–40. Cambridge: Cambridge University Press.

McGann, Anthony J., and Herbert Kitschelt. 2005. "The Radical Right in the Alps: Evolution of Support for the Swiss SVP and Austrian FPÖ." *Party Politics* 11 (2): 147–171.

Modood, Tariq, and Riva Kastoryano. 2006. "Secularism and the Accommodation of Muslims in Europe." In *Multiculturalism, Muslims and Citizenship: A European Approach*, edited by Tariq Modood, Anna Triandafyllidou, and Ricard Zapata-Barrero, 1–23. New York: Routledge.

Monsma, Stephen V., and Christopher Soper. 2009. *The Challenge of Pluralism: Church and State in Five Democracies*. Plymouth: Rowman & Littlefield.

Moshammer-Mischkof, Stefanie Elisabeth. 2011. "Postkoloniale Kritik der Repräsentation muslimischer Frauen in ausgewählten Tageszeitungen während der Wien Wahl 2010." Master's thesis, University of Vienna.

Mudde, Cas. 2004. "The Populist Zeitgeist." *Government and Opposition* 39 (4): 541–563.

Muno, Wolfgang. 2009. "Fallstudien und die vergleichende Methode." In *Methoden der vergleichenden Politik-und Sozialwissenschaft*, edited by Gert Pickel, Joachim Lauth, and Detlef Jahn, 113–132. Wiesbaden: Verlag für Sozialwissenschaften.

North, Douglass C. 1990. *Institutions, Institutional Change and Economic Performance*. Cambridge: Cambridge University Press.

North, Douglass C. 1993. "Institutions and Credible Commitment." *Journal of Institutional and Theoretical Economics* 149 (1): 11–23.

Nye, Joseph, Jr. 2004. *Soft Power: The Means to Success in World Politics*. New York: Public Affairs.

Obinger, Herbert. 2002. "Veto Players, Political Parties, and Welfare-State Retrenchment in Austria." *International Journal of Political Economy* 32 (2): 44–66.

Odmalm, Pontus. 2011. "Political Parties and 'the Immigration Issue': Issue Ownership in Swedish Parliamentary Elections 1991–2010." *West European Politics* 34 (5): 1070–1091.

Osman, Alexander. 2009. "Darstellung des Islam und der MuslimInnen in österreichischen Tageszeitungen." Master's thesis, University of Vienna.

Paster, Thomas. 2013. "Business and Welfare State Development: Why Did Employers Accept Social Reforms?" *World Politics* 65 (3): 416–451.

Pelinka, Anton. 2002. "Die FPÖ in der vergleichenden Parteienforschung: Zur typologischen Einordnung der Freiheitlichen Partei Österreichs." *Österreichische Zeitschrift für Politikwissenschaft* 31 (3): 281–290.

Pelinka, Anton, Hubert Sickinger, and Karin Stögner. 2008. *Kreisky—Haider: Bruchlinien österreichischer Identitäten*. Vienna: Braumüller Verlag.

Pelinka, Anton, and Ruth Wodak, eds. 2002. *"Dreck am Stecken": Politik der Ausgrenzung*. Vienna: Czernin Verlag.

Permoser, Julia Mourão, and Sieglinde Rosenberger. 2012. "Integration Policy in Austria." In *International Perspectives: Integration and Inclusion*, edited by James Frideres and John Biles, 39–58. Montreal: McGill-Queens University Press.

Pernegger, Maria. 2019. *Frauen—Politik—Medien. Jahresstudie 2018 Schwerpunkt Frauen der Wirtschaft*. Media Affairs, May 2019. https://www.contentadmin.de/contentanlagen/contentdatei9762.pdf.

Peters, B. Guy. 1999. *Institutional Theory in Political Science: The "New Institutionalism."* London: Continuum.

Peters, B. Guy, Jon Pierre, and Desmond S. King. 2005. "The Politics of Path Dependency: Political Conflict in Historical Institutionalism." *Journal of Politics* 67 (4): 1275–1300.

Petritsch, Wolfgang. 2010. *Bruno Kreisky: Die Biografie.* Vienna: Residenz Verlag.

Pierson, Paul. 2000. "Increasing Returns, Path Dependence, and the Study of Politics." *American Political Science Review* 94 (2): 251–267.

Plasser, Fritz, and Peter A. Ulram. 1995. "Akzeptanz und Unterstützung Sozialpartnerschaftlicher Interessenvertretung in Österreich." In *Kammern auf dem Prüfstand: Vergleichende Analysen institutioneller Funktionsbedingungen,* edited by Anton Pelinka and Christian Smekal, 75–109. Vienna: Signum Verlag.

Potz, Richard. 1996. "State and Church in Austria." In *State and Church in the European Union,* edited by Gerhard Robbers, 435–460. Baden-Baden: Nomos Verlag.

Potz, Richard. 2007. "Die öffentlich-rechtliche Stellung von Religionsgemeinschaften im säkularen Staat." In *Religion im öffentlichen Raum: Religiöse Freiheit im neuen Europa,* edited by Friedrich Gleißner, Hanspeter Ruedl, Heinrich Schneider, and Ludwig Schwarz, 169–171. Vienna: Böhlau.

Potz, Richard. 2010. "Das Islamgesetz 1912 und der religionsrechtliche Diskurs in Österreich zu Beginn des 20. Jahrhunderts." In *Grundlagen der österreichischen Rechtskultur: Festschrift für Werner Ogris zum 75. Geburtstag,* edited by Thomas Olechowski, Christian Neschwara, and Alina Lengauer, 385–408. Vienna: Böhlau.

Potz, Richard, and Brigitte Schinkele. 2014. *Stellungnahme zum Entwurf eines Bundesgesetzes, mit dem das Gesetz betreffend die Anerkennung der Anhänger des Islam als Religionsgesellschaft geändert wird* (69/ME XXV. GP). https://www.parlament.gv.at/PAKT/VHG/XXV/SNME /SNME_02154/imfname_372284.pdf.

Potz, Richard, and Brigitte Schinkele. 2016. *Religion and Law in Austria.* Alphen aan den Rijn, Netherlands: Wolters Kluwer.

Potz, Richard, Brigitte Schinkele, and Wolfgang Wieshaider, eds. 2001. *Schächten: Religionsfreiheit und Tierschutz.* Freistadt, Austria: Kovar.

Potz, Richard, and Wolfgang Wieshaider, eds. 2004. *Islam and the European Union.* Leuven: Peeters.

Prainsack, Barbara. 2006. "Politik und Religion." In *Politik in Österreich,* edited by Herbert Dachs, Peter Gelich, Herbert Gottweis, Helmut Kramer, Volkmar Lauber, Wolfgang C. Müller, and Emmerich Tálos, 538–549. Vienna: Mainz Verlag.

Pratt Ewing, Katherine. 2000. "Legislating Religious Freedom: Muslim Challenges to the Relationship between 'Church' and 'State' in Germany and France." *Daedalus* 129 (4): 39–55.

Pyrah, Robert. 2007. "Enacting Encyclicals? Cultural Politics and 'Clerical Fascism' in Austria, 1933–1938." *Totalitarian Movements and Political Religions* 8 (2): 369–382.

Reiterer, Albert F. 1996. *Kärntner Slowenen: Minderheit oder Elite? Neuere Tendenzen der ethnischen Arbeitsteilung.* Klagenfurt: Drava Verlag.

Ronneberger, Klaus, and Vassilis Tsianos. 2015. "Panische Räume: Das Ghetto und die 'Parallelgesellschaft.'" In *No Integration?!,* edited by Sabine Hess, Jana Binder, and Johannes Moser, 137–152. Bielefeld: Transcript Verlag.

Rosenberger, Siegliende. 2013. "Das Staatssekretariat für Integration: Von der 'Integration durch Leistung' zur 'Vorintegration.'" In *Gaismair-Jahrbuch 2014,* edited by Elisabeth Hussl, Elisabeth Gensluckner, Martin Haselwanter, Monika Jarosch, and Horst Schreiber, 59–66. Vienna: Studienverlag.

Rosenberger, Sieglinde, and Birgit Sauer, eds. 2013. *Politics, Religion and Gender: Framing and Regulating the Veil.* London: Routledge.

Rovny, Jan. 2012. "Who Emphasizes and Who Blurs? Party Strategies in Multidimensional Competition." *European Union Politics* 13 (2): 269–292.

Rovny, Jan. 2013. "Where Do Radical Right Parties Stand? Position Blurring in Multidimensional Competition." *European Political Science Review* 5 (1): 1–26.

Rustemović, Rifat. 2019. "Von der Malkontentenbewegung bis zur gesetzlichen Anerkennung: Die Rolle der Autonomiebewegung der bosnischen Muslime bei der Anerkennung des Islams in der Habsburgermonarchie." In *Die Islamische Glaubensgemeinschaft in Österreich. 1909–1979–2019: Beiträge zu einem neuen Blick auf ihre Geschichte und Entwicklung*, edited by Farid Hafez and Rijad Dautović, 19–44. Vienna: New Academic Press.

Ryan, Ben. 2022. "Christianism." In *The Routledge Handbook of Religion, Politics and Ideology*, edited by Jeffrey Haynes, 211–226. London: Routledge.

Saad, Karim. 2009. "Islamophobie in österreichischen Tageszeitungen." In *Islamophobie in Österreich*, edited by John Bunzl and Farid Hafez, 199–209. Vienna: Studienverlag.

Said, Edward. 1978. *Orientalism*. New York: Pantheon Books.

Said, Edward. 1981. *Covering Islam: How the Media and the Experts Determine How We See the Rest of the World*. New York: Pantheon Books.

Salchegger, Silvia, Iris Höller, Manuela Pareiss, and Romana Lindemann. 2017. "Kompetenzentwicklung im Kontext familiärer Faktoren." In *PIRLS 2016. Die Lesekompetenzen am Ende der Volksschule. Erste Ergebnisse*, edited by Christina Wallner-Paschon, Ursula Itzlinger-Bruneforth, and Claudia Schreine, 67–82. Graz: Leykam.

Scharpf, Fritz W. 1991. *Crisis and Choice in European Social Democracy*. Ithaca, NY: Cornell University Press.

Scharpf, Fritz W. 1993. *Games in Hierarchies and Networks: Analytical and Empirical Approaches to the Study of Governance Institutions*. Frankfurt am Main: Campus Verlag.

Scheu, Harald Christian. 2021. "The Austrian Islam Law between Religion and Security." *Bezpieczeństwo: Teoria i Praktyka / Security: Theory and Practice* 3:21–31.

Schiffer, Sabine. 2005. *Die Darstellung des Islams in der Presse: Sprache, Bilder, Suggestionen; eine Auswahl von Techniken und Beispielen*. Mannheim: Ergon-Verlag.

Schiffer, Sabine and Wagner Constantin. 2009. *Antisemitismus und Islamophobie: Ein Vergleich*. Wassertrüdingen: HWK-Verlag.

Schmiedel, Ulrich. 2021. "The Cracks in the Category of Christianism: A Call for Ambiguity in the Conceptualization of Christianity." In *Contemporary Christian-Cultural Values: Migration Encounters in the Nordic Region*, edited by Cecilia Nahnfeldt and Kaia S. Rønsdal, 164–182. New York: Routledge.

Schönberger, Thomas. 2010. Über die Notwendigkeit Vorbehalte und Ängste zu erforschen." In *Jahrbuch für Islamophobieforschung 2010*, edited by Farid Hafez, 86–99. Vienna: Studienverlag.

Sedlak, Maria. 2000. "You Really Do Make an Unrespectable Foreigner Policy . . . Discourse on Ethnic Issues in the Austrian Parliament." In *Racism at the Top: Parliamentary Discourses on Ethnic Issues in Six European States*, edited by Ruth Wodak and Teun A. Van Dijk, 107–168. Klagenfurt: Drava-Verlag.

Shachar, Ayelet. 2007. "The Worth of Citizenship in an Unequal World." *Theoretical Inquiries in Law* 8 (2): 367–388.

Shakir, Amena. 2019. "Islamischer Religionsunterricht in Österreich—ein Modell für Europa?" In *Die Islamische Glaubensgemeinschaft in Österreich. 1909–1979–2019: Beiträge zu einem neuen Blick auf ihre Geschichte und Entwicklung*, edited by Farid Hafez and Rijad Dautović, 189–215. Vienna: New Academic Press.

Silvestri, Sara. 2009. "Islam and Religion in the EU Political System." *West European Politics* 32 (6): 1212–1239.

Skenderovic, Damir. 2006. "Feindbild Muslime—Islamophobie in der radikalen Rechten." In *Der Islam in Europa: Zwischen Weltpolitik und Alltag*, edited by Urs Altermatt, Mariano Delgado, and Guido Vergauwen, 79–95. Stuttgart: Kohlhammer.

Skenderovic, Damir. 2008. "Einleitung: Konturen des Rechtspopulismus." In *Rechtspopulismus und Migrationspolitik in der Schweiz seit den 1960er Jahren*, edited by Damir Skenderovic and Gianni D'Amato, 15–29. Zurich: Chronos Verlag.

Skowron-Nalborczyk, Agata. 2015. "A Century of the Official Legal Status of Islam in Austria: Between the Law on Islam of 1912 and the Law on Islam of 2015." In *Muslim Minority-State Relations: Violence, Integration, and Policy*, edited by Robert Mason, 61–82. Basingstoke, UK: Palgrave Macmillan.

Sonnleitner, Barbara. 2009. "Der Karikaturenstreit in den österreichischen Printmedien am Beispiel des Nachrichtenmagazins *Profil*." In *Islamophobie in Österreich*, edited by John Bunzl and Farid Hafez, 190–198. Vienna: Studienverlag.

Sorensen, Andre. 2015. "Taking Path Dependence Seriously: A Historical Institutionalist Research Agenda in Planning History." *Planning Perspectives* 30 (1): 17–38.

Spielhaus, Riem, and Martin Herzog. 2015. *Die rechtliche Anerkennung des Islams in Deutschland: Ein Gutachten für die Friedrich-Ebert-Stiftung*. Berlin: Friedrich-Ebert-Stiftung.

Spivak, Gayatri Chakravorty. 2010. "'Can the Subaltern Speak?' Revised Edition, from the 'History' Chapter of Critique of Postcolonial Reason." In *Can the Subaltern Speak? Reflections on the History of an Idea*, edited by Rosalind C. Morris, 171–219. New York: Columbia University Press.

Statistik Austria. 2022. "Bevölkerung nach Staatsangehörigkeit/Geburtsland." Statistik Austria. https://www.statistik.at/statistiken/bevoelkerung-und-soziales/bevoelkerung/bevoelkerungsstand/bevoelkerung-nach-staatsangehoerigkeit/-geburt.

Steininger, Rolf. 2008. *Austria, Germany, and the Cold War: From the Anschluss to the State Treaty, 1938–1955*. New York: Berghahn Books.

Sticker, Maja. 2008. *Sondermodell Österreich? Die Islamische Glaubensgemeinschaft in Österreich*. Klagenfurt: Drava Verlag.

Strasser, Sabine. 2008. "Europe's Other: Nationalism, Transnationals and Contested Images of Turkey in Austria." *European Societies* 10 (2): 177–195.

Strobl, Anna. 2005. "Der österreichische Islam: Entwicklung, Tendenz und Möglichkeiten." *SWS-Rundschau* 45 (4): 520–543.

Sturm, Roland. 2004. "Politische Kultur." In *Politische Theorie und Regierungslehre. Eine Einführung in die politikwissenschaftliche Institutionenforschung*, edited by Ludger Helms and Uwe Jun, 302–323. Frankfurt am Main: Campus Verlag.

Tálos, Emmerich. 1993. "Entwicklung, Kontinuität und Wandel der Sozialpartnerschaft." In *Sozialpartnerschaft: Kontinuität und Wandel eines Modells*, edited by Emmerich Tálos, 11–34. Vienna: Verlag für Gesellschaftskritik.

Tálos, Emmerich, and Bernhard Kittel. 2001. *Gesetzgebung in Österreich. Netzwerke, Akteure und Interaktionen in politischen Entscheidungsprozessen*. Vienna: WUV Universitätsverlag.

Taylor, Charles. 2007. *A Secular Age*. Cambridge, MA: Belknap Press of Harvard University Press.

Teczan, Levent. 2012. *Das muslimische Subjekt. Verfangen im Dialog der Deutschen Islam Konferenz*. Konstanz: Konstanz University Press.

Thelen, Kathleen. 1999. "Historical Institutionalism in Comparative Politics." *Annual Review of Political Science* 2:369–404.

Thurner, Ingrid. 2012. "Die dunkle Seite des Postens: Diskursmuster und Diskursstrategien bei Islamthemen." In *Islamophobia Studies Yearbook 2012*, edited by Fariz Hafez, 154–176. Vienna: Studienverlag.

Tibi, Bassam. 2001. "Leitkultur als Wertekonsens. Bilanz einer missglückten deutschen Debatte." *Aus Politik und Zeitgeschichte* no. 1/2, 23–26.

Traunmüller, Richard. 2014. "National Path Dependence or International Convergence? A Quantitative Comparative Analysis of Changes in Religious Policy in 31 European Democracies, 1990–2011." *Zeitschrift für Politik* 61 (2) (June): 160–181.

Triadafilopoulos, Triadafilos, and Joachim Rahmann. 2016. "Making Room for Islam in Germany's Public Schools: The Role of the Länder." In *Staat und Islam*, edited by Uwe Hunger and Nils Johann Schröder, 131–157. Wiesbaden: Verlag für Sozialwissenschaften.

Tschiggerl, Martin. 2021. "Significant Otherness Nation-Building and Identity in Postwar Austria." *Nations and Nationalism* 27 (3): 782–796.

Ulram, Peter A. 2009. "Integration in Österreich. Einstellungen, Orientierungen und Erfahrungen von MigrantInnen und Angehörigen der Mehrheitsbevölkerung." Wein: GfK Austria GmbH. https://publikationen.uni-tuebingen.de/xmlui/bitstream/handle/10900/72353/Integrationsstudie.pdf?sequence=1&isAllowed=y.

Unger, Brigitte, and Heitzmann, Karin. 2003. "The Adjustment Path of the Austrian Welfare State: Back to Bismarck?" *Journal of European Social Policy*, no. 13, 371–387.

Van Dijk, Teun A. 2000. "On the Analysis of Parliamentary Debates on Immigration." In *The Semiotics of Racism. Approaches in Critical Discourse Analysis*, edited by Ruth Wodak and Martin Reisigl, 85–103. Vienna: Passagen Verlag.

Van Dijk, Teun A. 2002. "Knowledge in Parliamentary Debates," *Journal of Language and Politics* 2 (1): 93–129.

Van Dijk, Teun A. 2004. "Text and Context of Parliamentary Debates." In *Cross-cultural Perspectives on Parliamentary Discourse,* edited by Paul Bayley, 339–372. Amsterdam: John Benjamins, 339–372.

Van Dijk, Teun A. 2011. "Discourse, Knowledge, Power and Politics: Towards Critical Epistemic Discourse Analysis," In *Critical Discourse Studies in Context and Cognition*, edited by Christopher Hart, 27–63. Amsterdam: John Benjamins.

Van Dijk, Teun A., and Ruth Wodak. 2000. *Racism at the Top: Parliamentary Discourses on Ethnic Issues in Six European States*. Klagenfurt: Drava.

Van Schendelen, M.P.C.M. 1984. "The Views of Arend Lijphart and Collected Criticisms." *Acta Politica* 19, no. 1 (January): 19–55.

Vidino, Lorenzo. 2017. "The Muslim Brotherhood in Austria." Program on Extremism, George Washington University, and University of Vienna. August 2017. https://extremism.gwu.edu/sites/g/files/zaxdzs5746/files/MB%20in%20Austria-%20Print.pdf.

Vocelka, Karl. 1993. "Das Osmanische Reich und die Habsburgermonarchie 1848–1918." In *Die Habsburgermonarchie im System der Internationalen Beziehungen*, vol. 6, pt. 2, edited by Adam Wandruszka, 247–278 Vienna: VÖAW.

Volk, Ewald, and Theo Wieser. 1986. "Die Entwicklung der österreichischen Industriepolitik und ihrer Bestimmungsgründe seit 1945." Unpublished expert opinion for the Federal Ministry of Science and Research, Vienna.

Völker, Michael. 2015. "Islamgesetz: Grüne sehen, Generalverdacht gegen Muslime." *Der Standard*, 13 February 2015.

Vrankić, Petar. 1998. *Religion und Politik in Bosnien und der Herzegowina (1878–1918)*. Paderborn: Ferdinand Schöningh.

Wald, Kenneth D., and Clyde Wilcox. 2006. "Getting Religion: Has Political Science Rediscovered the Faith Factor?" *American Political Science Review* 100 (4): 523–529.

Walter, Franz. 1999. "Katholisches Milieu und politischer Katholizismus in säkularisierten Gesellschaften: Deutschland, Österreich und die Niederlande im Vergleich." In *Solidarge-*

*meinschaft und fragmentierte Gesellschaft: Parteien, Milieus und Verbände im Vergleich*, edited by Tobias Dürr and Franz Walter, 43–71. Wiesbaden: Verlag für Sozialwissenschaften.

Wandruszka, Adam. 1985. "Katholisches Kaisertum und multikonfessionelles Reich. In: *Die Habsburgermonarchie 1848–1918. Band IV; Die Konfessionen*, edited by Adam Wandruszka and Peter Urbanitsch, xi–xvi. Vienna: Verlag der Österreichischen Akademie der Wissenschaften.

Weaver, Kent, and Bert Rockman, eds. 1993. *Do Institutions Matter? Government Capabilities in the United States and Abroad*. Washington, DC: Brookings Institution Press.

Weiss, Hilde. 2000. "Alte und neue Minderheiten: Zum Einstellungswandel in Österreich (1984–1998)." *SWS-Rundschau* 40 (1): 25–42.

Wieshaider, Wolfgang. 2013. "Zur Rechtspersönlichkeit gesetzlich anerkannter Religionsgesellschaften," *Österreichisches Archiv für Recht und Religion* 60 (2): 336–346.

Wlezien, Christopher. 2005. "On the Salience of Political Issues: The Problem with 'Most Important Problem.'" *Electoral Studies* 24 (4): 555–579.

Woditschka, Elisabeth. 2015. "Der Betriebsrat als Showstar." *Forbes Austria*, July 2015, 44–45.

Wolinetz, Steven B. 2002. "Beyond the Catch-All Party: Approaches to the Study of Parties and Party Organization in Contemporary Democracies." In *Political Parties: Old Concepts and New Challenges*, edited by Richard Gunther, José Ramón Montero, and Juan Linz, 136–165. Oxford: Oxford University Press.

Yazdiha, Haj. 2014. "Law as Movement Strategy: How the Islamophobia Movement Institutionalizes Fear through Legislation." *Social Movement Studies* 13 (2): 267–274.

## PRESS RELEASES AND GOVERNMENT DOCUMENTS

Amnesty International Austria. 2021. Stellungnahme zum Gesetzespaket betreffend das Bundesgesetz (Terror-Bekämpfungs-Gesetz—TeBG). 25 January 2021. https://www.amnesty.at/media/8087/amnesty_oesterreich_stellungnahme_bundesgesetze_anti-terrorismus-massnahmen_jan-2021.pdf.

Association of Austrian Female Lawyers. 2017. Stellungnahme zum Entwurf eines Anti-Gesichtsverhüllungsgesetzes. 103/SN-290/ME. XXV. GP, 8 March 2017. https://www.parlament.gv.at/PAKT/VHG/XXV/SNME/SNME_09566/imfname_621715.pdf.

Austrian Bar Association. 2021. Stellungnahme zu dem Ministerialentwurf betreffend Bundesgesetz, mit dem das Strafgesetzbuch, die Strafprozeßordnung 1975, das Strafvollzugsgesetz und das Gerichtsorganisationsgesetz zur Bekämpfung von Terror geändert werden (Terror-Bekämpfungs-Gesetz—TeBG). 23/SN-83/ME. XXVII. GP, 29 January 2021. https://www.parlament.gv.at/PAKT/VHG/XXVII/SNME/SNME_36504/index.shtml.

Austrian Bishops' Conference. 2021. Entwurf eines Bundesgesetzes, mit dem das Strafgesetzbuch, die Strafprozeßordnung 1975, das Strafvollzugsgesetz und das Gerichtsorganisationsgesetz zur Bekämpfung von Terror geändert werden (Terror- Bekämpfungs-Gesetz—TeBG). 54/SN-83/ME. XXVII. GP, 2 February 2021. https://www.bischofskonferenz.at/dl/lMtmJmoJKNKmJqx4KJKJKJKLLKoO/2021_02_02_BMJ_Terror-Bek_mpfungs-Gesetz_Stellungnahme_PDF_pdf.

BGBl (Bundesgesetzblatt für Die Republik Österreich). 1955. Verordnung des Bundesministeriums für Unterricht vom 27. September 1955, betreffend die Anerkennung der Anhänger des Religionsbekenntnisses der "Kirche Jesu Christi der Heiligen der Letzten Tage" (Mormonen) als Religionsgesellschaft. Nr. 339/1955.

BGBl. 1973. Verordnung: Anerkennung der Anhänger der Armenisch-apostolischen Kirche in Österreich als Religionsgesellschaft. 1973 4/6.

BGBl. 1998. Bundesgesetz über die Rechtspersönlichkeit von religiösen Bekenntnisgemein- schaften. I Nr. 19/1998. https://www.ris.bka.gv.at/GeltendeFassung.wxe?Abfrage=Bundes normen&Gesetzesnummer=10010098.

BGBl. 2003. Bundesgesetz über äußere Rechtsverhältnisse der orientalisch-orthodoxen Kirchen in Österreich (Orientalisch-orthodoxes Kirchengesetz; OrientKG). BGBl. I Nr. 20/2003. https://www.ris.bka.gv.at/GeltendeFassung.wxe?Abfrage=Bundesnormen&Gesetzes nummer=10009290.

BGBl. 2014. Bundesgesetz: Symbole-Gesetz (NR: GP XXV RV 346 AB 412 S. 53. BR: AB 9291 S. 837.). 29 December 2014, Teil I 103. 103.https://www.ris.bka.gv.at/Dokumente /BgblAuth/BGBLA_2014_I_103/BGBLA_2014_I_103.pdfsig.

BGBl. 2019. Bundesgesetz: Änderung des Symbole-Gesetzes. 9 January 2019, Teil I 2. https:// www.ris.bka.gv.at/Dokumente/BgblAuth/BGBLA_2019_I_2/BGBLA_2019_I_2.pdfsig.

BGBl. 2021a. Bundesgesetz: Änderung des Bundesgesetzes über die Rechtspersönlichkeit von religiösen Bekenntnisgemeinschaften und des Islamgesetzes 2015. 26 July 2021, Teil I 146. https://www.ris.bka.gv.at/Dokumente/BgblAuth/BGBLA_2021_I_146/BGBLA_2021 _I_146.pdfsig.

BGBl. 2021b. Bundesgesetz: Änderung des Staatsbürgerschaftsgesetzes 1985 und des Symbole- Gesetzes. 27 July 2021, Teil I 162. https://www.ris.bka.gv.at/Dokumente/BgblAuth/BGBLA _2021_I_162/BGBLA_2021_I_162.pdfsig.

BKA (Bundeskanzleramt). 2020a. "Bundeskanzleramt: Bundeskanzler Kurz: Terrorismus und politischen Islam mit allen Mitteln bekämpfen." 11 November 2020. https://www .bundeskanzleramt.gv.at/bundeskanzleramt/nachrichten-der-bundesregierung/2020 /bundeskanzler-kurz-terrorismus-und-politischen-islam-mit-allen-mitteln-bekaempfen .html.

BKA. 2020b. "Pressestatements zur Präsentation der Dokumentationsstelle Politischer Islam." 15 July 2020. https://www.youtube.com/watch?v=INb1HzZrFVQ.

BKA. 2021. "Integrationsministerin Raab: Europäischer Schulterschluss gegen den poli- tischen Islam." 28 October 2021. https://www.bundeskanzleramt.gv.at/bundeskanzleramt /nachrichten-der-bundesregierung/2021/10/integrationsministerin-raab-europaeischer -schulterschluss-gegen-den-politischen-islam.html.

BKA. 2023. "Vienna Forum on Countering Segregation and Extremism in the Context of Inte- gration." September 2023. https://www.bundeskanzleramt.gv.at/agenda/integration/vienna -forum-on-countering-segregation-and-extremism-in-the-context-of-integration.html.

BMEIA (Bundesministerium für Europäische und Internationale Angelegenheiten). 2003. "Ferrero-Waldner at the Conference of Chairmen of Islamic Centres and Imams in Europe." Ministry of European and International Affairs. Graz, 13 June 2006. https://www.bmeia .gv.at/en/the-ministry/press/speeches/2003/ferrero-waldner-at-the-conference-of -chairmen-of-islamic-centres-and-imams-in-europe/.

BMEIA. 2006a. "Foreign Minister Plassnik and Professor Schakfeh: 'Trust in the Power of Dialogue.'" Ministry of European and International Affairs. Vienna, 7 February 2006. https://www.bmeia.gv.at/en/the-ministry/press/news/2006/foreign-minister-plassnik -and-professor-schakfeh-trust-in-the-power-of-dialogue/.

BMEIA. 2006b. 180 Degrees East and West—Muslims in Austria. Exhibition. Austrian Federal Ministry for Foreign Affairs. https://www.bmeia.gv.at/fileadmin/user_upload/Zentrale /Publikationen/muslims_in_austria.pdf.

BMEIA. 2009. "Islam in Europe: The Austrian Cultural Forum in New York Is Part of 'Mus- lim Voices.'" Ministry of European and International Affairs. New York, 4 June 2009. https://www.bmeia.gv.at/en/the-ministry/press/news/2009/islam-in-europe-the -austrian-cultural-forum-in-new-york-is-part-of-muslim-voices/.

BMEIA. 2011. "Spindelegger: 'Inter-Religious Dialogue Is Essential for Combating Discrimination and Xenophobia.'" Ministry of European and International Affairs. Vienna, 21 September 2011. https://www.bmeia.gv.at/en/the-ministry/press/news/2011/spindelegger -inter-religious-dialogue-is-essential-for-combating-discrimination-and-xenophobia/.

BMEIA. 2018. "Karin Kneissl: 'Das Kopftuch ist ein Symbol für die Unterdrückung der Frauen.'" OTS. Vienna, 12 July 2018. https://www.ots.at/presseaussendung/OTS_20180712 _OTS0126/karin-kneissl-das-kopftuch-ist-ein-symbol-fuer-die-unterdrueckung-der -frauen.

BMI (Bundesministerium für Inneres). 1998. *Staatsschutzbericht 1997.* Ministry of Interior. Vienna, 1998. https://www.dsn.gv.at/501/files/VSB/Verfassungsschutzbericht_1997.pdf.

BMI. 2000. *Staatsschutzbericht 1999.* Ministry of Interior. Vienna, June 2000. https://www .dsn.gv.at/501/files/VSB/Verfassungsschutzbericht_1999.pdf.

BMI. 2012a. "'Dialogforum Islam' soll 'Versachlichung' Bringen." *Kleine Zeitung,* 23 January 2012. https://www.kleinezeitung.at/politik/3916712.

BMI. 2012b. "'Dialogforum Islam': Präsentation der Ergebnisse aus dem ersten Jahr." Ministry of Interior. Vienna, 3 December 2012. https://www.ots.at/presseaussendung/OTS_20121203 _OTS0118/dialogforum-islam-praesentation-der-ergebnisse-aus-dem-ersten-jahr Dialogfo rum Islam.

BMI. 2012c. "Integration: 'Dialogforum Islam' im Staatssekretariat gestartet." Ministry of Interior, 23 January 2012. https://www.ots.at/presseaussendung/OTS_20120123_OTS0080 /integration-dialogforum-islam-im-staatssekretariat-gestartet.

BMI. 2017. "Stimmenstärkste Partei pro Bundesland." Ministry of Interior. https://bundes wahlen.gv.at/2017/.

BMI. 2018. "Schlag gegen Muslimbruderschaft und Graue Wölfe." Ministry of Interior, Artikel Nr: 16437. 19 November 2018. https://www.bmi.gv.at/news.aspx?id=57567834466641794 F59303D.

BMUK. 1978. Geschäftszahl 9076/1-9c/78, Bundesministerium für Unterricht und Kunst.

BR. 2013. *Arbeitsprogramm der österreichischen Bundesregierung 2013–2018* [Working Program of the Federal Government 2013–2018]. Vienna: Federal Chancellery.

BR. 2015. "Stenographisches Protokoll, 839. Sitzung des Bundesrates der Republik Österreich." Austrian Parliament. 12 March 2015.

Bundespressedienst. 2018. "AVISO: Pressekonferenz Kurz, Strache, Kickl und Blümel." 7 June 2018. https://www.ots.at/presseaussendung/OTS_20180607_OTS0227/aviso-press ekonferenz-kurz-strache-kickl-und-bluemel.

BVT. 2004. *Verfassungsschutzbericht 2004.* Office for the Protection of the Constitution and Counterterrorism, Ministry of the Interior. Vienna. https://www.dsn.gv.at/501/files/VSB /Verfassungsschutzbericht_2004_Berichtszeitraum_2003.pdf.

BVT. 2005. *Verfassungsschutzbericht 2005.* Office for the Protection of the Constitution and Counterterrorism, Ministry of the Interior. Vienna. https://www.dsn.gv.at/501/files/VSB /Verfassungsschutzbericht_2005_Berichtszeitraum_2004.pdf.

BVT. 2006. *Verfassungsschutzbericht 2006.* Office for the Protection of the Constitution and Counterterrorism, Ministry of the Interior. Vienna. https://www.dsn.gv.at/501/files/VSB /Verfassungsschutzbericht_2006_Berichtszeitraum_2005_und_erstes_Halbjahr_2006.pdf.

BVT. 2007. *Verfassungsschutzbericht 2007.* Office for the Protection of the Constitution and Counterterrorism, Ministry of the Interior. Vienna. https://www.bvt.bmi.gv.at/401/files /Verfassungsschutzbericht_2006_Berichtszeitraum_2005_und_erstes_Halbjahr_2006.pdf.

BVT. 2013. *Verfassungsschutzbericht 2013.* Office for the Protection of the Constitution and Counterterrorism, Ministry of the Interior. Vienna. https://www.dsn.gv.at/501/files/VSB /Verfassungsschutzbericht_2013_Berichtszeitraum_2012.pdf.

BVT. 2014. *Verfassungsschutzbericht 2014*. Office for the Protection of the Constitution and Counterterrorism, Ministry of the Interior. Vienna. https://www.bvt.bmi.gv.at/401/files /Verfassungsschutzbericht_2013_Berichtszeitraum_2012.pdf.

BVT. 2016. *Verfassungsschutzbericht 2016*. Office for the Protection of the Constitution and Counterterrorism, Ministry of the Interior. Vienna. https://www.dsn.gv.at/501/files/VSB /Verfassungsschutzbericht_2016.pdf.

BVT. 2017. *Verfassungsschutzbericht 2017*. Office for the Protection of the Constitution and Counterterrorism, Ministry of the Interior. Vienna. https://www.dsn.gv.at/501/files/VSB /Verfassungsschutzbericht_2017.pdf.

BVT. 2019. *Verfassungsschutzbericht 2018*. Office for the Protection of the Constitution and Counterterrorism, Ministry of the Interior. Vienna. https://www.bvt.gv.at/bmi_documents /2344.pdf.

BZÖ. 2006. *Deinetwegen. Österreich. Das Wahlprogramm des BZÖ*. Vienna. http://www.erhoert .at/wahlprogramm_BZOE.pdf.

BZÖ. 2008. Deinetwegen. Österreich. Das Wahlprogramm des BZÖ. https://www.vol.at/2008 /09/BZOE_Wahlprogramm_2008.pdf.

Coalition Program. 2013. *Erfolgreich. Österreich. Arbeitsprogramm der österreichischen Bundesregierung für die Jahre 2013 bis 2018*. Vienna: Bundeskanzleramt, Bundespressedienst. https:// www.politik-lernen.at/dl/OkopJKJKonmKNJqx4KJK/131216_Regierungsprogramm _Barrierefrei_pdf.

Council of Europe. 2021. "Publication of Austria's 'Islam Map' Is Hostile to Muslims and Potentially Counterproductive." Strasbourg, 31 May 2021. https://www.coe.int/en/web /antisemitic-anti-muslim-hatred-hate-crimes/-/publication-of-austria-s-islam-map-is -hostile-to-muslims-and-potentially-counterproductive.

Dialogforum Islam. 2012. *Bericht*. Bundesministerium für Inneres, December 2012. https:// www.bmeia.gv.at/fileadmin/user_upload/Zentrale/Integration/Publikationen/DFI _Bericht_Web.pdf.

Die Grünen. 2008. *Neu beginnen! Das grüne programm für einen neubeginn*. http://www .erhoert.at/Politinfos/Parteiprogramme/GRUENES_PR_WAHL08.pdf.

Die Grünen. 2017. *Das ist Grün. Wahlprogramm der Grünen. Nationalratswahl 2017*.

Diyanet. 1972. Din İs.Y.Krl.Bşk.D/1-3/72. 18 December 1972.

*Europe News*. 2008. "Wiener Akademikerbund stellt 15 Forderungen an österreichische Muslime." 22 November 2008. http://europenews.dk/de/node/16427.

FEYKOM. 2018. Stellungnahme zu einem Bundesgesetz, mit dem das Symbole-Gesetz geändert wird. 11/SN-81/ME. XXVI. GP, 31 October 2018. http://www.parlament.gv.at/PAKT /VHG/XXVI/SNME/SNME_02951/imfname_717319.pdf.

FPÖ. 2005. *The Freedom Party Program for 1997 (with amendments from 2005)*. https://www.fbi -politikschule.at/fileadmin/user_upload/www.fpoe-bildungsinstitut.at/dokumente /Programm_der_FPOE_2005.pdf.

FPÖ. 2008a. "Mölzer: Freiheitliche Positionen zum Islam." 22 January 2008. https://www.ots.at /presseaussendung/OTS_20080122_OTS0109/moelzer-freiheitliche-positionen-zum-islam.

FPÖ. 2008b. *Wahlprogramm der Freiheitlichen Partei Österreichs FPÖ Nationalratswahl 2006*. https://www.erhoert.at/Wahlprogramm_FP__2006.pdf.

FPÖ. 2008c. "Wir und der Islam. Freiheitliche Positionen zur Religionsfreiheit, zur islamischen Welt und zur Problematik des Zuwanderungs-Islam in Europa." 22 January 2008. https://rfjfreistadt.files.wordpress.com/2009/02/wir_und_der_islam_-_freiheitliche _positionen1.pdf.

FPÖ. 2015. "FPÖ-Steger: Kopftuchverbot an Schulen, Universitäten und im öffentlichen Dienst ist in Österreich längst überfällig." 5 February 2015. https://www.ots.at/presseaussen

dung/OTS_20150205_OTS0176/fpoe-steger-kopftuchverbot-an-schulen-universitaeten
-und-im-oeffentlichen-dienst-ist-in-oesterreich-laengst-ueberfaellig.

FPÖ. 2016. "FPÖ-Ullmann: Richtungsentscheidung Verschleierungsverbot—eine Chance für die Zukunft!" 29 September 2016. https://www.ots.at/presseaussendung/OTS_20160929 _OTS0027/fpoe-ullmann-richtungsentscheidung-verschleierungsverbot-eine-chance-fuer -die-zukunft.

FPÖ. 2017a. "Haimbucher zu EuGH-Kopftuchverbot: Auch im öffentlichen Dienst verbieten." 13 March 2017. https://www.ots.at/presseaussendung/OTS_20170314_OTS0102 /haimbuchner-zu-eugh-kopftuchverbot-auch-im-oeffentlichen-dienst-verbieten.

FPÖ. 2017b. Österreicher verdienen Fairness. Freiheitliches Wahlprogramm zur Nationalratswahl 2017. https://www.fpoe.at/fileadmin/user_upload/Wahlprogramm_8_9_low.pdf.

FPÖ. 2017c. "Raml: Freiheitliche Jugend unterstützt Forderung nach Kopftuchverbot in schuen." 31 January 2017. https://www.ots.at/presseaussendung/OTS_20170131_OTS0083 /raml-freiheitliche-jugend-unterstuetzt-forderung-nach-kopftuchverbot-in-schulen.

FPÖ. 2017d. "Strache: Kopftuchverbot in allen Bildungseinrichtungen mit Öffentlichkeitsrecht!" 6 March 2017. https://www.ots.at/presseaussendung/OTS_20170306_OTS0099 /strache-kopftuchverbot-in-allen-bildungseinrichtungen-mit-oeffentlichkeitsrecht.

FPÖ. 2017e. "Strache zu Integrationspaket: Asyl ist Schutz auf Zeit!" 7 February 2017. https:// www.ots.at/presseaussendung/OTS_20170207_OTS0079/strache-zu-integrationspaket -asyl-ist-schutz-auf-zeit.

FPÖ. 2017f. "Terrorismus: FPÖ-Kickl fordert von Kurz Islam- und Integrationsgesetz mit Substanz." 23 May 2017. https://www.ots.at/presseaussendung/OTS_20170523_OTS0170 /terrorismus-fpoe-kickl-fordert-von-kurz-islam-und-integrationsgesetz-mit-substanz.

FPÖ. 2018a. "FPÖ-Gudenus: Mit Kopftuchverbot in Kindergärten wird zentrales freiheitliches Wahlversprechen umgesetzt." 24 August 2018. https://www.ots.at/presseaussendung /OTS_20180824_OTS0069/fpoe-gudenus-mit-kopftuchverbot-in-kindergaerten-wird -zentralesfreiheitliches-wahlversprechen-umgesetzt.

FPÖ. 2018b. "FP-Schmidt: Kopftuchverbot in Kindergärten und Schule gerade in Wien dringend notwendig." 3 April 2018. https://www.ots.at/presseaussendung/OTS_20180403 _OTS0119/fp-schmidt-kopftuchverbot-in-kindergaerten-und-schule-gerade-in-wien -dringend-notwendig.

FPÖ. 2018c. "FP-Krauss: Endlich grünes Licht für Kopftuchverbot in Kindergärten," OTS, 15 July 2018. https://www.ots.at/presseaussendung/OTS_20180715_OTS0021/fp-krauss -endlich-gruenes-licht-fuer-kopftuchverbot-in-kindergaerten.

FPÖ. 2019. "FPÖ-Schimanek: Verbot des Kopftuches an Volksschulen ist eine richtige und wichtige Maßnahme zum Schutz unserer Kinder." 16 May 2019. https://www.ots.at/presse aussendung/OTS_20190516_OTS0085/fpoe-schimanek-verbot-des-kopftuches-an -volksschulen-ist-eine-richtige-und-wichtige-massnahme-zum-schutz-unserer-kinder.

H.-C. Strache. 2013. "Politik der 'Nächstenliebe' heißt." Wayback Machine. https://web .archive.org/web/20130818012658/hcstrache.at/themen/.

Hesse, Gerhard. 2010. Entwurf eines Bundesgesetzes, mit dem das Israelitengesetz 1890 geändert wird; Begutachtung; Stellungnahme. https://www.parlament.gv.at/PAKT/VHG /XXIV/SNME/SNME_04516/fname_202095.pdf.

IGGÖ. 2012. Der Islam. Monthly magazine of the Islamic Religious Society in Austria.

IGGÖ. 2014. "Oberster Rat lehnt Entwurf zur Novellierung des Islamgesetzes in der jetzigen Form ab." 20 October 2014. http://www.derislam.at/?f=news&shownews=1917&kid=70.

IGGÖ. 2015. Stellungnahme des Schurarates der IGGÖ zum Bundesgesetz über die äußeren Rechtsverhältnisse Islamischer Religionsgesellschaften—Islamgesetz [Answer to draft of Islam Act] 2015. 16 February 2015. http://derislam.at/?f=news&shownews=1960&kid=70.

IGGÖ. 2016. "Verfassung der IGGÖ—genehmigt am 26.02.2016." 26 February 2016. http://
www.derislam.at/deradmin/news/Verfassung%20der%20IGG%C3%96%20-%20Gene-
hmigt%20am%2026.6.2016.pdf.

IGGÖ. 2017. Stellungnahme zum Anti-Gesichtsverhüllungsgesetz. 48/SN-290/ME. XXV.
GP, 5 March 2017. http://www.parlament.gv.at/PAKT/VHG/XXV/SNME/SNME_09487
/imfname_621450.pdf.

IGGÖ. 2018. Stellungnahme zu dem Ministerialentwurf betreffend Bundesgesetz, mit dem
das Symbole-Gesetz geändert wird. 15/SN-81/ME. XXVI. GP. https://www.parlament.gv
.at/PAKT/VHG/XXVI/SNME/SNME_03004/imfname_717457.pdf.

IGGÖ. 2020. "IGGIÖ zum türkis-grünen Regierungsübereinkommen." OTS, 3 January 2020.
https://www.ots.at/presseaussendung/OTS_20200103_OTS0113/iggoe-zum-tuerkis
-gruenen-regierungsuebereinkommen.

Institut für Rechts- und Kriminalsoziologie. 2021. Stellungnahme zu dem Ministerialentwurf
betreffend Bundesgesetz, mit dem das Strafgesetzbuch, die Strafprozeßordnung 1975, das
Strafvollzugsgesetz und das Gerichtsorganisationsgesetz zur Bekämpfung von Terror geändert
werden (Terror-Bekämpfungs-Gesetz—TeBG). 36/SN-83/ME. XXVII. GP, 1 February 2021.
https://www.parlament.gv.at/PAKT/VHG/XXVII/SNME/SNME_36533/index.shtml.

Institut für Strafrecht und Kriminologie. 2021. Stellungnahme zum Entwurf eines Bundesgesetzes, mit dem das Strafgesetzbuch, die Strafprozessordnung 1975, das Strafvollzugsgesetz und das Gerichtsorganisationsgesetz zur Bekämpfung von Terror geändert werden
(Terror-Bekämpfungs-Gesetz—TeBG). 83/ME. XXVII. GP. https://www.parlament.gv
.at/PAKT/VHG/XXVII/SNME/SNME_36543/index.shtml.

JVP. 2010. "JVP-Kurz: Nicht Konflikte schüren, sondern Integration ermöglichen," OTS.
4 September 2010. https://www.ots.at/presseaussendung/OTS_20100904_OTS0016
/jvp-kurz-nicht-konflikte-schueren-sondern-integration-ermoeglichen.

Khol, Andreas. 2006. "Nationalratspräsident Khol bei Europäischer Imamekonferenz Friedliches
Zusammenleben in Österreich als Vorbild für Europa." Parlamentskorrespondenz Nr. 309.
7 April 2006. http://www.parlament.gv.at/PAKT/PR/JAHR_2006/PK0309/index.shtml.

KIJA. 2018. Stellungnahme der Kinder- und Jugendanwaltschaften Österreichs zum Entwurf
eines Bundesgesetzes mit dem das Symbole-Gesetz geändert wird. 14/SN-81/ME. XXVI.
GP, 31 October 2018. https://www.parlament.gv.at/PAKT/VHG/XXVI/SNME/SNME
_02975/imfname_717343.pdf.

Klagsverband. 2018. Entwurf eines Bundesgesetzes, mit dem Symbolegesetz geändert wird.
7/SN-81/ME. XXVI. GP, 29 October 2018. https://www.parlament.gv.at/PAKT/VHG
/XXVI/SNME/SNME_02852/imfname_716837.pdf.

Mohr, Martin. 2016. "Anzahl der Muslime in Österreich von 1971 bis 2016." Statista, 9 August
2019. https://de.statista.com/statistik/daten/studie/312152/umfrage/anzahl-der-muslime
-in-oesterreich/#:~:text=Im%20Jahr%202016%20lebten%20in,1971%20auf%208%20
Prozent%202016.

Mohr, Martin. 2022a. "Anzahl der katholischen Gottesdienstbesucher in Österreich von 2010
bis 2020." Statista, 20 April 2022. https://de.statista.com/statistik/daten/studie/304784
/umfrage/katholische-gottesdienstbesucher-in-oesterreich/#:~:text=Im%20Jahr%20
2020%20nahmen%20in,fiel%20in%20diesem%20Jahr%20aus.

Mohr, Martin. 2022b. "Anzahl der Gläubigen von Religionen in Wien." Statista, 9 December 2022. https://de.statista.com/statistik/daten/studie/1087721/umfrage/religionszuge
hoerigkeit-in-wien/.

Mohr, Martin. 2023. "Anteil der Ausländer an der Bevölkerung in Österreich von 2012 bis
2022." Statista, 16 February 2023. https://de.statista.com/statistik/daten/studie/293102
/umfrage/auslaenderanteil-in-oesterreich/.

NAI. 2018. "Network Against Islamophobia (NAI) Statement on Proposed Muslim Brother-hood Bill and Related Executive Order." Jewish Voice for Peace, 8 February 2018. https://jewishvoiceforpeace.org/network-islamophobia-nai-statement-proposed-muslim-brotherhood-bill-related-executive-order/.

NEOS. 2018a. "NEOS: Kopftuchverbot alleine löst Versäumnisse bei Integration nicht." 4 April 2018. https://www.ots.at/presseaussendung/OTS_20180404_OTS0084/neos-kopftuchverbot-alleine-loest-versaeumnisse-bei-integration-nicht.

NEOS. 2018b. "NEOS: Schwarz-blaue Gesprächsverweigerung zeigt Geringschätzung gegenüber Parlament." 22 November 2018. https://www.ots.at/presseaussendung/OTS_20181122_OTS0176/neos-schwarz-blaue-gespraechsverweigerung-zeigt-geringschaetzung-gegenueber-parlament.

NEOS. 2018c. "NEOS: Unredliches Verknüpfen des Kopftuchverbots für Kinder mit Fördermittel zum Ausbau von Kinderbetreuungseinrichtungen." 9 July 2018. https://www.ots.at/presseaussendung/OTS_20180709_OTS0083/neos-unredliches-verknuepfen-des-kopftuchverbots-fuer-kinder-mit-foerdermittel-zum-ausbau-von-kinderbetreuungseinrichtungen.

NEOS. 2019a. "NEOS: Schwarz-Blau geht es beim Kopftuchverbot nicht um Lösungen." 16 January 2019. https://www.ots.at/presseaussendung/OTS_20190116_OTS0110/neos-schwarz-blau-geht-es-beim-kopftuchverbot-nicht-um-loesungen.

NEOS. 2019b. "NEOS zu Kopftuchverbot: Es braucht ein Gesamtkonzept, keine populistische Einzelmaßnahme." 19 March 2019. https://www.ots.at/presseaussendung/OTS_20190319_OTS0168/neos-zu-kopftuchverbot-es-braucht-ein-gesamtkonzept-keine-populistische-einzelmassnahme.

NEOS. 2019c. "NEOS zu Kopftuchverbot: Es braucht endlich Schulpolitik und keine Wahlkampfgags." 23 August 2019. https://www.ots.at/presseaussendung/OTS_20190823_OTS0075/neos-zu-kopftuchverbot-es-braucht-endlich-schulpolitik-und-keine-wahlkampfgags.

NR. 2015. "Steneographisches Protokoll, 61. Sitzung des Nationalrates der Republik Österreich, XXV. Gesetzgebungsperiode." 25 February 2015. Austrian Parliament.

NR. 2019. "Steneographisches Protokoll, 74. Sitzung des Nationalrates der Republik Österreich, XXVI. Gesetzgebungsperiode." 15 May 2019. Austrian Parliament, https://www.parlament.gv.at/dokument/XXVI/NRSITZ/74/fnameorig_779563.html.

oe24. 2018. "Strache: 'War erst der Beginn.'" Austria, 10 June 2018. https://www.oe24.at/oesterreich/politik/Strache-ueber-Moschee-Schliessungen-War-erst-der-Beginn/336725536.

Ombud for Equal Treatment. 2021. Stellungnahme zu dem Ministerialentwurf betreffend Bundesgesetz, mit dem das Strafgesetzbuch, die Strafprozeßordnung 1975, das Strafvollzugsgesetz und das Gerichtsorganisationsgesetz zur Bekämpfung von Terror geändert werden (Terror-Bekämpfungs-Gesetz—TeBG). 53/SN-83/ME. XXVII. GP. 2 February 2021. https://www.parlament.gv.at/PAKT/VHG/XXVII/SNME/SNME_36561/index.shtml.

OSCE. 2015. "Opinion on the Draft Federal Law of Austria Amending the Law on the Recognition of Adherents to Islam a Religious Society." 7 November 2014. http://www.osce.org/odihr/126575?download=true.

OSCE. 2021. Stellungnahme zu dem Ministerialentwurf betreffend Bundesgesetz, mit dem das Strafgesetzbuch, die Strafprozeßordnung 1975, das Strafvollzugsgesetz und das Gerichtsorganisationsgesetz zur Bekämpfung von Terror geändert werden (Terror-Bekämpfungs-Gesetz—TeBG). 59/SN-83/ME. XXVII. GP. 29 January 2021. https://www.parlament.gv.at/PAKT/VHG/XXVII/SNME/SNME_36584/index.shtml.

Österreichischer Integrations Fonds. 2017. "Anti-Gesichtsverhüllungsgesetz tritt in Kraft." Integrationsfonds, 21 September 2017.

Österreich Konvent. 2003. Tonbandabschrift 5. Sitzung, Freitag, 21 November 2003. http://www.konvent.gv.at/K/DE/KSITZ/KSITZ_00005/fnameorig_012803.html.

ÖVP. 2008. *Neustart für Österreich* (website discontinued).

ÖVP. 2013. *Zukunftsweisend Österreich 2013: Das Programm der ÖVP zur Nationalratswahl 2013*.Wein: Österreichische Volkspartei. https://www.vienna.at/die-oevp-praesentiert-ihr -programm-zur-nationalratswahl/3664751.

ÖVP. 2017a. "Blümel: Unterstützung für Kopftuchverbot im öffentlichen Dienst." 6 January 2017. https://www.ots.at/presseaussendung/OTS_20170106_OTS0025/bluemel-unter stuetzung-fuer-kopftuchverbot-im-oeffentlichen-dienst.

ÖVP. 2017b. "Der neue Weg. Ordnung & Sicherheit 3/3." In *Das Programm der Liste Sebastian Kurz—die neue Volkspartei zur Nationalratswahl 2017*. Wien: Österreichische Volkspartei.

ÖVP. 2017c. "Gerstl: Integration bedingt Anerkennung kultureller Identität des Gastlandes." 7 January 2017. https://www.ots.at/presseaussendung/OTS_20170107_OTS0013/gerstl -integration-bedingt-anerkennung-kultureller-identitaet-des-gastlandes.

ÖVP. 2017d. "VP-Gaggl: Gemeinsam für mehr Sicherheit in Kärnten." 21 March 2017. https:// www.ots.at/presseaussendung/OTS_20170321_OTS0178/vp-gaggl-gemeinsam-fuer -mehr-sicherheit-in-kaernten.

ÖVP. 2018a. "Wölbitsch/Hungerländer zu ATIB-Moschee: Preis für rot-grüne Politik des Weg-schauens." 17 April 2018. https://www.ots.at/presseaussendung/OTS_20180417_OTS0183 /woelbitschhungerlaender-zu-atib-moschee-preis-fuer-rot-gruene-politik-des-wegschauens.

ÖVP. 2018b. "Wölbitsch/Schwarz ad Czernohorszky: Gegen Radikalisierung an Wiens Schulen ist weiterhin niemand erreichbar." 20 November 2018. https://www.ots.at/presse aussendung/OTS_20181120_OTS0111/woelbitschschwarz-ad-czernohorszky-gegen -radikalisierung-an-wiens-schulen-ist-weiterhin-niemand-erreichbar.

ÖVP. 2019a. "Nehammer ad SÖZ: 'Lehrerinnen müssen neutral sein.'" 27 August 2019. https://www.ots.at/presseaussendung/OTS_20190827_OTS0141/nehammer-ad-soez -lehrerinnen-muessen-neutral-sein.

ÖVP. 2019b. "Neue Volkspartei Wien unterstützt Kopftuchverbot: Kinder vor Stigmatisier-ung schützen." 23 August 2019. https://www.ots.at/presseaussendung/OTS_20190823 _OTS0037/neue-volkspartei-wien-unterstuetzt-kopftuchverbot-kinder-vor-stigmatisie rung-schuetzen.

ÖVP. 2019c. "Schwarz/Hungerländer: Kopftuchverbot richtige und wichtige Entscheidung." 8 May 2019. https://www.ots.at/presseaussendung/OTS_20190508_OTS0201/schwarz hungerlaender-kopftuchverbot-richtige-und-wichtige-entscheidung.

ÖVP. 2019d. "VP-Frauen-Chefin Juliane Bogner-Strauß appelliert bei Kopftuchverbot an Frauen in anderen Parteien." 24 August 2019. https://www.ots.at/presseaussendung/OTS _20190824_OTS0006/vp-frauen-chefin-juliane-bogner-strauss-appelliert-bei-kopftuch verbot-an-frauen-in-anderen-parteien.

ÖVP. 2019e. Nehammer zu Kopftuchverbot: Expertenhearing bestätigt Notwendigkeit des Kopftuchverbots in der Volksschule," OTS. 19 March 2019. www.ots.at/presseaussendung /OTS_20190319_OTS0183/nehammer-zu-kopftuchverbot-expertenhearing-bestaetigt -notwendigkeit-des-kopftuchverbots-in-der-volksschule.

ÖVP. 2020. "VP-Integrationssprecher ad IGGIÖ: 'Politischer Islam' ist eine Gefahr." OTS, 3 January 2020. https://www.ots.at/presseaussendung/OTS_20200103_OTS0119/vp-inte grationssprecher-ad-iggoe-politischer-islam-ist-eine-gefahr.

ÖVP Club Vienna. 2018. "Wölbitsch/Hungerländer zu ATIB-Moschee: Preis für rot-grüne Politik des Wegschauens." 17 April 2018. https://www.ots.at/presseaussendung/OTS _20180417_OTS0183/woelbitschhungerlaender-zu-atib-moschee-preis-fuer-rot-gruene -politik-des-wegschauens.

Parlament Österreich. 2003. "Schönborn, Christoph: Keine Norm garantiert Schutz der Men-schenwürde. Vertreter der Kirchen und Religionsgemeinschaften im Ö-Konvent." Parla-

mentskorrespondenz Nr. 882. 21 November 2003. http://www.parlament.gv.at/PAKT
/PR/JAHR_2003/PK0882/index.shtml.

Parlament Österreich. 2010. Israelitengesetz 1890, Änderung (199/ME). 199/ME. XXIV. GP.
https://www.parlament.gv.at/gegenstand/XXIV/ME/199.

Parlament Österreich. 2014a. Ministerialentwurf Gesetz. Islamgesetz 1912, Änderung (69/
ME. 69/ME. XXV. GP. https://www.parlament.gv.at/gegenstand/XXV/ME/69.

Parlament Österreich. 2014b. Terror-Symbole-Gesetz 2014. 64/ME. XXV. GP. https://www
.parlament.gv.at/PAKT/VHG/XXV/ME/ME_00064/index.shtml#tab-Stellungnahmen.

Parlament Österreich. 2015. "Neues Islamgesetz: Verfassungsausschuss empfiehlt Beschlussfas-
sung." Parliamentskorrespondenz Nr. 105. 12 February 2015. https://www.parlament.gv.at
/aktuelles/pk/jahr_2015/pko105.

Parlament Österreich. 2019a. Ministerialentwurf—Erläuterungen. 81/ME. XXVI. GP. https://
www.parlament.gv.at/PAKT/VHG/XXVI/ME/ME_00081/fname_712103.pdf.

Parlament Österreich. 2019b. 74. Sitzung. 15 May 2019. https://www.parlament.gv.at/PAKT
/VHG/XXVI/NRSITZ/NRSITZ_00074/A_-_19_51_39_00201778.html.

Parlament Österreich. 2021. Nationalrat beschließt Anti-Terror-Paket Einstimmigkeit für den
Punkt Führerscheinentzug für Terrorismus-Verurteilte. Parlamentskorrespondenz Nr.
852. 7 July 2021. https://www.parlament.gv.at/PAKT/PR/JAHR_2021/PK0852/.

Potz, Richard. 2012. "100 Years of Austrian Legislation on Islam." Ministry for European and
International Affairs. https://www.bmeia.gv.at/fileadmin/user_upload/Zentrale/Kultur
/Publikationen/Islamgesetz_EN.pdf.

Potz, Richard, and Brigitte Schinkele. 2010. Stellungnahme zum Entwurf eines Bundesgesetzes, mit dem das Gesetz von 21. März 1890 betreffend die Regelung des äußeren Rechtsverhältnisse der israelitischen Religionsgesellschaft (IsraelitenG) geändert wird (199/ME.
XXIV. GPr Regierungsvorlage). https://www.parlament.gv.at/PAKT/VHG/XXIV/SNME
/SNME_04510/imfname_201929.pdf.

Protestant Church. 2021. Stellungnahme zu dem Ministerialentwurf betreffend Bundesgesetz,
mit dem das Strafgesetzbuch, die Strafprozeßordnung 1975, das Strafvollzugsgesetz und
das Gerichtsorganisationsgesetz zur Bekämpfung von Terror geändert werden (Terror-
Bekämpfungs-Gesetz—TeBG). 50/SN-83/ME. XXVII. GP, 2 February 2021. https://
www.parlament.gv.at/PAKT/VHG/XXVII/SNME/SNME_36553/index.shtml.

Republik Österreich. 2013. Erfolgreich Österreich. Arbeitsprogramm der österreichischen Bundesregierung 2013–2018. December 2013. https://images.derstandard.at/2013/12/12/regierungs
programm%202013%20-%202018.pdf.

Republik Österreich. 2017. Zusammen. Für unser Österreich. Regierungsprogramm 2017–2022.

Republik Österreich. 2020. Aus Verantwortung für Österreich. Regierungsprogramm 2020–2024.
https://www.dieneuevolkspartei.at/Download/Regierungsprogramm_2020.pdf.

RGBl (Reichsgesetzblatt). 1874. Gesetz vom 20. Mai 1874, betreffend die gesetzliche Anerkennung von Religionsgesellschaften. RGBl. Nr. 68/1874. https://www.ris.bka.gv.at/Gelten
deFassung.wxe?Abfrage=Bundesnormen&Gesetzesnummer=10009173.

RIV. 2021. Stellungnahme zu dem Ministerialentwurf betreffend Bundesgesetz, mit dem das
Strafgesetzbuch, die Strafprozeßordnung 1975, das Strafvollzugsgesetz und das Gerichtsorganisationsgesetz zur Bekämpfung von Terror geändert werden (Terror-Bekämpfungs-
Gesetz—TeBG). 39/SN-83/ME. XXVII. GP, 1 February 2021.https://www.parlament.gv
.at/PAKT/VHG/XXVII/SNME/SNME_36537/index.shtml.

Rosenkranz, Walter, Karl Nehammer, Rudolf Taschner, and Wendelin Mölzer. 2018. 495/A
XXVI. GP—Initiativantrag, eingebracht am 22.11.2018.

Schima, Stefan. 2014. "Gutachten zum Entwurf zum Bundesgesetz, mit dem das Gesetz betreffend die Anerkennung der Anhänger des Islam als Religionsgesellschaft geändert wird."

Vienna, 28 October 2014. https://www.parlament.gv.at/PAKT/VHG/XXV/SNME/SNME _02194/imfname_372317.pdf.

Schima, Stefan. 2015. "Staat und Religionsgemeinschaften in Österreich—Wo stehen wir heute? (Ein Versuch eines Vergleichs mit der Zeit Konstantins, genannt 'der Große')." In *Kirchen und Staat am Scheideweg? 1700 Jahre Mailänder Vereinbarung*, edited by Christian Wagnsonner, Karl-Reinhart Trauner, and Alexander Lapin, 111–161. Vienna: Bundesminister für Landesverteidigung und Sport.

Schwaighofer, Klaus, and Andreas Venier. 2021. Stellungnahme zu dem Ministerialentwurf betreffend Bundesgesetz, mit dem das Strafgesetzbuch, die Strafprozeßordnung 1975, das Strafvollzugsgesetz und das Gerichtsorganisationsgesetz zur Bekämpfung von Terror geändert werden (Terror-Bekämpfungs-Gesetz—TeBG). 35/SN-83/ME. XXVII. GP, Rechtswissenschaftliche Fakultaet an der Universitaet Innsbruck. 1 February 2021. https://www.parlament.gv.at/PAKT/VHG/XXVII/SNME/SNME_36531/index.shtml.

SPÖ. 2008. *Wahlmanifest der Sozialdemokratischen Partei Österreichs. Nationalratswahl 2008*. 40. Ordentlichen Bundesparteitag. 8 August 2008. http://www.erhoert.at/Politinfos/SPOE _wahlmanifest08.pdf.

SPÖ. 2016. "SP-Berger-Krotsch ad FP-Ullmann: Frauen sollen ihr Leben selbstbestimmt gestalten können." OTS. Vienna, 11 August 2016. https://www.mycity24.at/2016/08/sp -berger-krotsch-ad-fp-ullmann-frauen-sollen-ihr-leben-selbstbestimmt-gestalten -koennen/.

SPÖ. 2018a. *Grundsatzprogram*. Beschlossen am 44. Ordentlichen Bundesparteitag. Wels, 2018.

SPÖ. 2018b. "Königsberger-Ludwig zu Kinderbetreuung: Rücknahme der Kürzungen ist Sieg der Vernunft." 24 August 2018, OTS. https://www.ots.at/presseaussendung/OTS_20180824 _OTS0095/koenigsberger-ludwig-zu-kinderbetreuung-ruecknahme-der-kuerzungen-ist -sieg-der-vernunft.

SPÖ. 2018c. "Kopftuch—Lercher: Um von dieser Regierung wahrgenommen zu werden, müssten sich Österreichs Arbeitnehmer kollektiv ein Kopftuch umbinden." OTS. Vienna, 8 July 2018. https://www.ots.at/presseaussendung/OTS_20180708_OTS0028/kopftuch -lercher-um-von-dieser-regierung-wahrgenommen-zu-werden-muessten-sich-oesterreichs -arbeitnehmer-kollektiv-ein-kopftuch-umbinden.

SPÖ. 2018d. "SP-Schindele: 'Nachhaltiges pädagogisches Gesamtpaket notwendig.'" OTS. St. Pölten, 21 November 2018. https://www.ots.at/presseaussendung/OTS_20181121 _OTS0087/sp-schindele-nachhaltiges-paedagogisches-gesamtpaket-notwendig.

SPÖ NO 2018. "Kocevar/Kögl/Buljubasic: Sozialdemokratie leistet Widerstand gegen soziale Fehlentwicklungen." OTS. 26 June 2018. https://www.ots.at/presseaussendung/OTS _20180426_OTS0143/kocevarkoeglbuljubasic-sozialdemokratie-leistet-widerstand -gegen-soziale-fehlentwicklungen.

VfGH. 2020. Verfassungsgerichtshof G 4/2020-27. Vienna, 11 December 2020. https://www .vfgh.gv.at/downloads/VfGH-Erkenntnis_G_4_2020_vom_11.12.2020.pdf.

## NEWSPAPER PUBLICATIONS

AFP. 2018. "Turkey Furious as Austria Plans to Expel up to 60 Imams." *The Local*, 8 June 2018. https://www.thelocal.at/20180608/austria-will-expel-several-foreign-funded-imams-and -shut-seven-mosques-chancellor-says/.

Alkan, Güler. 2017. "Sie müssen sich Kulturchristen nennen!" *Der Standard*, 7 March 2011. http://derstandard.at/1297819743799/daStandardat-Reportage-Sie-muessen-sich -Kulturchristen-nennen.

APA. 2008. "Umfrage: Große Mehrheit in Türkei für Verbotsaufhebung" *Der Standard,* 20 March 2008. https://www.derstandard.at/story/1200563201586/umfrage-grosse-mehrheit -in-tuerkei-fuer-verbotsaufhebung.

Arbeiter Zeitung. 1979. "Erste Moschee Österreichs und islamisches Zentrum eröffnet" [First Mosque and Islamic Center in Austria Opened]. *Arbeiter Zeitung,* 21 November 1979.

Bischof, Daniel. 2018. "Graue Wölfe, Erdogan und das Islamgesetz." *Wiener Zeitung,* 8 June 2018. https://www.wienerzeitung.at/nachrichten/oesterreich/politik/969933_Graue-Woelfe -Erdogan-und-das-Islamgesetz.html.

*Der Standard.* 2014. "Höchstgericht: Pädophilie-Vorwurf gegen Mohammed beleidigt Islam." 13 January 2014. https://www.derstandard.at/story/1388650792132/hoechstgericht-paedo philie-vorwurf-gegen-mohammed-beleidigt-islam.

*Der Standard.* 2019. "Gudenus will Gesetz Gegen Politischen Islam bis Mitte 2019." 16 December 2018. https://mobil.derstandard.at/2000094068620/Gudenus-will-Gesetz-gegen -politischen-Islam-bis-Mitte-2019.

*Die Presse.* 2016. "Warum Österreich das EU-Lager der USA-Skeptiker anführt." 6 September 2016. https://www.diepresse.com/5007322/warum-oesterreich-das-eu-lager-der-usa -skeptiker-anfuehrt.

*Die Presse.* 2018a. "BVT-Affäre: Vorwürfe der NS-Wiederbetätigung." 4 November 2018. https:// diepresse.com/home/innenpolitik/5524032/BVTAffaere_Vorwuerfe-der-NSWieder betaetigung.

*Die Presse.* 2018b. "Kopftuchverbot in Volksschulen SPÖ und Neos gesprächsbereit." 18 November 2018. https://diepresse.com/home/bildung/schule/5531932/Kopftuchverbot -in-Volksschulen_SPOe-und-Neos-gespraechsbereit.

*Die Presse.* 2018c. "Regierung plant kein Kopftuch-Verbot bis an die Universitäten." 6 April 2018. https://diepresse.com/home/innenpolitik/5401207/Regierung-plant-kein-Kopftuch Verbot-bis-an-die-Universitaeten?direct=5405505&_vl_backlink=/home/innenpolitik /5405505/index.do&selChannel=.

*Die Presse.* 2019. "Nationalrat beschloss Kopftuchverbot für Volksschülerinnen." 16 May 2019. https://diepresse.com/home/innenpolitik/5629006/Nationalrat-beschloss-Kopftuch verbot-fuer-Volksschuelerinnen.

Euro News. 2008. "Wiener Akademikerbund stellt 15 Forderungen an österreichische Muslime," 22 November 2008. https://web.archive.org/web/20110831101511/http:/europenews .dk/de/node/16427

Farzan, Antonia Noori. 2021. "Muslim Groups in Austria Fear Attacks after Government Publishes Map of Mosques." *Washington Post,* 29 May 2021. www.washingtonpost.com/world /2021/05/29/austria-islam-map/.

Gaigg, Vanessa, and Colette M. Schmidt. 2020. "Antiterrorpaket: Neuer Straftatbestand Zielt auf Religiöse extremistische Verbindungen ab." *Der Standard,* 16 December 2020. www .derstandard.at/story/2000122537911/ministerrat-will-umstrittenes-anti-terror-paket -beschliessen.

Gigler, Claudia, and Michael Jungwirth. 2018. "Regierung Überprüft 61 Imame und Schließt sieben Moscheen." *Kleine Zeitung,* 8 June 2018. https://www.kleinezeitung.at /politik/innenpolitik/5442906/Jetzt-live_Regierung-plant-Ausweisung-von-40-Imamen -und.

Ichner, Bernd. 2019a. "Analyse: Das schwere Erbe der Milli Görüs." *Kurier,* 25 February 2019. https://kurier.at/chronik/wien/das-schwere-erbe-der-milli-goerues/400414436.

Ichner, Bernhard. 2019b. "Höchstgericht soll über Arabische Kultusgemeinde entscheiden." *Kurier,* 14 February 2019. https://kurier.at/politik/inland/hoechstgericht-soll-ueber -arabische-kultusgemeinde-entscheiden/400406888.

Karnitschg, Mattthew. 2021. "Austria's Sebastian Kurz Steps Down amid Corruption Probe." *Politico*, 9 October 2021. https://www.politico.eu/article/austrias-sebastian-kurz-resigns/.

Kocina, Erich. 2019. "Moscheen rechtswidrig geschlossen." *Die Presse*, 14 February 2019. https://diepresse.com/home/innenpolitik/5579752/Moscheen-rechtswidrig-geschlossen.

*Kronen Zeitung*. 2018. "Politischer Islam Darf Bürger Nicht Gefährden." 1 October 2018. https://www.krone.at/1780687.

*Kronen Zeitung*. 2020. "Dokumentationsstelle Nimmt Extremismus Ins Visier." 15 July 2020. https://www.krone.at/2192166.

*Kurier*. 2014a. "Kurz für einheitliche Koran-Übersetzung." *Kurier*, 20 September 2014. http://kurier.at/politik/inland/kurz-fuer-einheitliche-koran-uebersetzung/86.827.235.

*Kurier*. 2014b. "Neues Islamgesetz: Mehr Rechte, deutscher Koran." *Kurier*, 26 September 2014. http://kurier.at/politik/inland/neues-islamgesetz-mehr-rechte-deutscher-koran/87.840.832.

*Kurier*. 2017. "'Burka-Rebell' in Wien abgeführt." 9 October 2017. https://m.kurier.at/chronik/wien/burka-rebell-in-wien-abgefuehrt/290.945.740.

Kurz, Sebastian. 2015. "Islam europäischer Prägung—Muslime mitten in der Gesellschaft," *Fisch+Fleisch*, 3 July 2015. https://www.fischundfleisch.com/sebastian-kurz/islam-europaeischer-praegung-muslime-mitten-in-der-gesellschaft-8528.

Lauxmann, Bernhard. 2020. "Diese Regierung neigt zur Religionsfeindlichkeit." *Die Presse*, 17 January 2020. https://www.diepresse.com/5753886/diese-regierung-neigt-zur-religionsfeindlichkeit.

Liphshiz, Cnaan. 2020. "Sebastian Kurz Has Totally Shifted Austria's Treatment of Israel. Is It Because of a Bromance with Benjamin Netanyahu?" *Jewish Telegraphic Agency*, 19 June 2020. https://www.jta.org/2020/06/19/global/sebastian-kurz-has-totally-shifted-austrias-treatment-of-israel-is-it-because-of-a-bromance-with-benjamin-netanyahu.

Metzger, Ida. 2014. "Höhlenmenschen—Sager laut Kurz 'einfach dumm.'" *Kurier*, 16 November 2014. http://kurier.at/politik/inland/integrations-gipfeltreffen-strache-gegen-kurz-streitgespraech-ueber-asyl-und-islam/97.260.998.

Mittelstaedt, Katharina. 2018. "Warum die geschlossenen Moscheen offen sind." *Der Standard*, 22 June 2018. https://mobil.derstandard.at/2000082025668/Warum-die-geschlossenen-Moscheen-offen-sind.

Murphy, Francois. 2018. "Austria's Police Raid on Intelligence Agency Was Legal, Officials Say." *Reuters*, 16 March 2018. https://www.reuters.com/article/us-austria-politics-intelligence/austria-says-intelligence-raids-were-legal-but-political-storm-rolls-on-idUSKCN1GQ2R5.

Neuhold, Clemens. 2014. "Wir brauchen den Islam." *Wiener Zeitung*, 9 November 2014. http://www.wienerzeitung.at/nachrichten/oesterreich/politik/700481_Wir-brauchen-den-Islam.html.

Noack, Rick, and Souad Mekhennet. 2019. "Austrian Chancellor Calls for New Elections after Leader of Far-Right Ally Resigns in Scandal." *Washington Post*, 18 May 2019. https://www.washingtonpost.com/world/2019/05/18/austrias-vice-chancellor-announces-resignation-amid-leak-video-purported-graft/?utm_term=.667c07d31c97.

Nowak, Rainer. 2010. "Laura Rudas: Kopftuch-Gegnerin als Staatssekretärin?" *Die Presse*, 13 October 2010. http://diepresse.com/home/innenpolitik/kulisse/601936/Laura-Rudas_KopftuchGegnerin-als- Staatssekretaerin.

ORF (Austrian Broadcasting Corporation). 2015. "IGGÖ-Präsident Sanaç gibt sich versöhnt mit Islamgesetz." 26 July 2015. http://religion.orf.at/stories/2723325/.

ORF. 2018a. "Regierung schließt islamistische Moscheen." 8 June 2018.

ORF. 2018b. "Weiter keine Moscheen der Arabischen Gemeinde." 18 June 2018.

ORF. 2019a. "Gericht: Moscheenschließung Rechtswidrig." 14 February 2019. https://wien
.orf.at/v2/news/stories/2964549/.

ORF. 2019b. "Offenbar Beobachtungsstelle Gegen Extremismus Geplant." 12 January 2019.

ORF. 2019c. "Regierung plant Schließung von sieben Moscheen." 8 June 2018. http://orf.at
/stories/2441928/.

ORF. 2020a. "IGGÖ-Kritik an Dokustelle für politischen Islam." 15 July 2020. https://religion
.orf.at/v3/stories/3004988/.

ORF. 2020b. "Raab: Islamismus-Dokumentationsstelle und Kopftuchverbot Zuerst." 6 January 2020. https://orf.at/stories/3150355/.

OTS. 2010. "Presseaussendung: FPÖ Winter kritisiert Schweinefleischverbannung aus Steirischer Schule." 21 October 2010. https://www.ots.at/presseaussendung/OTS_20101021
_OTS0058/fpoe-winter-kritisiert-schweinefleisch-verbannung-aus-steirischer-schule.

Pándi, Claus. 2018. "Strache will jetzt Kopftuchverbot in Kindergärten." *Kronen Zeitung*,
31 March 2018. http:// www.krone.at/1682481.

Pipes, Daniel. 2018. "The Sound of Debate in Austria." *Washington Times*, 4 April 2018. https://
www.washingtontimes.com/news/2018/apr/4/immigration-islamization-are-more
-urgent-than-neo-/.

Postl, Elisabeth. 2019. "BVT: Kickl spricht von 'ÖVP-Geheimdienst.'" *Die Presse*, 1 July 2019.
https://www.diepresse.com/5652808/bvt-kickl-spricht-von-ovp-geheimdienst.

Potz, Richard. 2017. "Islamgesetz: Eine 'Polizei' für die Religion(en)?" *Die Furche*, 13 July 2017.
https://www.furche.at/religion/islamgesetz-eine-polizei-fuer-die-religionen-1248351.

*Profil.* 2003. "Diese Peanuts sind für Gott kein Thema. Interview mit Wolfgang Schüssel." *Profil*, 15 November 2003.

*Profil.* 2019. "Jedem Kind sein Schnitzel." 17 August 2019. https://www.profil.at/oesterreich
/jedem-kind-sein-schnitzel/400908809.

Renner, Georg. 2019a. "Beobachtungsstelle neu. Ein DÖW für Islamisten! Oder: Wie die
Regierung Schnell Zurück zu ihrem Lieblingsthema Kommt." *Kleine Zeitung*, 3 March 2019.
https://www.kleinezeitung.at/meinung/5588894/Beobachtungsstelle-neu_Ein-DOeW
-fuer-Islamisten-Oder_Wie-die.

Renner, Georg. 2019b. "Regierung lässt Kultusamt Moscheen kontrollieren." *Kleine Zeitung*,
1 April 2019. https://www. kleinezeitung.at/politik/innenpolitik/5605062/Muslime
-protestieren_Regierung-laesst-Kultusamt-Moscheen-kon- trollieren.

Sablatnig, Wolfgang. 2023. "Radikalisierung im Netz: Terrorexperte Stockhammer arbeitete
den Anschlag von Wien auf." Tiroler Tageszeitung. 27 October 2023. https://www.tt.com/
artikel/30867885/radikalisierung-im-netz-terrorexperte-stockhammer-arbeitete-den
-anschlag-von-wien-auf.

Schneiders, Thorsten Gerald. 2009. *Islamfeindlichkeit*. Wiesbaden: VS Verlag für
Sozialwissenschaften.

Schreiber, Dominik, and Kid Möchel. 2019. "Causa BVT: Neos zeigen Ex-Innenminister Herbert Kickl an." *Kurier*, 24 July 2019. https://kurier.at/politik/inland/causa-bvt-neos
-zeigen-ex-innenminister-herbert-kickl-an/400560092.

Temel, Peter, Lukas Kapeller, and Bernhard Ichner. 2018. "Sieben Moscheen müssen geschlossen werden: Wie geht es weiter?" *Kurier*, 8 June 2018. https://kurier.at/politik/inland/die
-wichtigsten-fragen-rund-um-die-moscheen- schliessung/400047758.

*Wiener Zeitung.* 2020. "Job Advertisement for the Board of the Documentation Center for
Political Islam." 16 July 2020.

# INDEX

Page numbers in *italics* denote tables.

# ABOUT THE AUTHORS

FARID HAFEZ has been the Class of 1955 Distinguished Visiting Professor of International Studies at Williams College since 2021 and also, since 2017, a non-resident researcher at Georgetown University's Bridge Initiative. He was a senior researcher at the University of Salzburg, from 2014 to 2021. In 2017, he was Fulbright-Botstiber Visiting Professor of Austrian-American Studies at the University of California, Berkeley's Center for Race and Gender. In 2014, he was a visiting scholar at the Middle East Institute at Columbia University, New York. Since 2010, Hafez has been the (founding) editor of the *Islamophobia Studies Yearbook*, and since 2015 coeditor of the annual *European Islamophobia Report*. He has received the Bruno Kreisky Award for the political book of 2009 for his anthology Islamophobia in Austria (coedited with John Bunzl) and has published more than 150 books and academic articles. His research has appeared in journals such as *Politics and Religion, German Politics and Society, Journal for Religion, Society and Politics, Oxford Journal of Law and Religion, Patterns of Prejudice,* and many others. Since 2020, Hafez also has been an editorial board member of the *Journal of Austrian-American History* (Pennsylvania State University Press). Hafez has taught and studied race, far-right politics in Europe, Muslim minorities, and political thought. His latest books include the anthology *The Rise of Global Islamophobia in the War on Terror: Coloniality, Race, and Islam,* with Naved Bakali.

REINHARD HEINISCH has been professor of comparative Austrian politics at the University of Salzburg since 2010. He received his academic training in the United States, where he completed his PhD at Michigan State University in 1994 and then taught at the University of Pittsburgh at Johnstown and the University of Pittsburgh from 1994 to 2009, last as professor of political science. He has remained an affiliated member of the European Studies Center at the University of Pittsburgh. Heinisch's research focuses on the rise of the radical right, populism, democracy, voting, and survey research. His research has appeared in journals such as *European Journal of Political Research, Political Studies, Party Politics, West European Politics, Democratization, Comparative European Politics, Politics and Religion,* and many others. His book publications include *Populism Proporz Pariah: Austria Turns Right, Understanding Populist Party Organization: The Radical Right in Western Europe, The People and the Nation: Populism and Ethno-Territorial Politics in Europe,* and *Political Populism: A Handbook.* His research has been supported by various project grants including a European

Union Horizon 2020 grant and funding from the Austrian and Swiss Research Fund. He is the recipient of the Austrian National Science Prize from the Austrian Parliament. Drawing on survey experiments, he is currently undertaking a multicountry study of political conspiracy theories and voter behavior.